Biology

D1151929

Gareth Price

Jane Taylor

LORETO COLLEGE LIBRARY MANCHESTER

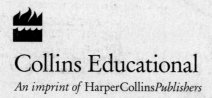

Collins Educational

An imprint of HarperCollinsPublishers

Published by Collins Educational
An imprint of HarperCollins*Publishers*
77–85 Fulham Palace Road
Hammersmith
London
W6 8JB

© HarperCollins*Publishers* 1997

First published 1997

ISBN 000 322387 6

Jane Taylor and Gareth Price assert their moral right to be identified as the authors of this work.

All rights reserved. No part of this publication may be reproduced, stored in a retrieval system, or transmitted in any form or by any means, electronic, mechanical, photocopying, recording or otherwise, without either the prior permission of the Publisher or a licence permitting restricted copying in the United Kingdom issued by the Copyright Licensing Agency, 90 Tottenham Court Road, London W1P 9HE.

British Library Cataloguing in Publication Data
A catalogue record for this book is available from the British Library.

Edited by Gina Walker and Jane Bryant
Design by Raynor Design
Illustrations by Barking Dog Art, Hardlines and Raynor Design
Picture research by Caroline Thompson
Production by Mandy Inness
Printed and bound by HarperCollins(HK)

769.

ACC No. 037575
CLASS No. 574 PRI
DATE REC'D 4|3|97
COPY No.

Acknowledgements

cover photographs: (top) R Campbell/Bruce Coleman Ltd, (bottom) G Price
title page: NHPA/ Stephen Dalton, contents page: (top) Petit Format/Nestlé/Science Photo Library, (bottom) Birds Eye Walls Ltd. theme 1 header: John Reader/Science Photo Library, theme 2 header: NHPA/ Christopher Ratier, theme 3 header: European Space Agency/Science Photo Library, theme 4 header: Gene Ahrens/Bruce Coleman Ltd., p7 (mid) Biophoto Associates, p7 (bottom) Keith Nels Swenson/Bruce Coleman Ltd., p8 NHPA/ Stephen Dalton, p12 Will and Deni McIntyre/ Science Photo Library, p13 (top) Philip Sayers/ Planet Earth Pictures, p13 (left) Eckart Pott/Bruce Ltd., p13 (centre) Petit Format/Nestlé/Science Photo Library, p13 (right) Hans reinhard/ Bruce Coleman Ltd., p14 (centre) Eric Grave/Science Photo Library, p14 (right) MI Walker/Science Photo Library, p15 (right) David Scharf/Science Photo Library, p15 (left) Alfred Pasieka/Science Photo Library, p16 Dr Jeremy Burgess/Science Photo Library, p17 Prof F Motta/Dept of Anatomy/University of La Sapienza, Rome/Science Photo Library, p19 (both) Carloine Thompson, p 23 Biophoto Associates/Science Photo Library, p24 CNRI/Science Photo Library, p27 (top) G Price, p27 (left) Peter A hinchliffe/Bruce Coleman Ltd., p27 (right) Adam Hart-Davis/Science Photo Library, p27 (centre) Gerard Vandestadt/Agence Vandestadt, p36 (top) AB Dowsett/Science Photo Library, p36 (centre)CNRI/Science Photo Library, p36 (bottom) Secchi-Lecaque/Roussel-Uclaf/Science Photo Library, p40 (left) GF Gennaro/Science Photo Library, p40 (right) Science Photo Library, p44 (mid) Eric Grave/Science Photo Library, p44 (bottom) Jane Burton/Bruce Coleman Ltd., p49 (top)Hattie young/Science Photo Library, p49 (centre) Adam Hart-Davis/Science Photo Library, p49 (left) CNRI/Science Photo Library, p50 David Parker/Science Photo Library, p52 Andrew Syred/Science Photo Library, p53 Biophoto Associates, p62 Advertising Archives, p64 David Scharf/Science Photo Library, p67 Mary Clay/ Planet Earth Pictures, p 68 Gunter Zeisler/Bruce Coleman Ltd., p70 MI Walker/Science Photo Library, p71 (top) EM Unit, CVL Weybridge/Science Photo Library, p71 (bottom) David Reed/Panos Pictures, p73 David Scharf/Science Photo Library, p75 Institut Pasteur, CNRI/Science Photo Library, p77 S Nagendra/Science Photo Library, p79 (top) Hulton Deutsch collection, p79 (mid) Hank Morgan/Science Photo Library, p81 John Birdsall Photography, p84 Heather Angel, p85 Andrew Syred/Science Photo Library, p86 (top) JC Revy/Science Photo Library, p86 (mid) Hans Reinhard/Brice Coleman Ltd., p87 Michael and Lois Warren/Photos Horticultural, p89 Eric Grave/Science Photo Library, p92 Simon Fraser, RVI, Newcastle-upon-Tyne/Science Photo Library, p94 (top) NHPA/ Anthony Bannister, p96 Ronald Grant Archive, p97 SHOUT, p98 G Price, p100 David Hisler/Tony Stone, p103 (top) J Croyle/Custom Medical Stock Photo/Science Photo Library, p103, (left) PM Motta and J Van Blerkom/Science Photo Library, p104 Adam Hart-Davis/Science Photo Library, p106 (top centre) Peter Davey/Bruce Coleman Ltd., p106 (left) Christian Zuber/Bruce Coleman Ltd., p106 (right) John Shaw/NHPA, p106 (bottom) Sally and Richard Greenhill, p111 (left) Micheal Tweedie/NHPA, p111 (right) Laurie Campbell/NHPA, , p114 Omikron/Science Photo Library, p115 (both) Stephen Dalton/NHPA, p117 (mid) Manfred Kage/Science Photo Library, p117 (top) CNRI/Science Photo Library, p119 Michael Vard/Bruce Coleman Ltd., p120 Barnaby's Picture Library, p121 (left) Stephen Dalton/NHPA, p121(mid) Jean-Pierre Zwaenepoel, p121 (bottom) Christer Fredriksson/Bruce Coleman Ltd., p128 (left) Anthony Bannister/NHPA, p128 (centre) Laurie Campbell/NHPA, p128 (right) Christope Ratier/NHPA, p135 (left) George McCarthy/Bruce Coleman Ltd., p135 (centre) Kim Taylor/Bruce Coleman Ltd., p135 (right) Dr Ivan Polunin/NHPA, p136 Sally and Richard Greenhill, p139 Willem Harinck/Holt Studios International, p140 Hans Reinhard/Bruce Coleman Ltd., p145 (top left) Francois Leroy, Biocosmos/Science Photo Library, p145 (top centre) Norbert Wu/NHPA, p145 (top right) Nigel Cattlin/Holt Studios International, p145 (bottom left) ANT/NHPA, p145 (bottom centre) Norbert Wu/Oxford Scientific Films, p145 (bottom right) Nigel Cattlin/Holt Studios International, p148 (top) Hans Reinhard/Bruce Coleman Ltd., p148 (bottom) G Price, p158 (left) Jane Burton/Bruce Coleman Ltd., p158 (centre) Frans Lanting/Bruce Coleman Ltd., p158 (right) Manfred Danneger/NHPA, p160 (top, both) Mark Burnett/Science Photo Library, p160 (bottom, both) Caroline Thompson, p161 CNRI/Science Photo Library, p163 Science Photo Library, p171 Will and Deni McIntyre/Science Photo Library, p172 (left) Michael and Lois Warren/Photos Horticultural, p172 (right) Gerard Lacz/NHPA, p174 (top) Nigel Cattlin/Holt Studios International, p174 (bottom) NASA/Science Photo Library, p177(both) Bruce Coleman Ltd. p178 (left) Janos Jurka/Bruce Coleman Ltd., p178 (right) Jeff Foot Production/Bruce Coleman Ltd., p189 (top left) Alfred Pasieka/Science Photo Library, p189 (top centre) Sinclair Stammers/Science Photo Library, p189 (bottom) John Lythgoe/Planet Eart Pictures, p190 Natural History Museum, p191 (top) B and C Alexander/NHPA, p191 (bottom) Kevin Schafer/NHPA, p193 Kim Taylor/Bruce Coleman Ltd., p194 (top) ANT/NHPA, p194 (bottom) Gordon Langsbury/Bruce Coleman Ltd. p198 (top) Mary Evans Picture Library, p198 (mid) Frans Lanting/Bruce Coleman Ltd., p198 (bottom) Daniel Heuclin/NHPA, p202 (left) Mark Edwards/Still Pictures, p202 (right) Harry Nor-Hansen/Science Photo Library, p206 (left) Heather Angel, p206 (right, both) Laurie Campbell/NHPA, p211 (top) European Space Agency/Science Photo Library, p211 (bottom) Herbert Girardet/Still Pictures, p214 Nigel Cattlin/Holt Studios International, p217 Stephen Dalton/NHPA, p220 Nigel Cattlin/Holt Studios International, p222 (top) Nigel Cattlin/Holt Studios International, p222 (bottom) Popperfoto, p224 (left) J Allan Cash Ltd., p224 (right) David Neele/Tony Stone, p225 Marcelo Brodsky/Science Photo Library, p226 Caroline Thompson, p228 Robert Dowling/Oxford Scientific Films, p229 Birds Eye Walls Ltd., p233(left and centre) Caroline Thompson, p233 (right) Sally and Richard Greenhill, p240 Sean Sprague/Panos Pictures, p241 Hulton Deutsch, p244 David Woodfall/Tony Stone, p245 PPL, p247 (top right) Colin Varndell/Bruce Coleman Ltd., p247 (centre right) Trevor Barrett/Bruce Coleman Ltd., p247 (bottm left) Erik Bjurstrom/Bruce Coleman Ltd., p247 (bottom right) Laurie Campbell/NHPA

Contents

LORETO COLLEGE LIBRARY MANCHESTER

From chemicals to organisms

Living processes

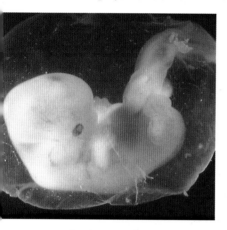

Organisms in their environment

Managing organisms

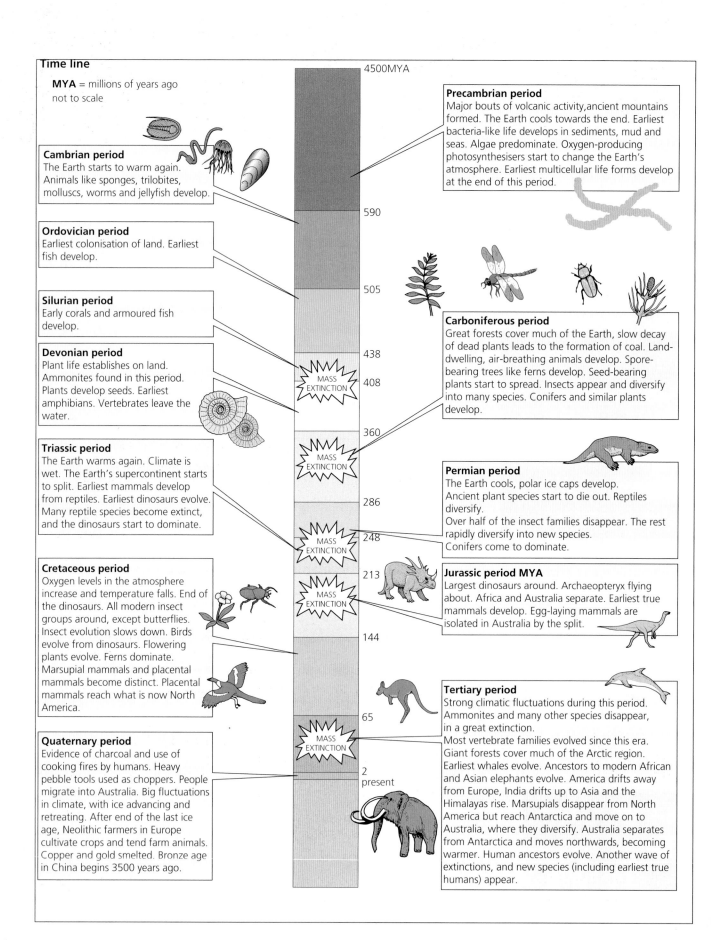

Time line

MYA = millions of years ago
not to scale

Cambrian period
The Earth starts to warm again. Animals like sponges, trilobites, molluscs, worms and jellyfish develop.

Ordovician period
Earliest colonisation of land. Earliest fish develop.

Silurian period
Early corals and armoured fish develop.

Devonian period
Plant life establishes on land. Ammonites found in this period. Plants develop seeds. Earliest amphibians. Vertebrates leave the water.

Triassic period
The Earth warms again. Climate is wet. The Earth's supercontinent starts to split. Earliest mammals develop from reptiles. Earliest dinosaurs evolve. Many reptile species become extinct, and the dinosaurs start to dominate.

Cretaceous period
Oxygen levels in the atmosphere increase and temperature falls. End of the dinosaurs. All modern insect groups around, except butterflies. Insect evolution slows down. Birds evolve from dinosaurs. Flowering plants evolve. Ferns dominate. Marsupial mammals and placental mammals become distinct. Placental mammals reach what is now North America.

Quaternary period
Evidence of charcoal and use of cooking fires by humans. Heavy pebble tools used as choppers. People migrate into Australia. Big fluctuations in climate, with ice advancing and retreating. After end of the last ice age, Neolithic farmers in Europe cultivate crops and tend farm animals. Copper and gold smelted. Bronze age in China begins 3500 years ago.

4500MYA

590

505

438

408

MASS EXTINCTION

360

MASS EXTINCTION

286

248

MASS EXTINCTION

213

MASS EXTINCTION

144

65

MASS EXTINCTION

2
present

Precambrian period
Major bouts of volcanic activity, ancient mountains formed. The Earth cools towards the end. Earliest bacteria-like life develops in sediments, mud and seas. Algae predominate. Oxygen-producing photosynthesisers start to change the Earth's atmosphere. Earliest multicellular life forms develop at the end of this period.

Carboniferous period
Great forests cover much of the Earth, slow decay of dead plants leads to the formation of coal. Land-dwelling, air-breathing animals develop. Spore-bearing trees like ferns develop. Seed-bearing plants start to spread. Insects appear and diversify into many species. Conifers and similar plants develop.

Permian period
The Earth cools, polar ice caps develop. Ancient plant species start to die out. Reptiles diversify.
Over half of the insect families disappear. The rest rapidly diversify into new species.
Conifers come to dominate.

Jurassic period MYA
Largest dinosaurs around. Archaeopteryx flying about. Africa and Australia separate. Earliest true mammals develop. Egg-laying mammals are isolated in Australia by the split.

Tertiary period
Strong climatic fluctuations during this period. Ammonites and many other species disappear, in a great extinction.
Most vertebrate families evolved since this era. Giant forests cover much of the Arctic region. Earliest whales evolve. Ancestors to modern African and Asian elephants evolve. America drifts away from Europe, India drifts up to Asia and the Himalayas rise. Marsupials disappear from North America but reach Antarctica and move on to Australia, where they diversify. Australia separates from Antarctica and moves northwards, becoming warmer. Human ancestors evolve. Another wave of extinctions, and new species (including earliest true humans) appear.

The *prebiotic* soup

Learning objectives

By the end of this chapter you should be able to:

- **explain** how scientists can estimate the age of the Earth
- **explain** the term 'prebiotic soup'
- **suggest** how complex chemicals may form from simple molecules
- **explain** what a biologist means by the term 'life'

1.1 The early Earth

What were conditions like on the early Earth?

Scientists think the Earth is roughly 4 500 000 000 (4.5 billion) years old. This figure has been estimated using data from the decay of radioactive elements found in meteorites. Current theories assume that meteorites and the Earth formed at roughly the same time. Since the oldest meteorites are about 4.5 billion years old, this suggests that the Earth is a similar age.

The Earth formed when millions of rocks and particles of dust from the Sun gathered together under the influence of gravity. As they fell together, they got hotter and produced a molten lump which became the Earth.

The Earth began to cool as heat radiated into space. The outer surface cooled to form a crust rather like the skin on a bowl of rice pudding. Radioactive decay of elements inside the Earth generated more heat in the central core. This pushed molten rock out through volcanoes.

Chemical reactions inside the Earth also produced a collection of gases which reached the surface and were held there by the Earth's gravitational field. Over millions of years an atmosphere rich in water vapour, hydrogen, carbon monoxide and nitrogen developed. This atmosphere was very different from our modern oxygen-rich air.

A visitor to the Earth just under 4 billion years ago would have found a planet with the beginnings of an atmosphere, oceans of liquid water and many active volcanoes. The atmosphere contained no oxygen and therefore no ozone, so ultraviolet light from the Sun passed straight through to the planet's surface. There would have been no signs of even the simplest forms of life.

Summary of the early Earth

- Scientists can estimate the age of the Earth from elements in meteorites.
- The atmosphere of the early Earth contained no oxygen.

1.2 The origin of life

What is life?

It is easy to distinguish between a living sheep, a dead sheep, a cardigan made of wool and a pair of plastic knitting needles. The living sheep is obviously the only thing that is alive – but what do we mean by alive?

The living sheep:
- takes in food
- uses oxygen to release energy from food (respires)
- produces wastes

- reproduces itself
- grows and develops
- responds to the environment
- dies

We can apply these simple characteristics to large complex organisms to distinguish between living, once-living (dead) and non-living. However, when life began, organisms were much simpler and this distinction would have been more difficult. Even today it can be difficult to decide whether simple micro-organisms are alive or dead.

For example, a sheep may suffer from a disease called scrapie. Scrapie is caused by a tiny virus-like organism that does not feed, take in oxygen, produce wastes or grow. It can only reproduce itself by using the chemical machinery of the sheep's cells. So is it alive? The scrapie prion is considered to be alive, because it can produce millions of copies of itself, even though it needs a living sheep cell to do it. This ability to copy itself, called **self-replication**, seems to be the essential feature of a living organism.

How did life begin?

In the early 1950s, two American scientists, called Stanley Miller and Harold Urey, created a model of the early Earth in their laboratory. This model contained water and the same mixture of gases as that present in the early atmosphere. The scientists passed an electric spark (see figure 1) through the mixture to mimic the effect of the many thunderstorms thought to be active in the early atmosphere.

After running their model for several days, Miller and Urey analysed the chemicals inside. To their surprise they found simple amino acids – the building blocks of proteins. The main surprise, however, was not that amino acids were present, but that many of the thousands of other chemicals that *could* have been produced were not. It seemed as though their model had produced exactly the chemicals needed for life, and ignored the rest. It may be that life developed using these chemicals because they were common.

Many researchers continued these early Earth experiments and produced a rich collection of chemicals over the years. The researchers assumed that this mixture was similar to the oceans of the early Earth. They called it the **prebiotic soup**.

If it formed today, the prebiotic soup would not last long in our oxygen-rich atmosphere. Most of the chemicals would be oxidised to water and carbon dioxide, and millions of bacteria would absorb any complex chemicals left.

1 **a** Why did the researchers call the mixture prebiotic?
b Do you think any of the chemicals in the flask were alive?
c What was the concentration of amino acids in the mixture after 125 hours?

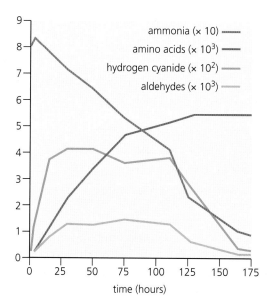

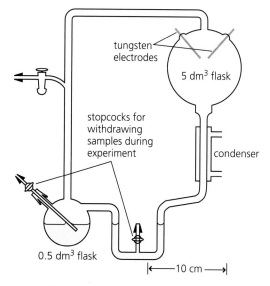

Source: *The Origins of Life on Earth*, by Stanley Miller and Leslie Orgel, Prentice Hall, 1974.

Figure 1

How did self-replication start?

Life is not just a soup of simple amino acids. Life is able to reproduce itself, or self-replicate. Self-replication needs a molecule to carry information from one generation to the next. In living things today, that molecule is DNA, deoxyribonucleic acid. You can read more about DNA in chapter 2, *Chemicals of life*. Just over 3.5 billion years ago, the oceans would have contained molecules of nucleic acids and proteins that could reproduce themselves. This could be defined as the beginning of life.

Chemical activities like self-replication depend on carefully controlled concentrations and suitable supplies of energy to drive reactions. The early self-replicating molecules were probably surrounded by a complex mixture of other chemicals. These chemicals were to develop into enzymes, cell membranes and other essential parts of the cell. At first these collections of chemicals would probably have been loosely bound to mineral particles, so that they could exchange materials easily with the prebiotic soup. Mineral ions may also have acted as catalysts to drive some of the chemical reactions needed for these early life forms.

How did the first cells develop?

At some point, a flat sheet of fatty molecules with lumps of protein stuck in it developed (figure 2). This would have been a random event, but it meant that the molecules of life could be held together inside a bag – the first cell was born. Enclosing the chemicals in a membrane was more efficient than allowing them to be washed around in the prebiotic soup. The first cell probably formed less than 3.5 billion years ago.

Life now consisted of a cell that had cut itself off from its environment with a membrane. A series of reactions within the cell provided energy for growth. These early reactions were probably similar to the reactions that became

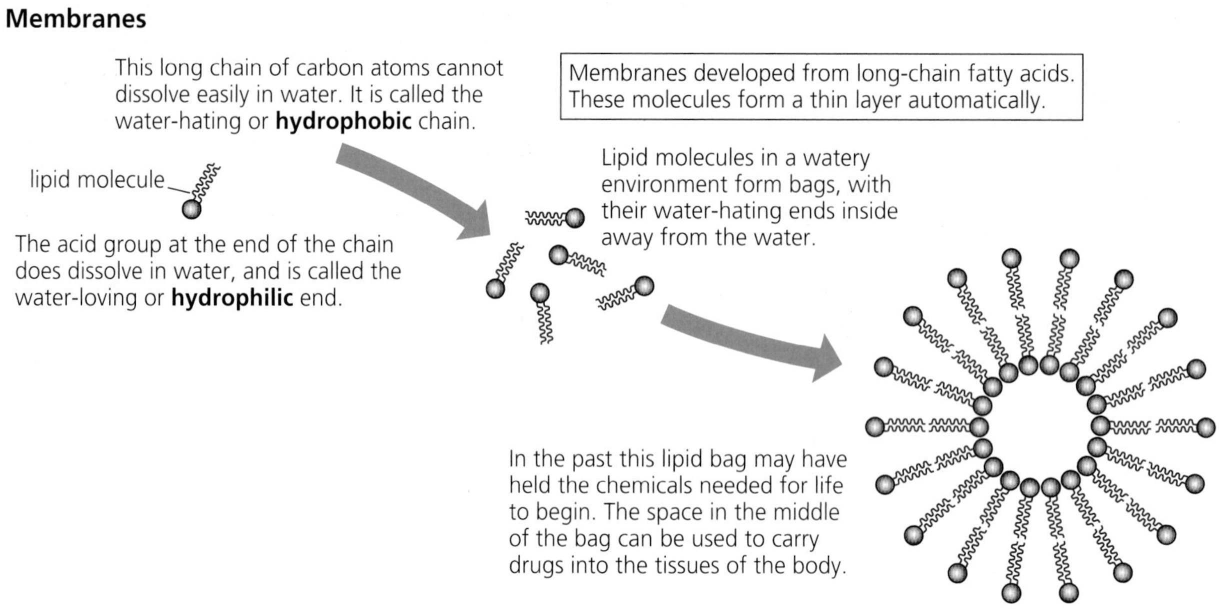

Membranes
This long chain of carbon atoms cannot dissolve easily in water. It is called the water-hating or **hydrophobic** chain.
Membranes developed from long-chain fatty acids. These molecules form a thin layer automatically.
lipid molecule
The acid group at the end of the chain does dissolve in water, and is called the water-loving or **hydrophilic** end.
Lipid molecules in a watery environment form bags, with their water-hating ends inside away from the water.
In the past this lipid bag may have held the chemicals needed for life to begin. The space in the middle of the bag can be used to carry drugs into the tissues of the body.

Figure 2

anaerobic respiration (see chapter 4, *Energy transfers*). As time went on, reactions within the cells became more sophisticated and enzymes replaced the mineral ion catalysts. The next significant step was to develop a way to use sunlight as a source of energy.

About 3 billion years ago, a type of **photosynthesis** came about that could release oxygen to the atmosphere. Life then developed in the oceans to produce a biotic soup of simple bacteria. Some could carry out photosynthesis and release oxygen. Others consumed the organic material left over from the prebiotic soup, or that produced by the photosynthetic types. Over the next 2 billion years the organisms became more complicated, and membrane structures developed to form cells with a membrane-bound nucleus. All this happened in the oceans, where the water protected the life forms from dangerous ultraviolet radiation.

It took over 2 billion years for oxygen levels to reach even 1% of the current atmospheric level (figure 3). We know this because iron-rich minerals absorbed oxygen and changed from iron (II) (ferrous) to iron (III) (ferric) forms. Geologists can follow these changes in rocks of particular ages (Table 1).

Table 1

Time (billions of years)	Nature of iron-containing rock
<1.8	all iron II
1.8 – 3.3	iron II and III, probably because of reaction with oxygen in solution
>3.2	all iron III

Oxygen rise on Earth
Oxygen concentration (fraction of present atmospheric level)
1
0.1
0.01
0.001
0.0001
27
20
10
8
6
4
2
Present
Time (1000 millions years ago)

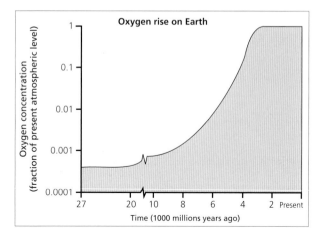

Figure 3

2 a Draw a flow chart showing the important stages in the development of life from 4.5 billion years ago to 400 million years ago.

b Australopithecus is probably one of the earliest human-like creatures. Skulls just over 2 million years old have been found in Africa. On a scale diagram of the Earth's life, Australopithecus is 2 cm from the present. Calculate the scale distance to each of the important stages on your flow chart.

Figure 4 The earliest living organisms were just one cell. These were the ancestors of modern bacteria, but they also gave rise to all multicellular animals and plants.

The ozone that formed from the oxygen began to screen out some of the dangerous ultraviolet radiation from the Sun. By the beginning of the Cambrian period, 590 million years ago, the surface waters were safe for life. Photosynthesising organisms could capture more light, so things then began to speed up – in geological terms. In less than 200 million years the level of oxygen in the atmosphere had increased ten-fold, and the land was now protected sufficiently from ultraviolet radiation for living organisms to survive there. The first land plants, made up of cells that contained a membrane-bound nucleus and many of the structures we see in modern plants, probably developed roughly 400 million years ago.

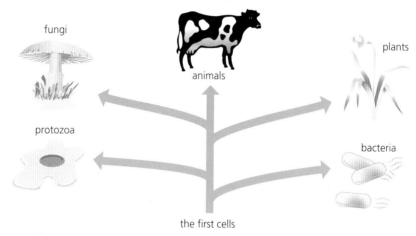

Summary of the origin of life

- Living things: take in food; respire; produce wastes; reproduce; grow and develop; respond to their environment and die.
- Electrical discharges in the early atmosphere probably produced the chemicals needed for life to begin. These chemicals formed the prebiotic soup.
- Self-replicating molecules were probably the start of living organisms on Earth.
- Photosynthetic organisms produced oxygen which gave rise to the ozone layer. This screened out ultraviolet light and made it safe for living organisms to colonise the land.

Chemicals of life

2

Learning objectives

By the end of this chapter you should be able to:

- **list** the chemicals that make up living materials
- **describe** the features that make them suitable for these roles
- **describe** their roles in living organisms
- **explain** what happens if there is a shortage of these molecules in the body

Living things are made of various chemicals. Each of these chemicals has properties that enable it to do its particular job. The chemicals that make up living things are sorted into groups:

- carbohydrates
- proteins
- fats
- vitamins
- minerals
- nucleic acids
- water.

2.1 Carbohydrates

Carbohydrates are very familiar substances to us. Some carbohydrates are easy to break down in the body and these are used as energy sources. A gram of carbohydrate releases about 17 kJ of energy. Other carbohydrates resist chemical or physical breakdown. These are useful for building cell walls and support structures (see figure 1 and table 1).

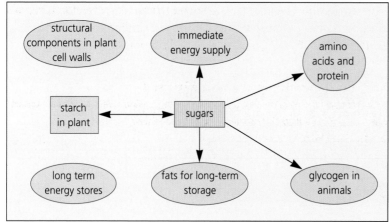

Figure 1

Table 1 *Carbohydrates and their uses.*

Carbohydrates used as energy sources	Carbohydrates used as structural materials
Glucose	Cellulose
Sucrose (cane sugar)	Agar
Lactose (sugar in milk)	
Starch	
Glycogen	

What are sugars?

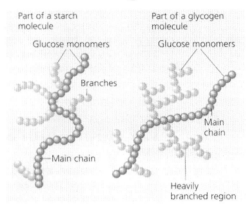

Part of a starch molecule

Glucose monomers

Branches

Main chain

Part of a glycogen molecule

Glucose monomers

Main chain

Heavily branched region

Figure 2

Carbohydrate molecules are made up of small sub-units called sugars. Their names end in '-ose'. Sugars are made from carbon, hydrogen and oxygen atoms arranged in a ring-shaped molecule. These molecules are small, taste sweet and dissolve in water. Sugars fuel respiration and provide cells with the energy they need. Dissolved sugars diffuse into cells from sap, blood and other fluids. Sugary fruits and nectar attract animals to plants, to aid pollination and seed dispersal. Groups of sugar molecules can link together to make larger molecules and long chain polymers called **polysaccharides** (figure 2).

How are polysaccharides used by organisms?

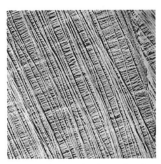

Cellulose fibres make plant cell walls strong, but slightly flexible.

Agar helps kelp survive at low tide by holding water which stops it drying out.

Polysaccharides do not dissolve easily because their molecules are so large. Cellulose and starch are made of straight chains of glucose sub-units with few branches (see figure 2). Glycogen is a polysaccharide found in animal cells. It is used as an energy source, not for building cells.

Plants make glucose during photosynthesis and convert it to starch. The starch accumulates as grains in chloroplasts and in specialised storage structures such as potato tubers. Starch is a useful storage molecule because it is insoluble and does not interfere with the water balance of the cell. It can be converted back to glucose easily and used for respiration when necessary.

Cellulose molecules are also chains of glucose sub-units, but linked slightly differently from those in starch. Cellulose molecules are rigid and resist squashing. In a plant cell wall, the cellulose molecules are linked together to make small fibres which form an open mesh. These cell walls are long-lasting because only a few microbes have the enzyme cellulase that can attack cellulose.

Agar is a polysaccharide found in algae. It traps water in a three-dimensional mesh and holds it, even in a dry environment. This trapped water prevents seaweeds drying out during low tides. The water-loaded agar molecules resist squashing, but are flexible and elastic which makes them ideal skeleton materials for large algae. Cartilage in joints contains a substance similar to agar, which makes it flexible while still acting as a cushion and support.

1 In which of the following plant organs might you expect to find starch?
a banana (fruit), carrot (root), a potato (underground storage stem), a stick of celery (leaf stem), a peanut (seed), a cabbage leaf (leaf), a Brussels sprout (bud), a cauliflower (flower)
2 What chemical elements do carbohydrates contain?

Summary of carbohydrates

- Carbohydrates contain carbon, hydrogen and oxygen. They include sugars and starches.
- Carbohydrates form good energy sources and support materials.

2.2 Fats

What are fats?

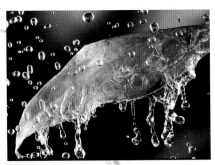

A waxy coating on the outer surface of a leaf stops moisture escaping from the interior, and repels rain.

Oils and fats are both types of **lipids**. Oils are liquid at room temperature, while fats are solid. Lipids contain carbon, hydrogen and oxygen, but the amount of oxygen is much less than in carbohydrates. Lipids are an excellent source and store of energy. They release 38 kJ of energy per gram when cells respire them, which is more than twice as much as carbohydrate.

Triglycerides, phospholipids and **steroids** are different types of lipids. These are excellent molecules for constructing barriers, such as cell membranes and waterproof coatings. Triglycerides are used as energy stores in plant seeds and in animals. Phospholipids are used in cell membranes. Steroids have many different roles. They include vitamins A and D, bile salts which help the body digest fats, and some hormones. Cholesterol is a raw material used to manufacture other steroids.

Triglyceride molecules are made of a 'backbone' of glycerol joined to three fatty acid sub-units (figure 3). The types of fatty acids affect the nature of the triglyceride. In a **saturated fat**, most of the carbon atoms in the fatty acid chains are joined to each other by just one bond, and the rest of the bonds are used to link with hydrogen atoms. In an unsaturated fat, some of the carbon atoms in the fatty acid chains are joined by double bonds.

Figure 3

Saturated fats

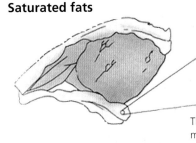

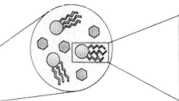

The fat in meat is a mixture of different fat molecules. It also contains a few other substances such as cholesterol and vitamins.

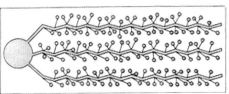

A fat molecule is made of glycerol with three fatty acids attached. The type of fatty acid can make the fat hard or oily. Most fats from animals are saturated.

Sunflower oil is a mixture of different fat molecules. Oils are fats that are liquid at room temperature.

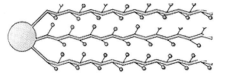

Plant fats are usually unsaturated. Fats containing the least hydrogen are called polyunsaturated fats.

3 Why do you think some fats are hard, like Cheddar cheese, but others are soft, like soft margarine?

Lipids with a high proportion of saturated fatty acids, such as lard or paraffin wax, are solid at room temperature, and are termed fats. Lipids containing a high proportion of unsaturated fatty acids, like sunflower oil, are liquid at room temperature.

Summary of fats

• Fats and oils are both types of lipids.

• Lipids are water barriers, and rich energy sources.

2.3 Proteins

The cytoplasm in a cell is largely protein and water, and the fluids around cells often contain **proteins** too. There are thousands of different types of protein, all doing different jobs (table 2). Some, such as those in cytoplasm, are used as building materials. **Enzymes** are proteins which catalyse chemical reactions in cells. Some hormones, for example insulin, are proteins.

Protein function	Example
Catalysing chemical reactions	Enzymes have pockets on the surface of the molecule. Other chemicals bind to the pockets and are brought close together, so that they react.
Changing shape	Proteins in muscle cell fibres move across each other and shorten the fibre, causing muscle contraction.
Trapping water molecules	Proteins in cytoplasm hold water within the cell.
Binding to other substances	Haemoglobin in red blood cells binds with oxygen and carries it round the body.
Coagulating	Blood-clotting proteins can be activated to produce a blood clot and seal a cut blood vessel. Antibodies bind to microbes and parasites that enter the body.

Table 2 Functions of proteins

Four polypeptide chains make up the haemoglobin molecule. Each chain contains 574 amino acids

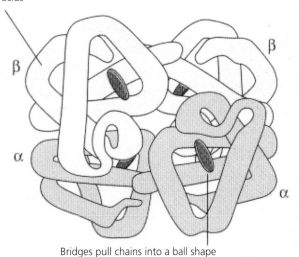

Bridges pull chains into a ball shape

Globular proteins have amino acid chains twisted into a loose bundle. The molecules are too large to dissolve in water, but they can form a suspension.

Figure 4 Globular proteins, like haemoglobin in red blood cells, are made of chains of amino acids, called polypeptide chains, held together in a ball shape by cross-linking bridges.

What are proteins?

Proteins are long chains made up of small units called **amino acids**. There are many different amino acids, and our bodies use about 20 of them to make proteins. We can make most of the amino acids we need, but we have to take in a few of them in food. These are called the essential amino acids.

4 List three important polymers in living things.

5 Which element is found in protein but not in carbohydrates?

Amino acids contain carbon, hydrogen, oxygen and nitrogen atoms. Plants make amino acids from sugars and nitrate ions absorbed from the soil. Proteins in the diet release about 17 kJ of energy per gram, but they are only used to provide energy when other sources are badly depleted by fasting.

Each type of protein has a particular arrangement of amino acids. The amino acids link together to make a long chain, which coils up into a complicated three-dimensional shape (figure 4).

A protein's three-dimensional shape is crucial. If it is changed, the protein may no longer function and is said to be **denatured**. High temperatures and pH changes can change the shapes of proteins. Ions of metals such as mercury, cadmium and lead can link to proteins, particularly enzymes, and prevent them from functioning effectively.

Summary of proteins

- Proteins have many functions, including acting as catalysts.
- Changes to the shape of a protein can adversely affect its activity.

- Proteins contain nitrogen atoms as well as carbon, hydrogen and oxygen.

2.4 Vitamins and minerals

Vitamins are various substances which we group together because they are all needed by the body in minute quantities. They play vital roles in the body, such as helping enzymes to work.

Minerals are simple inorganic compounds, usually used in the body as ions. They may have a specific chemical role, or they may be used in a compound which forms part of a structure. If one particular vitamin or mineral is lacking in the body, a whole process, such as respiration, is slowed down and may not match the body's demands. The effects can be severe enough to cause an illness, called a deficiency disease. For example, iron is used in haemoglobin, the substance which carries oxygen in red blood cells. People who are short of iron become anaemic. They cannot make enough red blood cells so they cannot carry enough oxygen to meet the body's needs. They appear pale because of the shortage of red blood cells and feel tired because they do not have enough energy. You can read more about the vitamins and minerals we need in chapter 7, *Feeding*.

Note

The fact that we need vitamins was discovered before the actual compounds were identified, and so they were named vitamin A, vitamin B and so on.

Summary of vitamins and minerals

- Vitamins and minerals are required by the body in very small amounts to do specific tasks.

- A shortage of vitamins or minerals in the diet leads to a deficiency disease.

2.5 Nucleic acids

Nucleic acids are substances found in the nuclei of cells, but some are active in cytoplasm as well. There are two sorts of nucleic acid, deoxyribonucleic acid (DNA) and ribonucleic acid (RNA).

Both DNA and RNA are made up of sub-units called nucleotides arranged in long chains. The nucleotides are themselves made up of three parts – a sugar, a phosphate and a nucleic base. In DNA the sugar is deoxyribose. In RNA it is ribose. There are four different nucleic bases used in DNA, called adenine (A), thymine (T), cytosine (C) and guanine (G).

A single DNA molecule is made of two long strands of nucleotides running parallel to each other. They are joined by a base on one strand linking to a base on the other. A base only links to one other base, cytosine always links to guanine, and andenosine always links to thymine. This is called **base pairing**. The nucleotides along the length of the chain interact with each other, making the molecule spiral into a double helix, which looks like a twisted ladder.

A chromosome is a very long DNA molecule, wound round 'beads' of protein. The string of beads coils back on itself many times, making coiled loops. These are arranged round a protein core to form the chromosome. This complex structure allows a very large molecule to be packaged into a small volume (see figure 5).

DNA carries the information that is needed for cell activities. When cells divide, DNA is copied so that the information is passed to the new cells. Cells divide time after time, so they have to be able to copy the DNA accurately every time.

A molecule that carries information needs to be stable, and the other molecules in the cell should not react with it or change its structure. The tight coils of DNA within the chromosomes keep it stable. Even so, there are chemicals called mutagens that can damage DNA or RNA. As a result of this damage, the information encoded in the molecule becomes scrambled which can lead to malfunctions. How DNA encodes information and is copied accurately is explained in chapter 3, *Cells*.

What does RNA do?

There are different forms of RNA, all of which help make proteins. In the nucleus, DNA carries a code which sets out the order in which amino acids have to be connected together to make proteins. mRNA carries information about this order of amino acids from the nucleus into the cytoplasm. tRNA brings amino acids to the growing protein molecule, and rRNA makes up ribosomes, which join the amino acids together. The details of how proteins are made in cells is explained in chapter 18, *Genetics*.

Summary of nucleic acids

- Nucleic acids carry the information needed to run a cell and manufacture its proteins.

DNA and RNA structures

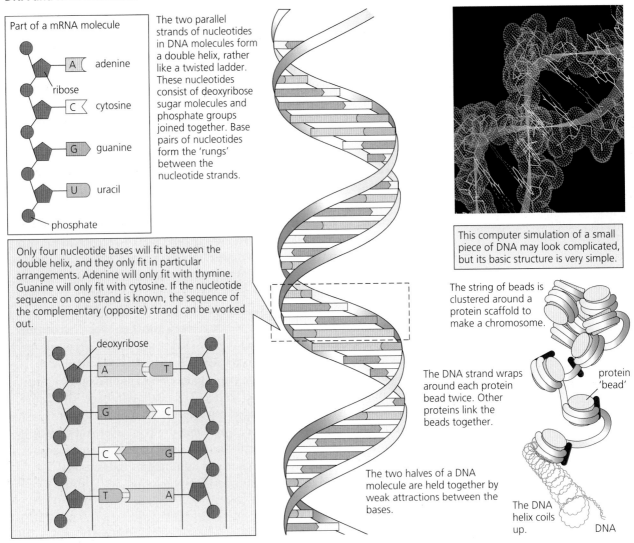

Part of a mRNA molecule

adenine

ribose

cytosine

guanine

uracil

phosphate

The two parallel strands of nucleotides in DNA molecules form a double helix, rather like a twisted ladder. These nucleotides consist of deoxyribose sugar molecules and phosphate groups joined together. Base pairs of nucleotides form the 'rungs' between the nucleotide strands.

Only four nucleotide bases will fit between the double helix, and they only fit in particular arrangements. Adenine will only fit with thymine. Guanine will only fit with cytosine. If the nucleotide sequence on one strand is known, the sequence of the complementary (opposite) strand can be worked out.

deoxyribose

This computer simulation of a small piece of DNA may look complicated, but its basic structure is very simple.

The string of beads is clustered around a protein scaffold to make a chromosome.

The DNA strand wraps around each protein bead twice. Other proteins link the beads together.

protein 'bead'

The two halves of a DNA molecule are held together by weak attractions between the bases.

The DNA helix coils up.

DNA

Figure 5

2.6 Water

Life evolved in water. The earliest organisms could use as much water as they needed, because they lived in the oceans. Their body fluids would have had a very similar composition to the sea water in which they lived. When living things colonised land, they kept their water-based life processes. Even now a large proportion of any living thing is water.

Water has many useful properties.

- Important biochemicals dissolve in the watery cytoplasm of a cell and are transported in watery body fluids or sap.
- The chemical reactions of the body take place in solution, so they need a watery environment.
- Water supports and cushions objects immersed in it. If organisms that live in water have air pockets or a moderate fat content, they are very buoyant and need very little in the way of a skeleton to support them. Even in land organisms, water is important for support. Because it does not compress easily, it makes plant cells rigid and thus supports the plant. Water also holds the shape of an earthworm, providing pressure inside the segments.
- Liquid water molecules attract each other, and it takes energy to separate them. In the summer, a lake can absorb a tremendous amount of heat energy from the Sun without its temperature rising much. This provides a thermally stable environment for water organisms. The attraction between water molecules at the surface of a pond or lake leads to surface tension, which is strong enough for lightweight insects to live on.
- When water freezes, it expands and becomes less dense. When ice forms in winter or in cold regions, the ice, being less dense, floats on top of the liquid water, where aquatic inhabitants can survive.

6   Why are frogs able to survive at the bottom of a pond, even when the pond is iced over?

The cold waters of the antarctic continental shelf support a rich ecosystem of plankton and fish, including this crocodile fish, under the floating ice.

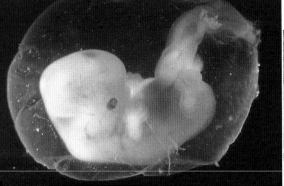

The amniotic fluid in the uterus supports the developing embryo.

Surface tension provides a 'skin' on a pond that will support a pond-skater, and can trap its prey.

Water evaporating from the dog's tongue provides an important cooling effect.

Summary of water

- Water has many functions inside cells. Living things take advantage of its properties in the environment.

Investigations

Vitamin C is destroyed when fruit and vegetables are chopped, cooked or kept in storage. The amount of vitamin C in a juice sample can be estimated by using it to decolourise a 1 cm^3 sample of 1% DCPIP. The more vitamin C there is the less it takes to change blue DCPIP to colourless. Plan an investigation to find out how the vitamin C content of stored juice is affected after it has been opened.

Cells

3

Learning objectives

By the end of this chapter you should be able to:

- **explain** how we can view and study cells
- **draw and label** a cell diagram
- **describe** the functions of cell components
- **list** the differences between animal and plant cells
- **describe** how cells are arranged in tissues and organs

- **explain** how materials enter and leave cells
- **explain** how enzymes work
- **describe** how new cells are made
- **explain** how cell reproduction sometimes goes wrong

3.1 Types of cells

What do cells look like?

Feeding, reproduction and all the other processes of life go on within single-celled organisms. The simplest cells are bacterial cells (see figure 1).

Plant and animal cells are more complex than bacterial cells, containing more structures and a network of membranes dividing the cytoplasm into compartments (see figure 2). Embedded in these membranes are enzymes that control all sorts of chemical reactions. The network of membranes gives a very large area for these chemical activities. Dividing the cytoplasm into compartments means that many different activities can take place at the same time without interfering with each other.

A typical bacterial cell

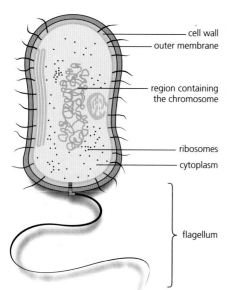

cell wall
outer membrane

region containing
the chromosome

ribosomes
cytoplasm

flagellum

Figure 1

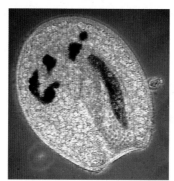

A small protozoan is digested inside the single cell of a larger one.

Single-celled organisms divide their cell contents by binary fission to make two new individuals.

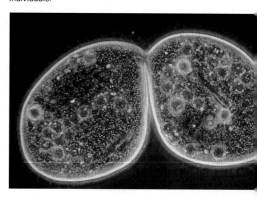

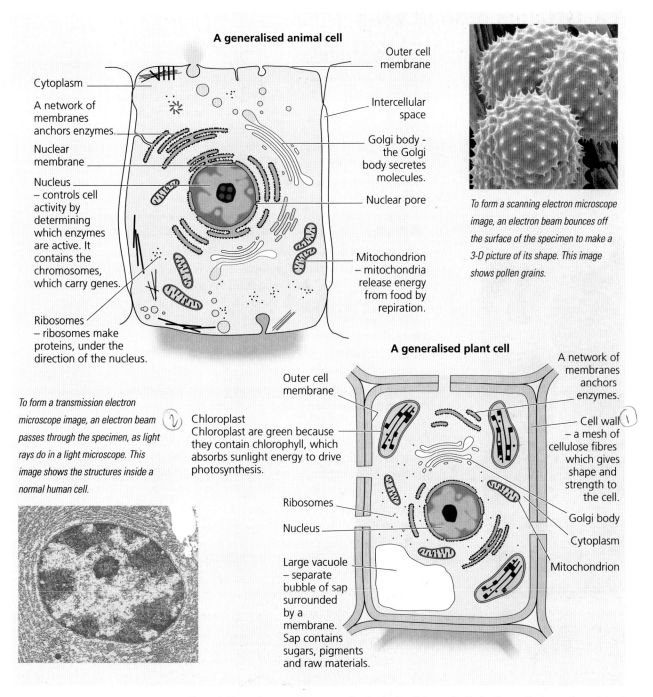

A generalised animal cell

Cytoplasm

A network of membranes anchors enzymes.

Nuclear membrane

Nucleus – controls cell activity by determining which enzymes are active. It contains the chromosomes, which carry genes.

Ribosomes – ribosomes make proteins, under the direction of the nucleus.

Outer cell membrane

Intercellular space

Golgi body - the Golgi body secretes molecules.

Nuclear pore

Mitochondrion – mitochondria release energy from food by repiration.

To form a scanning electron microscope image, an electron beam bounces off the surface of the specimen to make a 3-D picture of its shape. This image shows pollen grains.

To form a transmission electron microscope image, an electron beam passes through the specimen, as light rays do in a light microscope. This image shows the structures inside a normal human cell.

A generalised plant cell

Outer cell membrane

Chloroplast
Chloroplast are green because they contain chlorophyll, which absorbs sunlight energy to drive photosynthesis.

Ribosomes

Nucleus

Large vacuole – separate bubble of sap surrounded by a membrane. Sap contains sugars, pigments and raw materials.

A network of membranes anchors enzymes.

Cell wall – a mesh of cellulose fibres which gives shape and strength to the cell.

Golgi body

Cytoplasm

Mitochondrion

Figure 2 These diagrams show generalised animal and plant cells. Real cells vary in shape, size and detail.

Summary of types of cells

- Bacterial cells do not have a nucleus or separate structures for releasing energy from food.
- Animal and plant cells have a separate nucleus, mitochondria and chloroplasts.

- The cytoplasm in plant and animal cells is divided into compartments allowing different activities to take place simultaneously.
- Plant cells are surrounded by a rigid cell wall and contain chloroplasts.

3.2 Organisation of cells

How do different cells do different jobs?

1 List three differences between animal cells and plant cells.
2 What are the functions of:
   a the nucleus
   b the outer membrane?
3 Why are some plant cells green?

In multicellular organisms, all the functions of life are divided up between groups of cells, and each group of cells is specialised to do one job particularly well.

These specialised cells have adaptations to their structure which help them do their job more effectively, and which make them different from other cells. For example, red blood cells are specialised for carrying oxygen, and have a different structure from cells that carry nervous impulses.

Cells specialised for the same job are grouped together to make a **tissue**. The cells in a tissue are supplied with the particular materials they need. They are often linked together and their activity is co-ordinated. For example, muscle tissue is made of muscle cells which are specialised for contraction.

Tissues don't work in isolation. Several different kinds of cells may be needed to carry out a particular task. For example, to get water to a photosynthesising cell in a leaf, first the water must be taken in from the soil by root hair cells, and then other cells in the root make a path to the xylem transporting channels. In these channels, waterproof cells act as drainpipes up the plant, and then other cells distribute water to the photosynthesising tissue.

Groups of cells doing different jobs but contributing to a common purpose form organs. For example, the eye is an organ whose function is to sense changes in the environment by detecting changes in the pattern of light. The light patterns are converted into nervous impulses, which are interpreted by the brain. Several different tissues are needed to carry out this task. The retina is a tissue made of two types of light-sensitive cells. A layer of cells provides the retina with nutrients and a different set of cells carries the impulses generated by the retina to the brain. Other tissues focus light on the retina and regulate the amount of light entering the eye. Yet more tissues protect and support the eye.

Impulses from the eye are interpreted by visual centres in the brain. Appropriate responses to this information are brought about by other tissues and organs in the body. The nervous system carries all the information needed to co-ordinate responses in the body. Most organs are part of a system like this which carries out one of the functions of life. Living organisms are made up of many systems, co-ordinated together to produce an active functioning individual.

4 List the systems in the human body.
5 Which of the following are organs?
   leaf, petal, hair follicle, liver, root, muscle, brain, flower, pancreas, tongue
6 Name three parts of the human circulatory system.

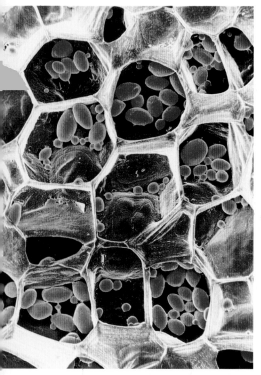

Potato tubers are made up of cells specialised for storage. Sugars from photosythesis are stored as starch grains.

How cells are organised

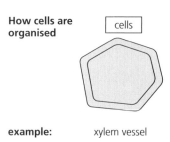

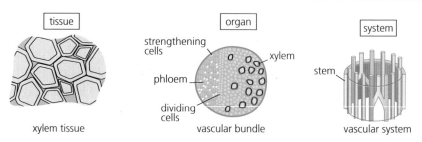

example: xylem vessel   xylem tissue   vascular bundle   vascular system

Figure 3 Cells are organised into systems.

Why are cells so small?

*These cells are specialised for cleaning and warming air entering the lungs The 'hairs' on their surface, called **cilia**, increase their surface area, trapping dirt and moving it up and out of the lungs.*

If cells carry out a function, such as making useful materials, surely bigger cells would do their job more efficiently than smaller cells. This may be true of factories, but it is not true of cells. The processes that take place within cells depend on the supply of materials from outside, and on the prompt removal of anything produced in the cell. Materials are exchanged through the outer cell membrane. The larger the surface area of the outer cell membrane, the more materials can be exchanged between the cell and its surroundings. But, in very large cells it may take too long for materials to pass from the surface to the cell's centre, or in the opposite direction. The critical factor is the relationship between the area of the cell's surface, where materials are exchanged, and the volume of the cell, where the materials are consumed and produced (see figure 4).

Cells can increase their surface area with long thin projections which have a large surface but a relatively small volume. Cells specialised for absorbing materials, such as the cells lining the gut, have projections called microvilli. Red blood cells have a very unusual adaptation which increases their surface area while reducing their volume. After they have developed, the nucleus collapses and the cell surfaces sink down, producing the familiar doughnut shape. It is thought that this enables the red blood cell to exchange more oxygen than a spherical cell.

Cell shapes

A sphere has the smallest surface area for a particular volume.

Making a sphere into a barrel shape enlarges the surface area. This shape is good for storage.

Flattening into a leaf shape gives a large surface area. This shape is efficient for exchanging materials.

A cube is a compact shape. Large cubes have a small surface area for their volume.

Narrow projections increase the surface area a huge amount. This shape is good fo absorbing.

Figure 4

7 Give two differences between a bacterial cell and a cell lining the airway to the lungs (as shown in the photo above).

Summary of organisation of cells

- Cells doing different jobs have different structures.
- Cells doing the same job are grouped together in tissues.
- Different tissues work together in an organ to perform a specific task.
- Organs within systems work together to carry out life functions.

3.3 Moving substances in and out of cells

Animal and plant cells are surrounded by a watery fluid. In mammals, this fluid is called **tissue fluid** and comes from the blood (see chapter 5, *Circulation*). In plants it comes from plant sap. The fluid contains a mixture of the ions and molecules that cells need, such as glucose, amino acids and oxygen. Waste materials, like carbon dioxide, are released from cells into the fluid, to be disposed of by specialised organs in the organism. Cells may also release useful materials into the fluid, to be used elsewhere in the body.

Everything that enters or leaves a cell passes through the outer cell membrane. This membrane influences how much of anything passes through it. Cell membranes are selectively permeable, because they allow some molecules to pass through but not others. They can even control the amount of some molecules that can pass through. Insulin, for example triggers a process in cell membranes that allows glucose to enter cells, though glucose cannot enter at other times.

How do substances move through membranes?

Diffusion is the main way in which dissolved substances (solutes) pass into cells. It is also the method by which gases move across the lung surface and through a leaf's surface, by which nutrients move from the gut into the blood and by which substances are filtered from the blood in the kidneys.

Particles (like atoms, molecules or ions) move randomly through their environment. This random movement spreads solutes out evenly through the whole solution. A concentration gradient exists where there is a difference in concentration of solute between different areas (figure 5). Particles tend to move along a concentration gradient from a region where there are many particles to a region where there are fewer.

Oxygen molecules diffuse from a high concentration in air in the lungs, to a lower concentration in the blood capillaries in the lungs. Substances move between and into cells in the same way. Small ions and molecules such as sodium, chloride, oxygen and carbon dioxide diffuse freely through fluids and membranes. Even medium sized nutrient molecules such as glucose readily diffuse through body fluids. However, large molecules such as proteins are too big to pass freely through cell membranes. Even small molecules cannot diffuse completely randomly inside organisms because they too may be restricted by cell membranes. Cell membranes can also prevent the diffusion of certain ions. For example, potassium ions are not often allowed to diffuse out of cells, because they are needed in larger amounts than is usually found in the surrounding fluid.

Figure 5

A concentration gradient

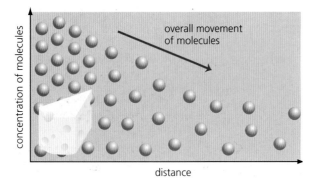

concentration of molecules

overall movement of molecules

distance

Figure 5

8 What controls the *direction* of diffusion of glucose between animal cells?

What affects the rate of diffusion?

The following factors influence the rate of diffusion along a concentration gradient.

- Small molecules diffuse faster than larger molecules.
- More soluble molecules diffuse faster than less soluble molecules.
- Diffusion works more efficiently if there is a large difference in concentrations: that is, the concentration gradient is steep.
- For diffusion through a membrane, the larger the surface, the more particles can pass through it.
- The further a substance has to travel, the longer it takes to diffuse. Diffusion is not a very effective way of moving materials over large distances.

Tissues that are specialised for the movement of materials by diffusion, like the alveoli of the lungs, are called **exchange surfaces**. Efficient exchange surfaces have:

- a large concentration gradient
- a large surface area. As the space inside the organism may be quite small, exchange surfaces are often tightly folded or highly branched to give a large surface area in a small volume
- a thin membrane, so that substances do not have to diffuse far
- a good transport system to ensure a continuous supply of the required substance at the surface
- another transport system which removes exchanged material quickly to keep a large difference in concentration.

9 Look at the photograph of the gut lining on page 64. Explain how its structure helps food molecules to diffuse from the gut into the lining cells as quickly as possible.

How does water move through membranes?

Osmosis is the diffusion of water molecules across a **partially-permeable membrane**. Water molecules will move from a high concentration of water, for example a dilute sugar solution, to a region where there are fewer water molecules, for example a more concentrated sugar solution, until the concentrations are equal.

Most cells are surrounded by watery solutions. Cells laden with sugars, ions, proteins and other soluble materials will draw water from the more dilute fluid around them. Cell membranes cannot control the movement of water, so if more and more water enters by osmosis, animal cells will expand and eventually burst.

Plant cell walls do not stretch much, so the cell wall will eventually resist the entry of any more water. A plant cell that is swollen with water is described as **turgid**. Turgid cells are important in holding a plant's shape.

If the fluid around cells is richer in solutes than the cell cytoplasm, water passes out from the cell. In this situation cells can become dehydrated. Dehydration damages animal cells and may kill them. For this reason, the concentration of animal body fluids is very tightly controlled. There is more about this in chapter 9, *Water balance*. The ability of a cell or fluid to draw water into itself from more dilute solutions is called its **water potential**. A concentrated sugar solution has a lower water potential than a dilute sugar solution, so water moves from the dilute sugar solution to the concentrated sugar solution. Water moves from regions of high water potential to regions of lower water potential.

What is active transport?

Sometimes diffusion is too slow, or the concentration gradient is not high enough or even the wrong way round to transport substances as cells require. For example, if a muscle cell has to work much harder than usual, diffusion cannot provide the extra glucose and oxygen it needs quickly enough. Instead, cells use energy to move materials through the membrane. This is **active transport**.

Sometimes substances cannot diffuse in the desired direction because the concentration gradient is unfavourable. This happens when cells need materials that are scarce in their environment. Cells can actively transport ions against a concentration gradient, and accumulate them within their cells. Root hair cells take up some mineral ions from soil water in this way.

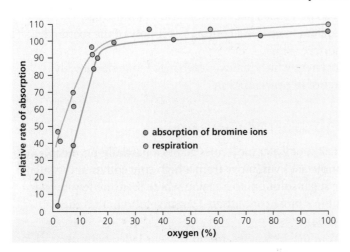

10 Give two differences between active transport and diffusion.

11 Slices of potato were placed in a solution of bromine. Oxygen was bubbled through in gradually increasing amounts and the relative rate of absorption recorded as shown in the graph on the left.

a What happens to the rate at which bromine is absorbed as the oxygen concentration increases?

b Why does this happen?

Summary of moving substances in and out of cells

- Cells have some control over substances entering or leaving them.
- Substances diffuse in or out of cells along a concentration gradient.
- In active transport, cells pump some chemicals against a concentration gradient.

- Osmosis is the movement of water by diffusion across a partially-permeable membrane.
- Substances diffuse from a region of high concentration to a region of lower concentration.

3.4 Making and breaking

Cells live by breaking substances down and making new ones. They use energy from respiration to drive these reactions. The chemical reactions in a living organism are called its **metabolism**.

Many biologically important reactions happen very slowly at room temperature. In a laboratory, a reaction can be speeded up by heating the reactants, but this isn't possible in a living cell. Instead, cell reactions are speeded up by enzymes.

How do enzymes work?

Enzymes are molecules that catalyse chemical reactions. They speed up the reaction without being permanently changed by it. All enzymes are proteins, and some need other molecules such as a B vitamin or a mineral ion before they can work. One enzyme molecule can catalyse the reaction of many thousands of reactant molecules each minute, so only a small number of enzyme molecules are needed to enable a reaction to go ahead smoothly.

Figure 6

The lock-and-key model

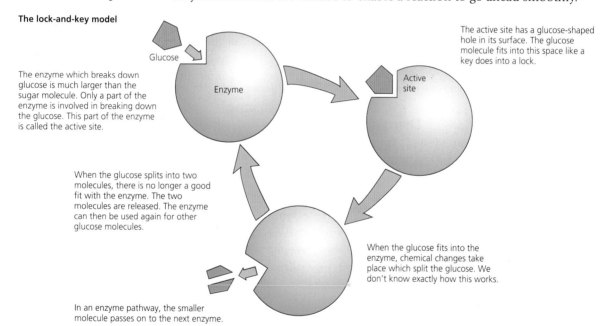

The enzyme which breaks down glucose is much larger than the sugar molecule. Only a part of the enzyme is involved in breaking down the glucose. This part of the enzyme is called the active site.

Glucose

Enzyme

The active site has a glucose-shaped hole in its surface. The glucose molecule fits into this space like a key does into a lock.

Active site

When the glucose splits into two molecules, there is no longer a good fit with the enzyme. The two molecules are released. The enzyme can then be used again for other glucose molecules.

When the glucose fits into the enzyme, chemical changes take place which split the glucose. We don't know exactly how this works.

In an enzyme pathway, the smaller molecule passes on to the next enzyme.

Enzymes bring molecules very close together so that reactions can take place (figure 6). They can also break molecules down, by straining them so that they split up. Any particular enzyme can only catalyse one or two similar reactions. Reactant molecules come in a range of sizes and shapes, so only one or two will fit into a particular enzyme's active site. If there is not an exact fit, the reaction does not happen. Each different reaction needs its own enzyme to catalyse it.

Making a substance within a cell usually involves three or four enzymes, working one after the other. The sequence of enzymes is called an enzyme pathway (figure 7). The molecules in the reaction do not have far to move

12 Why are there hundreds of different enzymes in a single cell?

Example of an enzyme pathway

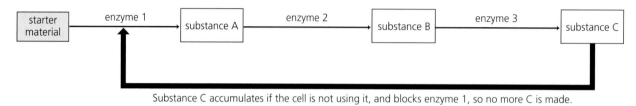

Substance C accumulates if the cell is not using it, and blocks enzyme 1, so no more C is made.

Figure 7

What factors affect an enzyme's activity?

Enzymes are protein molecules that have a particular three-dimensional shape. Enzyme activity is disrupted by factors that change the shape of the molecule's active site.

pH

Changes in acidity or alkalinity can change the shape of a protein molecule and so denature an enzyme. This sort of change is not permanent. When the pH reverts to normal, the protein will resume its normal shape.

Temperature

Usually, the warmer it is, the faster reactions go. This is because the reactant molecules move more quickly, bump into each other more often and so react together more frequently. However, the links that hold protein molecules in their three-dimensional shape are broken by temperatures over about 45 °C. The protein molecule **denatures** – it unravels and changes shape. The warmer it is, the more enzyme molecules are denatured. Reactant molecules no longer fit snugly into the active site, so the enzyme can no longer catalyse its reaction. The change is irreversible. You can see a protein being denatured when you fry an egg.

Inhibition

If you try to unlock a door with the wrong key, you often find that the key goes into the lock easily, but won't turn because it does not quite match. A similar thing can happen with enzymes. Some molecules can enter an active site and fit well enough to block entry to the desired reactant molecules. We say that the enzyme has been inhibited.

The inhibitors may be molecules formed later on in an enzyme pathway. If the cell is not using them up, they block the process that has produced them. This is an example of feedback inhibition (see figure 7).

Some substances block enzymes permanently. They bind to the active site, or to another part of the molecule, changing its shape. Such inhibitors include heavy metal ions such as lead, cadmium and mercury, and chemicals such as cyanide. They are cell poisons, because they stop vital processes irreversibly.

Summary of making and breaking

- Chemical reactions in cells are catalysed by enzymes.

- Changes in temperature and pH affect the rate of enzyme reactions.

3.5 Making new cells

How are new cells made?

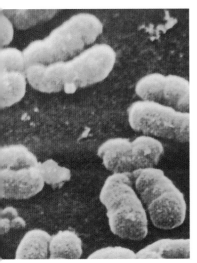

This is a scanning electron micrograph of human chromosomes, made of coiled DNA.

We all start life as a single fertilised egg, which divides to make many billions of cells. New cells are unspecialised, but they quickly become specialised. They are said to **differentiate**. As we grow larger, we make more cells. We also make new cells to replace worn out or damaged cells.

Plants have specialised regions for making new cells which you can read about in chapter 15, *Growing and developing*. Animals do not have specialised places for making new cells, but most tissues can generate new cells for growth and repair. Some tissues produce new cells constantly. Red blood cells are replaced as they reach the end of their useful life, and new cells are needed to repair the gut lining each day. Other cells are replaced more slowly as the need arises. Nervous tissue does not replace itself after the end of childhood growth.

The process by which most new cells are made is called **mitosis**. Sperm and eggs are made by a slightly different process called **meiosis**, explained in chapter 18, *Genetics*. In mitosis, the cell divides into two halves which go on to become two daughter cells. These cells then separate and become adapted for their particular purpose.

The events of mitosis begin before the cell starts to divide into two. It is easy enough to divide chloroplasts and mitochondria between two daughter cells, but it is not so straightforward to divide the nucleus into two parts.

Inside the nucleus are chromosomes, which carry the **genes** that cells need to work (figure 8). Genes are sequences of DNA (see chapter 2, *Chemicals of life*) that instruct the cell to make different proteins, and are responsible for inherited features such as your blood type, hair texture and eye colour. Each new cell needs a complete set of genes, not just half of them. Every gene has to be copied before cell division can take place. A duplicate set of genes is made before mitosis starts.

Figure 8

Chromosome structure

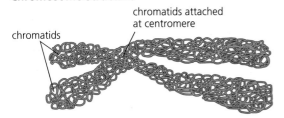

chromatids attached at centromere

chromatids

What happens during mitosis?

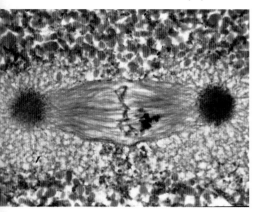

Mitosis is a long and complicated process as shown in figure 9. It may be summarised simply as follows:

1 The membrane surrounding the nucleus loses its structure and disappears. The chromosomes become visible.
2 The chromosomes, which consist of two identical chromatids, each containing identical sets of genes, are pulled apart, starting at the centromere.
3 The parted chromosomes are pulled to separate ends of the cell.
4 New cell membranes are made (and cell walls if it is a plant cell), and the cytoplasm is divided between the two daughter cells.

As this cell undergoes mitosis, the chromosomes in its nucleus become visible, down the centre.

Figure 9 Mitosis is a continuous process, although it is usually shown as a series of separate stages.

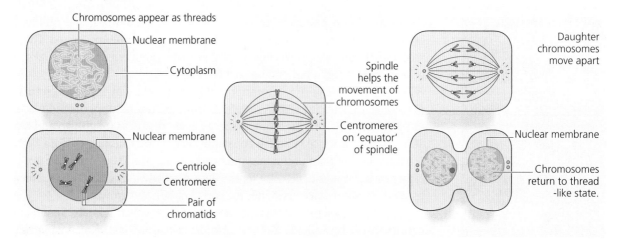

What happens when cell division goes wrong?

Cell division can go wrong in two ways:

• DNA molecules may be damaged by environmental factors so that copies made from it are wrong. These are **mutations**. To find out about mutations, read chapter 18, *Genetics*.
• The rate of cell division goes wrong. This can happen because something has damaged the genes that control cell division. This can lead to cancers.

When cell division goes wrong it makes unusual cells. Usually, the immune system quickly picks up and destroys 'rogue' cells, but sometimes rogue cells escape and result in cancer. Cancer is a general term covering many illnesses linked to over-active cell division. Cancers start with a change in just one or a few cells, which multiply faster than usual and produce a colony called a tumour. The tumour cells usually stop doing their normal job, and some even start to carry out different activities. The cells in a benign tumour stay in their tissue, like healthy cells, but form a growth or lump. The cells of a **malignant**

Table 1

Known carcinogens:

chemicals in cigarette smoke

radiation from nuclear waste

ultraviolet rays in strong sunlight

chemicals such as benzene

asbestos fibres

soot

tumour move away and settle somewhere else in the body. There they start new tumours.

The change in cell division rate is caused by factors called **carcinogens** which affect DNA in the cell's nucleus. Some carcinogens are linked to our environment, or lifestyle (table 1). Viruses may be linked with some cancers.

Cancers can form in any of our tissues. Cancers of tissues which normally divide rapidly anyway, such as skin and bone marrow, develop quickly. Others take much longer to develop, and it may be many years before the sufferer has symptoms.

13 The graph shows the number of skin cancers reported each year between 1973 and 1986.

a Calculate the percentage increase in skin cancers between 1973 and 1986. Show your working.

b Suggest a possible reason for this increase.

c Explain how a change in a skin cell can cause skin cancer to develop.

Summary of making new cells

- New cells are made by mitosis.

- Failures in the control of cell division can lead to cancer.

Investigations

1 Many important chemicals enter or leave cells by diffusion. A block of gelatine, used to make jellies, makes a good model for cells exchanging substances by diffusion. If a block of gelatine is immersed in a coloured solution the colour will gradually diffuse into the block.
Devise an investigation into how shape affects diffusion into a model animal.

2 In the 19th century Dr William Beaumont investigated digestion. One of his patients had a hole into his stomach as a result of an accident. Dr Beaumont could follow the progress of a piece of food as it was digested in the stomach, and could draw off digestive juices in order to investigate their activity. Dr Beaumont observed that food was digested faster inside the stomach than in a beaker.

a What factors are likely to influence the activity of an enzyme?

b Dr Beaumont thought that digestion in the stomach might be quicker because the body is warm, and because the food is churned up and mixed by the stomach muscles. Explain Dr Beaumont's idea in a scientific way. Plan an investigation to test this idea.

Energy transfers

Learning objectives

By the end of this chapter you should be able to:

- **recognise** energy transfers in living organisms
- **explain** why living organisms need a constant supply of energy
- **describe** the processes of photosynthesis and respiration
- **list** the factors that affect the rates of photosynthesis and respiration

- **describe** the adaptations of plants to photosynthesis
- **explain** the significance of aerobic and anaerobic respiration
- **describe** the way ATP transfers energy between reactions in cells

4.1 Energy transfer systems

What is energy?

Energy allows a system to *do* something. We cannot detect energy directly, we can only detect its effects. For example, electrical energy can make a light bulb glow. We notice the change in the bulb when the energy passes through the filament, but we cannot see the energy itself. Energy in sunlight can warm water in a solar panel. We notice the rise in temperature as the water absorbs energy. Transferring energy into something can have several effects, for example it could get hotter, change its velocity, make a noise, give out light or grow larger.

When a muscle cell contracts, it transfers some of the energy stored in food and oxygen into energy as movement.

Energy is not destroyed by these transfers, but some of it may be wasted. Contracting muscles get hot. The heat is wasted energy, because it does not help the muscle to move.

---

1 **a** Study the photographs on the next page. List the things that show each organism is using energy.

b Pick two of the photographs and draw system diagrams like the one above to show the energy transfers.

Green plants transfer light energy from the Sun into chemical energy in sugar molecules. When the plant cells respire, this energy is released to fuel life processes.

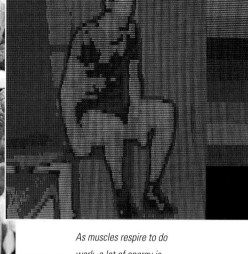

As muscles respire to do work, a lot of energy is released which warms the body. On this thermograph the hottest parts of the squash player show white.

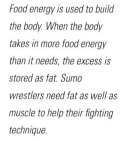

Food energy is used to build the body. When the body takes in more food energy than it needs, the excess is stored as fat. Sumo wrestlers need fat as well as muscle to help their fighting technique.

Glow worms transfer chemical energy to light energy, to send messages to others nearby.

Who needs energy?

Living things are more than just a collection of complicated chemicals gathered together in one place. All living things are constantly *doing* something with their chemicals. They build up large molecules, break them down and rearrange them. All these reactions involve energy transfers.

To build starch from glucose, the cell transfers energy *into* the chemicals.

glucose + energy → starch

When glucose is respired, that is, it reacts with oxygen to form carbon dioxide and water, energy is transferred *out*.

glucose + oxygen → carbon dioxide + water + energy

To control the reactions in the cell, a living organism must control these energy transfers. Reactions that need energy will not happen without an energy transfer, and reactions that release energy would make the body

27

overheat if the energy was not controlled. To manage energy transfers, living organisms must:

- collect energy from their environment
- store energy in their cells until it is needed
- transfer energy from these stores to other cell reactions.

Energy management in living things depends on two reactions:

- photosynthesis – transfers energy from light into cell chemicals
- respiration – transfers energy between reactions in the cell.

Summary of energy transfer systems

- Energy allows a system to do something.
- When energy is transferred, its effects might change.
- Energy transfers do not create or destroy energy, but do change its effects.
- Some effects of energy are more useful than others.

- Living things need to control energy transfers in order to control the chemical reactions in their cells.
- Living things use photosynthesis and respiration to manage energy transfers.

4.2 Photosynthesis

What is photosynthesis?

Plants collect the energy in sunlight and use it to drive reactions that make glucose and oxygen from carbon dioxide and water. We call this process **photosynthesis**.

carbon dioxide + water + energy → glucose + oxygen

Why do plants look green?

Sunlight is a mixture of lights with different wavelengths. Each wavelength has a different colour but the mixture appears white to our eyes. You can see the colours if you use a prism to spread out the different wavelengths and produce a spectrum. Light with shorter wavelengths looks blue, while the longest wavelengths look red. The energy carried by light also depends on its wavelength, so that blue light transfers more energy than red light.

Some chemicals can absorb certain wavelengths of light. When white light falls on these chemicals, the absorbed wavelengths stay behind in the chemical, and the other wavelengths are reflected. The reflected light is therefore coloured. For example, white light falls on to a red apple and the skin of the apple absorbs all the colours except red. The reflected light is red, so the apple looks red to our eyes.

2 a What wavelengths can
   chlorophyll absorb:
     i most efficiently
     ii least efficiently?
  b Which colour of light does a
   plant reflect?

Plants contain a package of chemicals called **pigments** which absorb light of particular wavelengths – some of these can be seen in figure 1. The most important pigment is **chlorophyll**.

Figure 1

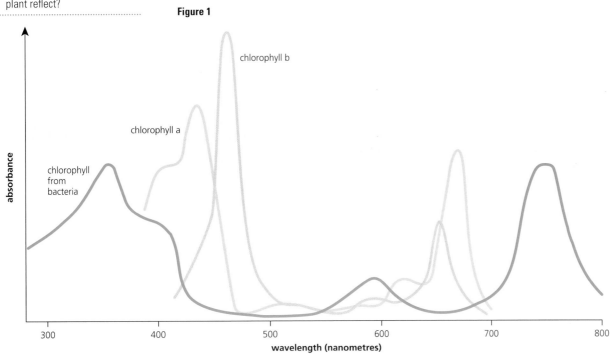

How do plants transfer energy from light?

When light hits a molecule of chlorophyll, the energy is transferred to an electron. This electron can then bounce around like a ball in a pinball machine. Enzymes in the plant cell use the energy in the bouncing electron to build energy-carrying chemicals. In this process, a water molecule is split into oxygen and hydrogen. This reaction needs light and so is called the **light-dependent reaction**.

The plant uses the hydrogen and the energy-carrying chemicals to react with a molecule of carbon dioxide. A series of reactions builds a molecule of glucose. These reactions do not need light, and so are called the **light-independent reaction**. They continue in the cell as long as energy, hydrogen and carbon dioxide are available.

Where does photosynthesis occur in the cell?

Chloroplasts are small, disc-shaped objects which contain the chlorophyll and **enzymes** needed for photosynthesis. Inside the chloroplasts are structures that look like stacks of green coins. These coin structures are made of membranes with chlorophyll and enzymes stuck on to them. This is where the light-dependent reaction takes place (see figure 2).

The light-independent reaction occurs in the clear areas of the chloroplasts. A mixture of enzymes here use the chemicals made by the light-dependent reaction to make glucose.

Glucose diffuses out of the chloroplasts into the rest of the cell. The plant uses the glucose to build a range of other chemicals, for example, starch which is often used as an energy store. In this way, photosynthesis builds up the mass of the plant.

Figure 2 The light-dependent reaction of photosynthesis takes place in the clear area of the chloroplast, called the stroma.

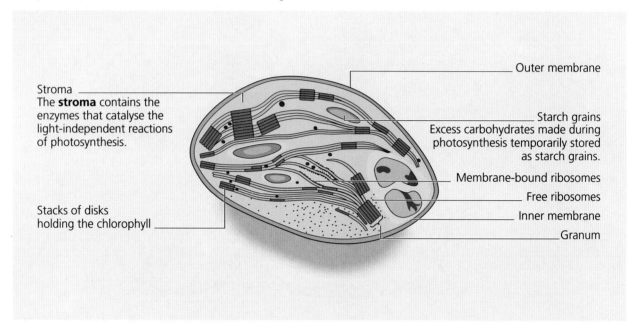

Stroma
The **stroma** contains the enzymes that catalyse the light-independent reactions of photosynthesis.

Stacks of disks holding the chlorophyll

Outer membrane

Starch grains
Excess carbohydrates made during photosynthesis temporarily stored as starch grains.

Membrane-bound ribosomes

Free ribosomes

Inner membrane

Granum

What affects the rate of photosynthesis?

Photosynthesis is a chain of reactions, and each of these reactions could slow down the whole process. To speed up photosynthesis we need to make sure every reaction is going as fast as possible.

The light-dependent reaction of photosynthesis needs light and water. Plants contain large amounts of water, so there is almost always a good supply of water for photosynthesis. In low light levels, the light-dependent reaction cannot absorb enough light and the reaction slows down. The light acts as a **limiting factor**, because it limits the speed of the reaction. If the level of light rises, the reaction rate increases. At a certain point, there is enough light and another factor now becomes limiting. An increase in light level will then have no effect.

3 Draw a system diagram to show the transfer of energy in photosynthesis.
4 List the factors needed by:
   a the light-dependent reaction   b the light-independent reaction.
5 a Some growers use fluorescent lights in greenhouses, others add carbon dioxide gas from small cylinders. Both of these things cost money, so why do they do this?
   b Plan an investigation to find out the most efficient balance of light, carbon dioxide and water for a grower.

6 Look at the table below. Draw a graph to show how the rate of photosynthesis for each of the plants, X and Y, varies with the light intensity. Add labels to show where:

a the light intensity, and **b** the carbon dioxide level,

is the limiting factor. Explain how you made your choices.

Light intensity	1	2	3	4	5	6
Plant X Rate of photosynthesis (arbitrary units)	1.7	1.9	2.1	2.1	2.2	2.2
Plant Y Rate of photosynthesis (arbitrary units)	0.9	1.5	2.4	2.9	3.3	3.6

c Which plant is more suitable for growing in a shady basement window? Explain your choice.

Summary of photosynthesis

- Photosynthesis uses chlorophyll to collect light energy to drive chemical reactions which build glucose from water and carbon dioxide.
- Carbon dioxide + water + energy → glucose + oxygen.
- The plant converts glucose into a range of other useful chemicals.
- The rate of photosynthesis depends on the light level, the carbon dioxide concentration and the availability of water and mineral salts.

- In the light-dependent reaction, light is absorbed, a molecule of water is split and oxygen is produced. The reaction can be limited by light levels.
- The light-independent reaction uses materials made by the light-dependent reaction to build glucose from carbon dioxide. The reaction can be limited by carbon dioxide levels.
- Photosynthesis is the only source of usable energy for most plants and animals.

5.3 Respiration

What is respiration?

Respiration is a process that transfers energy between chemical reactions in living organisms.

Billions of years ago, the first living organisms used energy transfer systems which did not need oxygen. Respiration that does not need oxygen is called **anaerobic respiration**. In this process, sugars are broken down into smaller organic molecules. Many micro-organisms use anaerobic respiration, and it still occurs sometimes in animals and plants. The products are different in animals and plants (see figure 3).

In animals: glucose → lactic acid + water + energy

In plants: glucose → ethanol + carbon dioxide + energy

As life evolved, new types of energy transfer systems developed. These needed oxygen, but could break down sugars completely to carbon dioxide and water.

Respiration

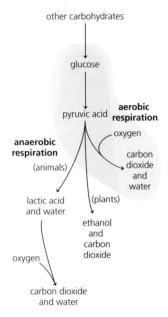

Figure 3

More energy was transferred from each molecule of sugar, allowing much more complex life forms to develop.

Respiration that needs oxygen is called **aerobic respiration**. It could only develop when the concentration of oxygen in the atmosphere reached a certain level. Living organisms needed to collect oxygen from their environment and get rid of the waste gas, carbon dioxide. This exchange of gases with the environment is called **gaseous exchange**.

Chemical reactions cannot create or destroy energy. The total amount of energy on each side of the respiration equation must be the same. It is the glucose and oxygen combination, not just the sugar alone, that stores the energy. For this reason, we say that living things use a **glucose–oxygen system** for energy storage.

Anaerobic respiration does not unlock all of the stored energy because it does not use oxygen. Organisms that can only carry out anaerobic respiration are now limited to areas where oxygen levels are low, for example at the bottom of stagnant ponds, inside the guts of animals or in badly polluted rivers. They survive there because the more efficient aerobic organisms cannot compete in these low oxygen areas.

7 a Write a sentence to explain the difference between respiration and gaseous exchange.

b What would happen to a cell if respiration stopped? Why?

c Why is the source of energy for aerobic respiration called a glucose–oxygen system?

8 a Respiration is similar to combustion, but organisms do not just 'burn' food. List the similarities and differences between aerobic respiration, anaerobic respiration and combustion.

b Look at the diagram of respiration in figure 3. How far can respiration go before it needs oxygen?

c Organisms that can only respire anaerobically are only found in areas where aerobic organisms cannot survive. Why?

What is an oxygen debt?

When a cell has enough oxygen and food, it can respire aerobically very efficiently. What happens if food or oxygen is in short supply? During a race, respiration is going as fast as it can in the muscle cells to supply energy for movement. This uses up lots of food and oxygen and produces large amounts of carbon dioxide, water and heat. The body tries to get more oxygen to the muscle cells by increasing the blood flow but sometimes this is not enough. The cells then use anaerobic respiration to supply the extra energy. This produces lactic acid.

Lactic acid is a toxic chemical and the body must get rid of it as soon as it can. The reaction that breaks it up needs oxygen, so it cannot occur while aerobic respiration is using all the available oxygen supplies. After the exercise is over, the need for energy drops dramatically and so aerobic respiration can slow down. This reduces the demand for oxygen so that some can be used to break down the lactic acid. The amount of oxygen needed to completely clear all the lactic acid made during heavy exercise is called the **oxygen debt**.

9 Runners continue to breathe deeply for some time after the race has finished. Why?

How does the body transfer energy between reactions?

10 Why does the supply of phosphate never run out in a cell?

Cells use a small molecule called **adenosine triphosphate (ATP)** to transfer energy between reactions. ATP is a bit like a rechargeable battery. When it is 'fully charged', it holds three phosphate groups. ATP can release one of its phosphate groups and become **adenosine diphosphate (ADP)**. The spare phosphate group sticks on to a molecule that needs the supply of extra energy. The molecule can then start reacting to form a useful product.

When the reaction is over, the phosphate group detaches from the product. The cell then has to use more energy from respiration to build fresh supplies of ATP out of ADP and the phosphate group. A cell can charge up 38 molecules of ATP from a single glucose molecule by aerobic respiration.

Respiration transfers energy from glucose–oxygen to ATP. How well does it do this job? We can work out the total energy stored in glucose by burning it in oxygen and measuring the energy given out as heat. The energy values found on many food packets and in dieting books depend on this method. We can also measure the energy when ATP molecules break down to ADP (table 1). One glucose molecule gives:

- 38 ATP molecules in aerobic respiration
- 2 ATP molecules in anaerobic respiration.

Table 1 *Energy released by glucose breakdown.*

Reaction	Energy per mole
glucose combustion	2800 kJ
ATP breakdown	30.66 kJ

11 a How much of the energy in one mole of glucose is transferred to ATP molecules during aerobic respiration?
b Why does the body only use anaerobic respiration when aerobic respiration is already going as fast as it can?
c Where does the 'lost' energy from respiration appear?

Where does respiration happen in the cell?

Respiration in the mitochondrion

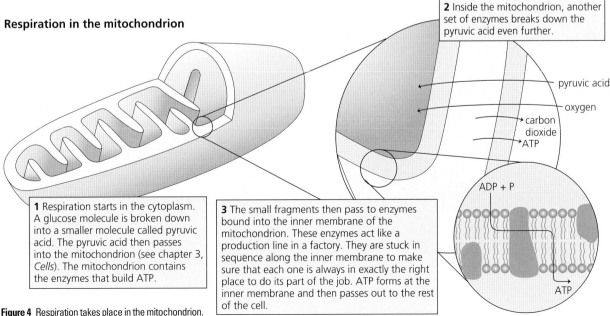

2 Inside the mitochondrion, another set of enzymes breaks down the pyruvic acid even further.

pyruvic acid
oxygen
carbon dioxide
ATP
ADP + P
ATP

1 Respiration starts in the cytoplasm. A glucose molecule is broken down into a smaller molecule called pyruvic acid. The pyruvic acid then passes into the mitochondrion (see chapter 3, *Cells*). The mitochondrion contains the enzymes that build ATP.

3 The small fragments then pass to enzymes bound into the inner membrane of the mitochondrion. These enzymes act like a production line in a factory. They are stuck in sequence along the inner membrane to make sure that each one is always in exactly the right place to do its part of the job. ATP forms at the inner membrane and then passes out to the rest of the cell.

Figure 4 Respiration takes place in the mitochondrion.

Can other chemicals give us energy?

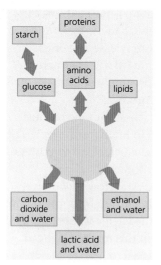

More complex carbohydrates are converted to glucose before respiration can start. However, if no glucose is available, fats or proteins can be used instead. Some of the steps in the glucose respiration pathway are the same as in fat or protein respiration. These steps act as junctions where chemicals can move between pathways (figure 5). So, a lipid molecule can be broken down until it reaches the junction, and can then be rebuilt as a sugar molecule. This allows the body to make a wide variety of different chemicals. The direction of the path depends on the chemicals available and whether energy is transferred into the molecule or out of it.

12 a Spare glucose is converted into fat. What is the advantage of this conversion to the body?
  b When people stop eating, fat and protein are broken down to release energy. List the stages that fat and protein go through to do this.

Figure 5 The direction of each set of reactions depends on the needs of the organism.

Do plants respire?

Plants use energy from sunlight to make glucose from carbon dioxide and water during photosynthesis. However, plants also need to respire because the energy they store in glucose must be linked to other cell reactions by respiration. Plants carry out photosynthesis in the daylight, and respiration at all times.

Since the chemicals needed by photosynthesis are produced by respiration, it is often difficult to tell if a plant is respiring in the daylight. The carbon dioxide produced in respiration is immediately taken up to use in photosynthesis.

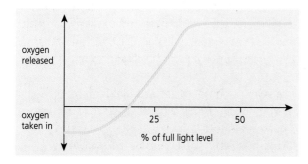

13 a Look at the graph. Describe the effect of light intensity on the release of carbon dioxide from a green plant.
  b At what light level is the oxygen produced by photosynthesis exactly balanced by the oxygen used up by respiration?
  c Nurses used to remove flowers and plants from hospital wards every evening and bring them back every morning. Why?

Summary of respiration

- Respiration is a process that transfers energy between reactions in all living cells.
- Energy transferred to a glucose–oxygen system by photosynthesis can be released by respiration.
- Aerobic respiration requires oxygen.
- Glucose + oxygen → carbon dioxide + water + energy.

- Anaerobic respiration does not need oxygen. It releases less energy than aerobic respiration.
- Respiration transfers energy from the glucose–oxygen system to ATP.
- Breakdown of glucose occurs in the cell cytoplasm. ATP is made in the mitochondria.

Learning objectives

By the end this chapter you should be able to:

- **explain** why large animals need a circulatory system
- **list** the substances blood transports around the body
- **describe** the different parts of blood
- **describe** how blood carries oxygen and carbon dioxide
- **work out** the amount of oxygen carried by a sample of blood

- **explain** why we need a heart
- **describe** the differences between single and double circulation
- **describe** the differences between arteries, veins and capillaries
- **explain** what the pulse rate shows about our fitness

Why do we need a circulatory system?

Living cells need a constant supply of food, oxygen, water and warmth. Cells produce wastes such as carbon dioxide and heat from chemical reactions. If these are not carried away the cell can become poisoned or overheat and die. All living cells are constantly exchanging things with their environment.

Small organisms such as bacteria and protozoa can get all the things they need quickly from the environment around them. Any wastes they produce pass easily out of the cell. Larger organisms need larger amounts of food and oxygen and produce more wastes. These organisms have gaseous exchange systems to collect gases, digestive systems to take in food and excretory systems to get rid of wastes.

Large organisms also have to move substances around inside their bodies. This needs a **circulatory system**. The first multicellular organisms had very simple circulatory systems compared with the most advanced systems in mammals today. Some of the most important changes in the evolution of these systems are described on page 43.

To move materials around inside a body, a circulatory system needs:

- a transport medium – this carries materials in solution or suspension
- a pump – this pushes the transport medium from one place to another
- a system of vessels – these make sure the transport medium flows in the right direction and reaches every part of the body.

5.1 The transport medium

What is blood made from?

Blood is a tissue made of cells, platelets and plasma.

Figure 1 The components of blood.

Blood cells
These make up 45% of blood.

Red blood cells
These cells:
- are made in the red bone marrow
- live for around 120 days
- are removed by the liver,
- have no nucleus, and are packed full of haemoglobin,
- have a smooth shape to allow them to slip along narrow capillaries.
  Their shape also helps to make gas exchange efficient.

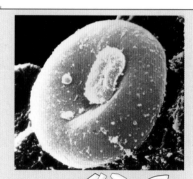

White blood cells
All white blood cells work together to protect the body against disease. During an infection, the level of these cells in the blood rises. There are many different types of white blood cell.

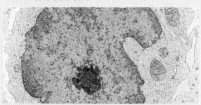

White blood cells without granules in the cytoplasm:
Lymphocytes:
- are made in the lymph glands,
- recognise invading cells and engulf them
- special lymphocytes called 'helper lymphocytes' are destroyed by AIDS.

Monocytes:
- are made in the yellow bone marrow,
- engulf invading cells.

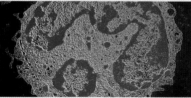

White blood cells with granules in their cytoplasm:
- are made in the yellow bone marrow
- reach damaged tissues first, and start to engulf invading cells
- some cells release chemicals to stimulate the body's defence system.

Platelets:
- are made in the red bone marrow
- help blood to clot

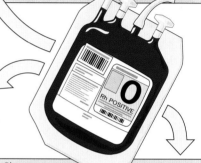

Plasma
This makes up 55% of blood. Plasma is the liquid part. It is 90% water.
The remaining 10% contains:

Sugar 0.248g/blood bag
- glucose (sugar) in the blood provides energy for all body cells,
- the level of glucose is carefully controlled by the body.

Salts 1.8 g/blood bag
- salts keep the blood at the right concentration, which helps blood cells to work properly,
- some salts help blood to clot.

Proteins 18 g/blood bag
- help to protect the body from invaders,
- help the blood to clot

Hormones (very small amount)
- these help to control the body

Wastes 0.135 g/blood bag
- carbon dioxide is carried to the lungs,
- urea is carried to the kidneys to make urine.

Fats 1.35 g/blood bag
- help to give blood the right thickness,
- some fats help to protect the body.

1 **a** What proportion of the blood is liquid?

b Assume one blood bag contains 1 dm³ of whole, normal blood. Work out the concentration of the following substances in the blood.
  i sugar
  ii protein.

2 **a** How many types of:
  i red blood cells
  ii white blood cells
are there?

b Explain this difference.

c Draw up a table to show the differences between red and white blood cells.

What does blood carry?

Table 1 *What the blood carries around the body.*

Substance carried	Taken from	Taken to	Notes
Oxygen	capillaries of the lungs	all tissues	All the body cells need oxygen for respiration.
Carbon dioxide	all tissues	capillaries of the lungs	Respiration in all body cells produces carbon dioxide.
Urea	liver	kidneys	To be passed out of the body in urine.
Food substances	gut	liver	The liver sorts the food substances absorbed during digestion. Some are passed back into the blood, while others are converted for other uses.
Water	all tissues	all tissues	Plasma is over 90% water. Cells use plasma as a water store.
Heat	all tissues	all tissues	The blood helps to regulate temperature in the body by carrying heat away from 'hot spots' and towards colder areas.
Antibodies	lymph nodes	infected areas	Antibodies act against any foreign chemicals in the body, for example bacterial cells.
Hormones	endocrine glands	target organs	A hormone changes the working of the target organ, usually slowing it down or speeding it up.

How does blood carry oxygen?

Red blood cells are packed full of **haemoglobin**. Haemoglobin is a protein wound around a group of atoms called the **haem group**. The haem group contains iron. When haemoglobin reacts with oxygen, the oxygen binds to the iron atoms in the haem group to make **oxyhaemoglobin**. However, oxyhaemoglobin is unstable and breaks down to give oxygen and haemoglobin again in certain conditions.

haemoglobin + oxygen → oxyhaemoglobin

In areas of high oxygen concentration, like the capillaries of the lungs, haemoglobin forms oxyhaemoglobin. 100 cm³ of fresh blood can absorb roughly 20 cm³ of oxygen. In areas of low oxygen concentration, like the cells of an active muscle, the oxyhaemoglobin breaks down and releases oxygen.

The blood carries carbon dioxide dissolved in the plasma as hydrogencarbonate ions (HCO_3^-). Haemoglobin helps carbon dioxide to dissolve. So haemoglobin controls the movement of both carbon dioxide and oxygen through the body.

3 Active cells produce large amounts of carbon dioxide, which dissolves in blood and makes it slightly more acidic. As the level of acidity rises, oxyhaemoglobin becomes more unstable. How does this help to transport oxygen to very active cells?

Summary of the transport medium

- All large organisms need a system to move materials around their bodies.
- The transport medium carries materials in solution (e.g. glucose, mineral salts) and suspended in liquid (e.g. large protein molecules, blood cells).
- Blood is a mixture. Different parts carry different substances around the body.
- Red blood cells are packed full of haemoglobin, which can bind with oxygen.
- Most of the carbon dioxide carried by the blood is dissolved in the plasma as hydrogencarbonate ions.

5.2 The pump

How does the heart work?

The heart has four chambers joined together within one large block of muscle (figure 2). In a resting adult human, it beats roughly 70 times per minute, and will complete 25 000 000 000 (25 billion) beats in an average lifetime. Despite this enormous task, a healthy heart can continue beating for many years after other body organs have worn out. Heart disease is one of the greatest killers in the Western world, but this is probably more to do with our abuse of the heart than design weakness. Heart disease seems to be one of the great preventable causes of death.

The heart has four major tasks:

- to collect blood at low pressure from the body
- to pump blood to the lungs
- to collect blood at low pressure returning from the lungs
- to push blood at high pressure into the **aorta** and from there to the rest of the body.

4 a Study the diagrams of the heart in figure 2 and identify the part of the heart that does each of the four tasks listed on the right.

b Explain how each of these parts is adapted to carry out its tasks.

Figure 2

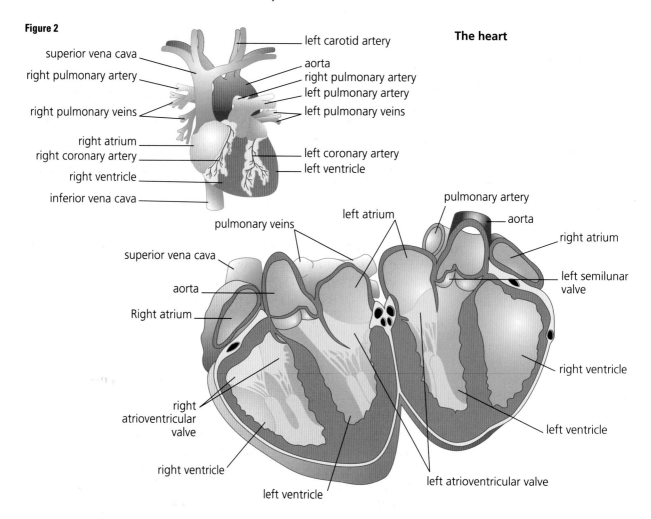

The heart

38

Why doesn't the heart get tired?

Figure 3 Pressure in the ventricles changes as the heart contracts and relaxes to pump blood around the body.

The heart is made of muscle. However, heart muscle is slightly different from other muscles in the body. It can contract and relax regularly without any nervous stimulation and seems able to go on for ever without tiring. An **electrocardiogram** (ECG) plots the electrical impulses that control the contraction of heart muscles (figure 3).

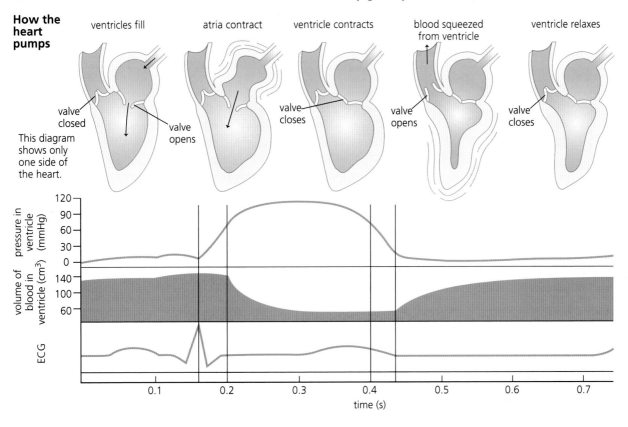

How the heart pumps

ventricles fill   atria contract   ventricle contracts   blood squeezed from ventricle   ventricle relaxes

valve closed   valve opens   valve closes   valve opens   valve closes

This diagram shows only one side of the heart.

pressure in ventricle (mmHg)

volume of blood in ventricle (cm³)

ECG

time (s)

5 a In figure 3, how much of the time is the muscle in the ventricle: **i** actively contracting, **ii** relaxed?

b In figure 3, the heart rate is 75 beats per minute. Sketch the shape of the graphs you would expect if the heart rate went up to 150 beats per minute.

c How would this affect the resting time available to the heart muscles?

Why is your pulse rate important?

The **pulse rate** is a measure of how often the heart beats. It has the same value as the heart rate. Trying to find a pulse is one of the first things a doctor or nurse will do after an accident.

When the heart beats, it pushes a surge of blood into the aorta. The arteries smooth out this surge to a gentle, continuous flow before it reaches the capillaries. However, where an artery lies near the surface of the body we can feel this surge as the pulse. Every beat of the heart produces a pulse in the artery. You can detect pulses in the wrists, ankles and neck.

Summary of the pump

- The heart is a muscular pump which pushes blood around the body. It has four chambers.
- The heart beats even without impulses from the brain.

- The atria collect blood from veins and push it into the ventricles. The ventricles are muscular chambers which push blood from the heart at high pressure.

5.3 The system of vessels

Where does the blood go?

In humans, the circulatory system moves the blood around the body, and also controls the blood distribution between different organs. A plan of the circulatory system is shown in figure 5. Every organ, except one, has a single blood supply which branches off from the main artery of the body, called the aorta. The one exception is the liver which has two blood supplies. The **hepatic portal vein** carries blood from the gut capillaries to the liver. This blood is rich in dissolved food substances, but low in oxygen because the oxygen has already been used by the gut cells. The **hepatic artery** carries oxygenated blood from the aorta to the liver. The liver is a metabolically very active organ, so it needs a good supply of oxygenated blood. One vein, the **hepatic vein**, drains the liver and returns blood to the heart.

The liver has the job of sorting the food substances in the blood. It is also able to break down a range of toxic chemicals.

Why are arteries and veins different?

Arteries, capillaries and veins have different jobs to do. Arteries and veins have to transport blood as quickly as possible from one place to another. Capillaries have to allow body cells to exchange materials with the blood.

Figure 4

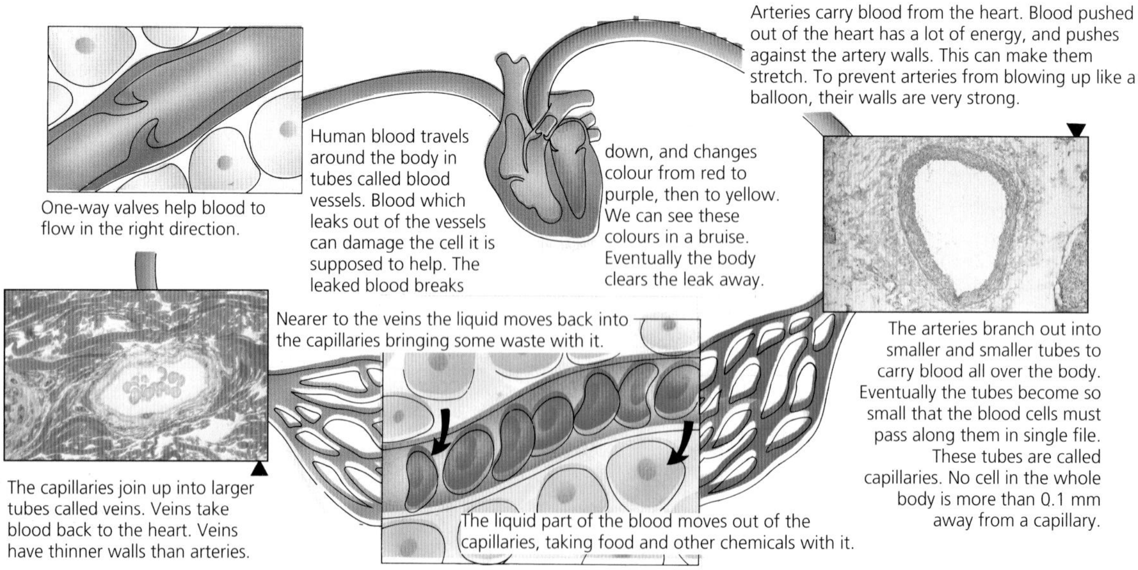

One-way valves help blood to flow in the right direction.

Human blood travels around the body in tubes called blood vessels. Blood which leaks out of the vessels can damage the cell it is supposed to help. The leaked blood breaks down, and changes colour from red to purple, then to yellow. We can see these colours in a bruise. Eventually the body clears the leak away.

Arteries carry blood from the heart. Blood pushed out of the heart has a lot of energy, and pushes against the artery walls. This can make them stretch. To prevent arteries from blowing up like a balloon, their walls are very strong.

The arteries branch out into smaller and smaller tubes to carry blood all over the body. Eventually the tubes become so small that the blood cells must pass along them in single file. These tubes are called capillaries. No cell in the whole body is more than 0.1 mm away from a capillary.

Nearer to the veins the liquid moves back into the capillaries bringing some waste with it.

The capillaries join up into larger tubes called veins. Veins take blood back to the heart. Veins have thinner walls than arteries.

The liquid part of the blood moves out of the capillaries, taking food and other chemicals with it.

Figure 5

Human circulation

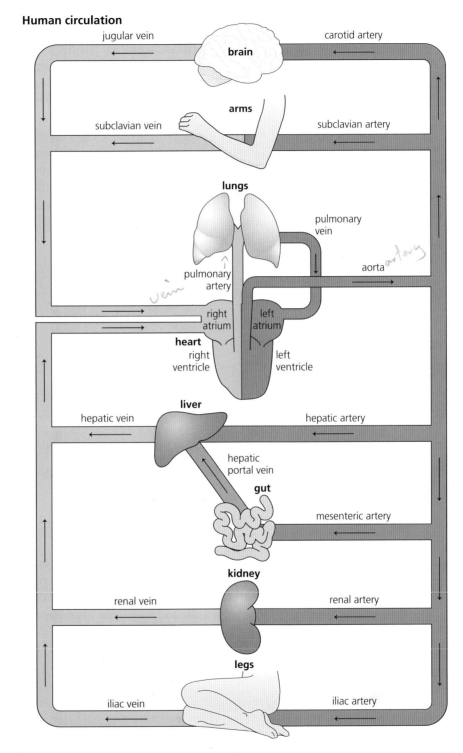

6 a List the structural similarities and differences between arteries and veins.

b Explain how these similarities and differences are linked to the jobs arteries and veins do .

7 Explain why it is important that the liver receives the blood supply from the gut before it passes into general circulation.

8 a Blood can only flow through the heart in one direction. Draw a flow chart to show the route a blood cell takes through the heart. The cell enters the heart through the body vein.

b Some people are born with a hole in the heart. This hole allows blood to move between the left and right ventricles. What effects would this have on:

i blood flow through the heart

ii the person's general health?

What are capillaries and lymph vessels?

The walls of arteries and veins are too thick for oxygen and food to pass from them to the cells. The blood is also travelling too fast for exchange to occur. As arteries divide to form arterioles and then capillaries, the total cross-sectional area of the system increases a thousand times. This means the blood slows down. The smaller capillary walls are also thin, to allow exchange of materials, and leaky, so that much of the liquid part of the blood passes out to form **tissue fluid** (figure 6). The red blood cells remain within the blood vessels. The cells of the body are bathed in tissue fluid, which moves back into the blood vessels as the capillaries begin to join up to form venules and veins. Tissue fluid which does not return to the blood is drained from the tissues in another set of vessels called the **lymph capillaries**.

Once the fluid gets into the lymph capillaries it is called **lymph**. Lymph capillaries join together to form larger lymph vessels which eventually return the fluid to the blood through openings in some of the larger veins. Muscle fibres in the lymph cappillaries squeeze the fluid along and one-way valves stop it from draining back into the tissues.

> **9 a** List the structural similarities and differences between blood capillaries and lymph capillaries.
> **b** Explain how these similarities and differences are linked to the jobs they do in the body.
> **c** People with high blood pressure often have puffy legs and ankles. Why?

Capillaries and lymph capillaries

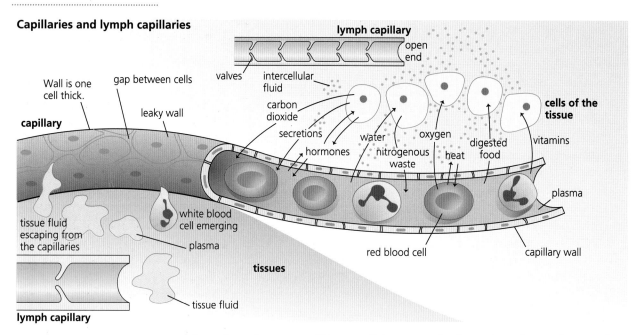

Figure 6

Lymph nodes are small knots of tissues on the larger lymph vessels. Lymph passes through these on the way back to the bloodstream. Lymph nodes contain cells which recognise foreign materials, such as invading disease-causing bacteria, and trigger the immune response (see chapter 8, *Disease and immunity*).

Summary of the system of vessels

- Blood vessels direct blood through the body. Arteries carry high pressure blood away from the heart. Capillaries are microscopic vessels which carry blood through body tissues. Veins drain blood from the tissues and carry it back towards the heart.

- The walls of blood vessels are adapted to cope with the pressure of the blood they contain and to allow exchange of materials between the body cells and the blood.

5.4 Circulatory systems

How have circulatory systems evolved?

The first circulatory systems probably moved substances by swirling a liquid around inside the body. This liquid was in close contact with body cells and flowed freely along cavities in the body. Movements of the whole body or specialised sections would keep the liquid moving. Modern insects use a system very similar to this. It is called an **open circulatory system**.

Two important developments helped to make transport around the bodies of other animals more efficient.

- A series of vessels guided the direction of flow around the body. The system changed from an open circulation to a **closed circulation**.
- The heart gave two pushes to the blood for every trip around the body. This shows a change from **single circulation** to **double circulation**.

Why do we have a double circulation?

Fish have a closed, single circulation. The heart gives a push to blood to send it to the capillaries of the gills. Here the blood picks up oxygen from the water and gives out carbon dioxide. The blood then passes on to the rest of the body.

The journey through the capillaries slows down the blood and makes it difficult for the blood to return to the heart. There are large open spaces in the fish's body through which the blood can more easily flow on the way back to the heart.

In frogs, the heart has three chambers. One powerful ventricle pushes blood towards the body and the lungs along the same artery. Blood going into the lungs returns directly to the heart and does not travel on to the rest of the body. This means the blood that passes to the body has not been slowed down by a trip through the lungs. Furthermore, blood from the lungs enters the heart through its own atrium and so gets an extra boost into the ventricle. Folds of tissue in the frog heart also seem to be able to keep most of the deoxygenated blood from the body separate from the oxygenated blood from the lungs.

In mammals, blood goes from the heart to the lungs and then back to the heart before it is pumped to the rest of the body. This means the blood is guaranteed two pushes for each trip around the body. This double circulation system moves blood more quickly around the body.

10 a Explain why a double circulation is much more efficient than a single circulation.
b Is a closed circulation much more efficient than an open one? Give reasons for your decision.

Summary of circulatory systems

- Circulatory systems have developed to make sure that blood travels through the gaseous exchange organs every time it passes around the body.
- Hearts in mammals have two pumps to keep lung circulation separate from the body circulation route.
- This separation is called double circulation.

Learning objectives

By the end of this chapter you should be able to:

- **recall** the composition of the atmosphere
- **explain** how the lungs work as an efficient exchange surface
- **describe** how breathing changes to match demands
- **explain** how some factors harm the lungs
- **explain** how plants exchange gases with their environment
- **explain** how plants regulate the exchange of gases

6.1 Gas exchange

How do gases enter living things?

This protozoan can absorb enough oxygen by diffusion. Carbon dioxide and other soluble wastes can diffuse out.

This axolotl uses external gas exchange organs, or gills. The water supports the finely divided gill filaments.

Gases diffuse from outside an organism, through its surface, into the interior. Similarly, waste gases diffuse out. This is called **gaseous exchange**.

In very small organisms, such as single-celled protozoa, gases diffuse directly into their cells across their cell membranes. The surface area of a protozoan is large compared to its volume, so it can get all the oxygen it needs by diffusion through its surface. As the organism respires, it uses up oxygen and more diffuses in from outside to replace it. Carbon dioxide builds up inside the cells, and diffuses out into the water. As long as there is plenty of oxygen and not much carbon dioxide in the water, gas exchange will carry on.

In larger animals and plants, the outer layers protect against water loss and the entry of micro-organisms which could cause disease. The waterproof outer layers are also 'gas-proof', and do not allow much gas exchange. So instead, large organisms have specialised structures, like lungs or gills, to exchange gases with the outside world (see figure 1). They are usually inside the organism's body, because they are fragile, and need to be kept moist, protected and supported. Enclosed gas exchange surfaces are also better at conserving water.

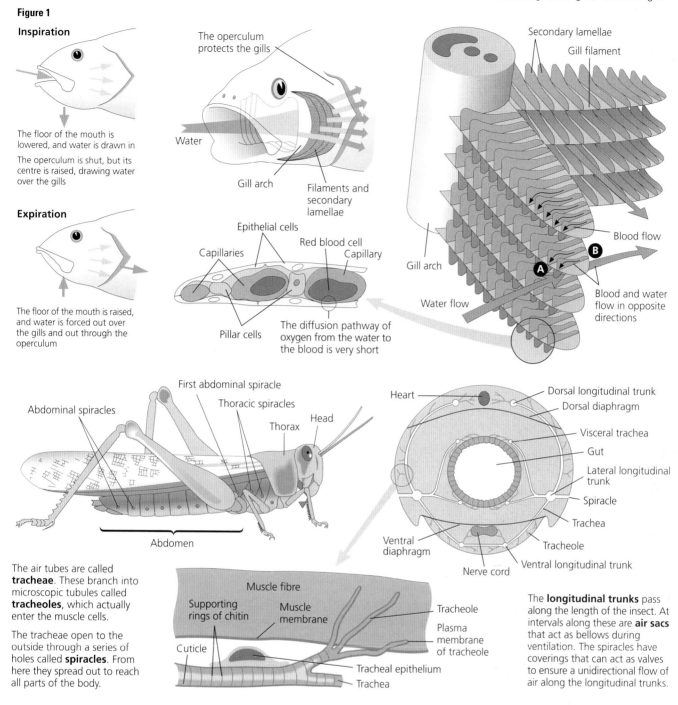

Figure 1

Inspiration

The floor of the mouth is lowered, and water is drawn in

The operculum is shut, but its centre is raised, drawing water over the gills

Expiration

The floor of the mouth is raised, and water is forced out over the gills and out through the operculum

The operculum protects the gills

Water

Gill arch

Filaments and secondary lamellae

Secondary lamellae

Gill filament

Gill arch

Water flow

Blood flow

A B

Blood and water flow in opposite directions

Epithelial cells

Capillaries

Red blood cell

Capillary

Pillar cells

The diffusion pathway of oxygen from the water to the blood is very short

Abdominal spiracles

First abdominal spiracle

Thoracic spiracles

Thorax

Head

Abdomen

Heart

Dorsal longitudinal trunk

Dorsal diaphragm

Visceral trachea

Gut

Lateral longitudinal trunk

Spiracle

Trachea

Tracheole

Ventral longitudinal trunk

Ventral diaphragm

Nerve cord

The air tubes are called **tracheae**. These branch into microscopic tubules called **tracheoles**, which actually enter the muscle cells.

The tracheae open to the outside through a series of holes called **spiracles**. From here they spread out to reach all parts of the body.

Muscle fibre

Supporting rings of chitin

Muscle membrane

Tracheole

Plasma membrane of tracheole

Cuticle

Tracheal epithelium

Trachea

The **longitudinal trunks** pass along the length of the insect. At intervals along these are **air sacs** that act as bellows during ventilation. The spiracles have coverings that can act as valves to ensure a unidirectional flow of air along the longitudinal trunks.

How quickly does gas exchange happen?

Gases diffuse across exchange surfaces. The efficiency of a surface depends on several factors:

- the concentration gradient across the surface
- the surface area of the surface
- the efficiency of the transport mechanism
- the thickness of the membrane

Figure 1 shows some exchange surfaces in different organisms. You will find more information on movement across membranes in chapter 3, *Cells*.

Summary of gas exchange

- Unicellular organisms carry out gas exchange by diffusion through cell membranes.
- Multicellular animals have specialised exchange surfaces to obtain the gases they need from their surroundings.
- Gases are exchanged by diffusion down concentration gradients.
- Exchange surfaces are adapted to ensure that gas exchange is as efficient as possible.

6.2 **Gas exchange in humans**
How do people breathe?

1 How are cells specialised to exchange gases in the lungs?

In humans, and many other animals, gas exchange takes place in the lungs. Your lungs are protected by a bony cage formed by your ribs, and your **diaphragm**, which is a sheet of muscle across your abdomen, just above your liver. Within your lungs, your main airway branches into smaller and smaller passages, which direct air to and from tiny air sacs, called **alveoli**. It is in the alveoli that gas exchange takes place (see figure 2).

Figure 2

Alveoli and gas exchange

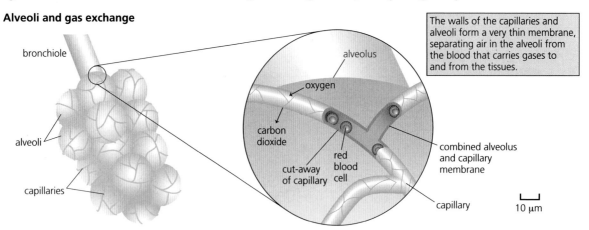

bronchiole

alveoli

capillaries

alveolus

oxygen

carbon dioxide

cut-away of capillary

red blood cell

The walls of the capillaries and alveoli form a very thin membrane, separating air in the alveoli from the blood that carries gases to and from the tissues.

combined alveolus and capillary membrane

capillary

10 μm

We move air in and out of our lungs all the time to maintain favourable concentration gradients. Moving air in and out of the chest is called **ventilation**. Breathing in, or **inhalation**, takes muscle action. Breathing out, or **exhalation**, happens when the muscles relax. Breathing is triggered by rising carbon dioxide concentrations in the blood (see figure 3).

Figure 3

Taking a breath

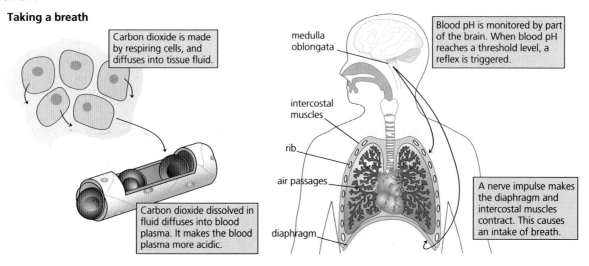

Carbon dioxide is made by respiring cells, and diffuses into tissue fluid.

Carbon dioxide dissolved in fluid diffuses into blood plasma. It makes the blood plasma more acidic.

medulla oblongata

intercostal muscles

rib

air passages

diaphragm

Blood pH is monitored by part of the brain. When blood pH reaches a threshold level, a reflex is triggered.

A nerve impulse makes the diaphragm and intercostal muscles contract. This causes an intake of breath.

As your diaphragm and intercostal muscles (between your ribs) contract, the chest capacity enlarges, as shown in figure 4. Your lungs are surrounded by moist membranes which stick them to the chest wall, so they are stretched by your expanding rib cage. The air pressure inside the lungs drops, and air is drawn in through your mouth and nose. At the end of the breath, the muscles relax, and air is gently expelled from the lungs.

Figure 4   Breathing

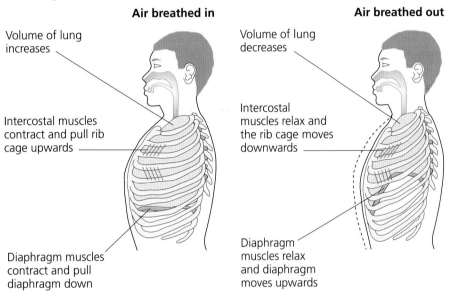

Air breathed in

Volume of lung increases

Intercostal muscles contract and pull rib cage upwards

Diaphragm muscles contract and pull diaphragm down

Air breathed out

Volume of lung decreases

Intercostal muscles relax and the rib cage moves downwards

Diaphragm muscles relax and diaphragm moves upwards

This expansion and contraction cycle flushes out a small volume of air from your lungs with each breath. Fresh air coming in dilutes the carbon dioxide-rich air left in your lungs. When you are resting, about 500 cm³ of air is pushed out and drawn in with each breath, but you can inhale or exhale far more than this if you need too.

Table 1

Gas	Atmosphere	Exhaled air, while carrying out moderate activity
Nitrogen	80%	80%
Oxygen	20%	17%
Carbon dioxide	0.03%	3%
Water vapour	variable	saturated

Occasionally you need to breathe out more fiercely than normal, when coughing, sneezing, or shouting, for example. To force air out, your internal intercostal muscles, which run along the inner surface of the rib cage, contract and pull it down. At the same time muscles in your abdomen wall contract, which pushes your liver and stomach against the diaphragm, and raises it up further than normal.

If you are very active, cell respiration goes faster than normal, and produces more carbon dioxide. The carbon dioxide levels in your blood reach the threshold level more quickly, and trigger you to breathe more often. At the same time, you push out more air with each breath, so you also breathe more deeply.

2 What pattern can you see in the data in the table below? Explain what this pattern shows.

Activity	Air breathed in (litres per minute)
Sitting	5.6
Standing still	7.8
Gentle walking	12.8
Fast walking	23.0
Running	45.2

How are the lungs protected?

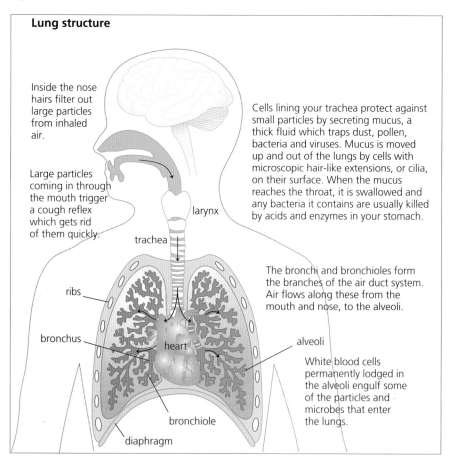

Lung structure

Inside the nose hairs filter out large particles from inhaled air.

Large particles coming in through the mouth trigger a cough reflex which gets rid of them quickly.

Cells lining your trachea protect against small particles by secreting mucus, a thick fluid which traps dust, pollen, bacteria and viruses. Mucus is moved up and out of the lungs by cells with microscopic hair-like extensions, or cilia, on their surface. When the mucus reaches the throat, it is swallowed and any bacteria it contains are usually killed by acids and enzymes in your stomach.

The bronchi and bronchioles form the branches of the air duct system. Air flows along these from the mouth and nose, to the alveoli.

White blood cells permanently lodged in the alveoli engulf some of the particles and microbes that enter the lungs.

larynx

trachea

ribs

bronchus

heart

alveoli

bronchiole

diaphragm

Figure 5

The warm, moist environment inside your lungs is ideal for growing harmful bacteria and viruses, and sharp air-borne particles could easily damage the thin alveolar walls. So your lungs must be protected against such infection and damage (see figure 5).

Microbial infections that inflame the main airways cause bronchitis. Bacterial infections are treated with a suitable **antibiotic**, but colds are caused by viruses which are not affected by antibiotics. Some microbes can also withstand attack from your white blood cells, and cause very serious infections such as tuberculosis. Cystic fibrosis is a genetic disease, which makes cells lining the lungs produce a sticky mucus (see chapter 18, *Genetics*). The mucus is difficult to clear from the air passages, and interferes with gas exchange. Sufferers have trouble breathing properly, and have problems with lung infections. Some have to take antibiotics all the time to prevent infections starting.

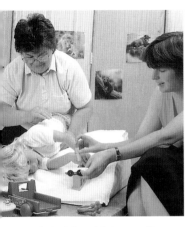

A physiotherapist gives a cystic fibrosis patient percussion treatment. This loosens mucus from the patient's airways, which is then coughed up.

3 List the ways your body protects your lungs against infections.

Years ago, asbestos was thought to be harmless, and was widely used for fireproofing. Now we know that asbestos fibres are extremely dangerous if inhaled. People who work with asbestos have to be rigorously protected.

Quarrying, timber processing and flour production generate large amounts of fine dust, which can cause breathing problems in workers. Small dust particles rub against the alveoli walls, scarring them. Frequent coughing makes the thin layers between neighbouring alveoli break down, leading to a disease called emphysema. The damage reduces the area available for exchanging gases, and sufferers cannot be as active as people with healthy lungs. Some solvents used in paint spraying, plastics and printing are thought to cause cancer. If workers must be exposed to dusts or solvents for long periods, they should work in well-ventilated areas with extractor fans, and wear protective masks, to minimise the risk of lung damage.

This white blood cell from the lung of an asbestosis sufferer has been speared by an inhaled asbestos fibre.

Can fumes from fossil fuels cause lung damage?

Fumes from burning fossil fuels can lead to respiratory problems. Exhaust fumes from cars and lorries contain a variety of irritant substances including carbon monoxide and hydrocarbon particles. Carbon monoxide is toxic: it diffuses into blood like oxygen and binds to **haemoglobin** (see chapter 5, *Circulation*, for more about haemoglobin). Haemoglobin linked to carbon monoxide does not break down, and so cannot carry oxygen to tissue cells. Burning coal and oil also releases sulphur dioxide into the air. This gas combines with moisture in the atmosphere, or in the lungs, to make a harmful acid. A combination of exhaust fumes, factory gases and sunlight can make a photochemical smog, which impairs breathing. People with respiratory problems such as asthma or bronchitis suffer particularly badly under these conditions.

Cyclists and joggers using heavily congested streets wear masks to reduce the noxious gases, and small particles from vehicle engines that go into their lungs. Here, the smog in Los Angeles, USA, is so thick that even close buildings are obscured.

How does smoking damage lungs?

Smoking damages lungs in many ways (figure 6), and causes more than 40 000 deaths from lung cancer in the UK each year. Even passive smokers, who inhale other people's cigarette smoke from their surroundings, are vulnerable.

Figure 6

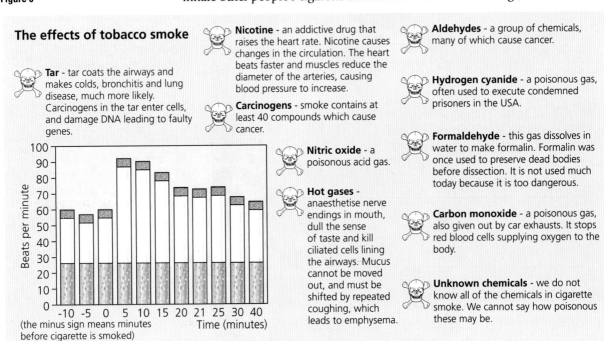

The effects of tobacco smoke

Tar - tar coats the airways and makes colds, bronchitis and lung disease, much more likely. Carcinogens in the tar enter cells, and damage DNA leading to faulty genes.

Nicotine - an addictive drug that raises the heart rate. Nicotine causes changes in the circulation. The heart beats faster and muscles reduce the diameter of the arteries, causing blood pressure to increase.

Carcinogens - smoke contains at least 40 compounds which cause cancer.

Nitric oxide - a poisonous acid gas.

Hot gases - anaesthetise nerve endings in mouth, dull the sense of taste and kill ciliated cells lining the airways. Mucus cannot be moved out, and must be shifted by repeated coughing, which leads to emphysema.

Aldehydes - a group of chemicals, many of which cause cancer.

Hydrogen cyanide - a poisonous gas, often used to execute condemned prisoners in the USA.

Formaldehyde - this gas dissolves in water to make formalin. Formalin was once used to preserve dead bodies before dissection. It is not used much today because it is too dangerous.

Carbon monoxide - a poisonous gas, also given out by car exhausts. It stops red blood cells supplying oxygen to the body.

Unknown chemicals - we do not know all of the chemicals in cigarette smoke. We cannot say how poisonous these may be.

4 Make a list of the ways that smoking damages your health.

Smoking has many more indirect effects on your health. If you smoke, your damaged, mucus-clogged lungs are more vulnerable to respiratory infections and take longer to recover. Your heart has to work harder to provide your tissues with enough oxygen for their needs. Women smokers who become pregnant are more likely to have miscarriages or low birth weight babies. Long term studies show that babies born to mothers who smoke can have impaired achievement levels for years after birth.

Summary of gas exchange in humans

- Human lungs are adapted to pack a large gas exchange surface area into a small volume by having a branching network of airways, ending in millions of tiny alveoli.
- Ventilation helps to maintain favourable concentration gradients across the gas exchange surfaces in the alveoli.

- Breathing rate is controlled by the concentration of carbon dioxide in the blood.
- Infections, dust particles and chemicals can damage the lung surface, reducing its capacity to exchange gases.

6.3 Gas exchange in plants

How does a leaf exchange gases?

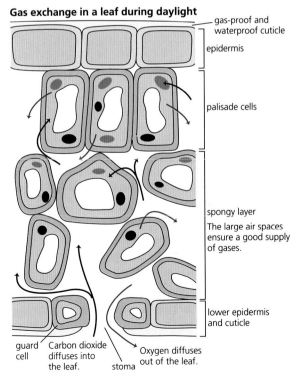

Gas exchange in a leaf during daylight

gas-proof and waterproof cuticle

epidermis

palisade cells

spongy layer

The large air spaces ensure a good supply of gases.

lower epidermis and cuticle

guard cell

Carbon dioxide diffuses into the leaf.

stoma

Oxygen diffuses out of the leaf.

Figure 7

A plant's **respiration** rate is much lower than that of an animal of similar size, so plants do not need to exchange gases at such a high rate. That means they do not need a system to pump air across an exchange surface. But plants do still need to exchange gases with their surroundings.

In bright daylight, when the rate of **photosynthesis** is greater than the rate of respiration, plants need:

- to take in carbon dioxide
- to get rid of excess oxygen
- a large surface area to absorb sunlight.

At night, when no photosynthesis occurs, plant cells need:

- oxygen for respiration
- to get rid of carbon dioxide.

The leaf structure of plants allows gases to be exchanged by diffusion between the air spaces within the leaf and cells.

Leaf surfaces are often smooth and shiny. This is because they are coated with a waterproof layer of waxes, called the cuticle, which stops water escaping from inside the leaf. Unfortunately this also prevents gas exchange. Small holes, or pores, called **stomata** in the leaf surface allow gases to pass through (see figure 7). Each pore is called a stoma.

As leaf cells photosynthesise, they remove carbon dioxide from the network of air spaces that surrounds them. Carbon dioxide from the atmosphere diffuses in through the stomata down the concentration gradient. Some oxygen from photosynthesis is used in respiration, but most accumulates in the leaf spaces, and then diffuses out into the atmosphere down the concentration gradient.

A pair of **guard cells** lie on either side of each stoma. They control the size of the pore. At night, and in low light intensities, the guard cells close the stoma because photosynthesis stops, so the interior cells no longer need to exchange gases with the atmosphere at a high rate. A leaf has enough oxygen in its air spaces to fuel respiration at night. Closing the stomata helps a plant to conserve water, which would otherwise diffuse out from the leaf interior.

5 Explain the following observations.
a Water lilies have stomata on the top surface only.
b Single-celled algae do not have stomata.

How do guard cells change the size of stomata?

Figure 8

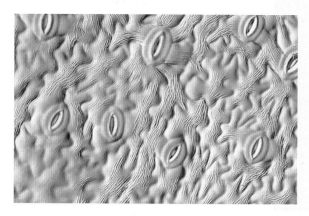

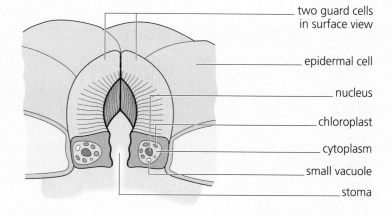

two guard cells in surface view

epidermal cell

nucleus

chloroplast

cytoplasm

small vacuole

stoma

Despite their tiny size, stomata are very effective at letting gases into and out of the leaf.

The stomata open and close as the size and shape of the guard cells change. This is done by changing by the amount of water in the guard cells. The cell wall next to the opening is thicker than the wall on the other sides, and there are cellulose strands running widthways across the cell. When a guard cell is full of water, or **turgid**, it is stretched into a banana shape (see figure 8). When the cells have less water in them they become floppy, or flaccid, and close together over the hole.

The plant changes the water content of guard cells by altering the concentration of ions inside them. If the concentration of ions in the guard cells is high, water moves into them from surrounding cells by **osmosis**. The guard cells expand and the stomata open. The energy needed to power ion movements comes from the respiration of starch stored in the guard cell chloroplasts.

If a plant is in very dry soil, conserving water is more important than gas exchange. A hormone travels from the roots to the shoots and causes a change in the guard cells, which means the alteration in ion concentrations cannot take place. The cells become flaccid and the stomata close.

6 How are guard cells specialised to regulate water loss in leaves?

Can plants survive where there is little oxygen?

The parts of a plant that are above ground have easy access to the gases they need in the atmosphere. Root cells must use oxygen from the air spaces in soil. If root cells do not have enough oxygen to fuel respiration, they cannot take up dissolved minerals from the soil, since this uses an energy-requiring process called **active transport** (see chapter 3, *Cells*).

Some plants are adapted to life in places where oxygen is short from time to time, such as in ponds, streams and waterlogged areas near to rivers. Some plants have large air spaces inside them, which allow vital gases to diffuse up and down the stem to reach root cells. The movement of gases is speeded up when the plant's leaves are warmed by the Sun. As air inside the leaf expands, some passes out through open stomata, but some is pushed down into the stem towards the roots. In other plants adapted to waterlogged conditions, dead shoots sticking up out of the water act as airways down to the submerged roots. Many water plants have carbohydrate stores in their roots and can respire anaerobically for some time using these stores (see chapter 4, *Energy transfers*, for more on **anaerobic respiration**).

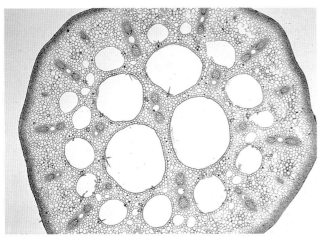

This micrograph of a water lily stem shows the large air spaces that allow gases to diffuse up and down the waterlogged plant.

7 How do root hair cells obtain the oxygen they need for respiration?

Summary of gas exchange in plants

- Plants do not need to exchange gases with their surroundings at the same high rate as animals, so they do not need to pump air across their gas exchange surfaces.

- Gases diffuse into and out of air spaces in the leaf through stomata. Gas exchange between cells and the air spaces happens directly by diffusion.
- The entry and exit of gases through stomata is controlled by guard cells.

Investigations

1 Mouth-to-mouth-resucitation relies on the rescuer breathing into the lungs of someone who cannot breathe for themselves. Even though the rescuer has already breathed the air there is still enough oxygen left to supply the victim. Devise an investigation into the amount of oxygen left in the air after breathing. How could you modify your investigation to find out how the oxygen and carbon dioxide content of breath changesx with activity?

2 Trumpet players and swimmers rely on a good supply of air to be able to carry out their activity well. Devise an investigation to find out if there is a link between these sorts of activity and lung capacity.

Feeding

Learning objectives

By the end of this chapter you should be able to:

- **list** the reasons why living organisms need food
- **explain** why food must be digested
- **explain** how teeth help to break down food
- **describe** how animals digest food
- **describe** some of the ways in which animals other than humans feed

7.1 Food

Why do living organisms need food?

All living organisms need materials to make new cells and to repair damaged tissues. They also need an energy source to fuel their activities. Plants make complex materials from simple substances in the air and soil, using sunlight to drive the reactions. They make glucose for energy, and then combine some of it with nitrates and other materials to make cellulose, fats and amino acids for building cells. You can find out more about **photosynthesis** in chapter 4, *Energy transfers*.

Animals take in energy-rich substances, and materials for growth and repair, by eating plants and other animals. This is called heterotrophic nutrition. The substances living things need for energy, growth and repair are called nutrients.

Single-celled animals engulf tiny food particles in a small bubble of fluid called a vacuole. They break the food down in the bubble and absorb the nutrients they need. Eventually, when the vacuole contains only indigestible material, it moves to the cell surface, and passes the waste to the outside.

Multicellular animals have developed specialised feeding organs. A structure that takes in food, breaks it down and absorbs nutrients, is called a gut.

Most animals are adapted to eat a particular diet. Animals may be classified into the following groups depending on what they eat:

- Herbivores, eat plants.
- Carnivores, kill and eat other animals.
- Omnivores eat both plants and animals.
- Parasites feed on other animals without killing them immediately.
- Detritus feeders feed on the remains of dead animals and plants.

Summary of food

- Animals need food to provide raw materials for growth and repair and as a source of energy for activities.

- The substances living things need for energy, growth and repair are called nutrients.

- Heterotrophic nutrition is eating animals and plants to obtain nutrients.

7.2 Balanced diets

What nutrients do humans need?

Humans are omnivorous, which means we can eat both vegetation and animal materials. The food we eat contains a mixture of nutrients, but they are often not in the right proportions for our needs. We have to eat a wide range of foods to get enough of each nutrient. We can store many nutrients if we eat more than we need, but we cannot store vitamin C or amino acids, so it is important to eat foods containing these each day. Vitamins and minerals are needed in tiny quantities but they play vital roles. If we do not have enough, the processes in which they are involved are hindered and a **deficiency disease** develops. Table 1 on the next page shows the wide range of nutrients the human body needs to live, grow and stay healthy.

Which foods provide the most energy?

Practically all foods provide some energy, but foods have different energy contents depending on the balance of nutrients in them. The main fuel for respiration is glucose, which is a simple carbohydrate. Complex carbohydrates in food are broken down to produce glucose and other simple sugars. Proteins and carbohydrates provide about the same amount of energy per gram of food, but our bodies use carbohydrate for energy and protein to build cells.

Sometimes we do not have access to all the energy in the food we eat, because some components are indigestible, or can only be partly broken down. For example, starch is an excellent energy source because our bodies can easily break it down, but we cannot break down cellulose so its energy remains unavailable to us.

Fats have the highest energy content of all nutrients: foods rich in fat supply the most energy per gram. Fats are stored in our bodies as emergency energy supplies. When carbohydrate reserves are exhausted fats are released from storage and converted to a form that can be respired.

How much energy do we need?

Any process that happens on top of just staying alive requires more energy. Growing children need more energy than adults of the same size would need. Pregnant and breastfeeding women need more energy than other women.

Table 1 *Nutrients required by the human body.*

Nutrient	Use	Food source	Deficiency disease
Protein	Amino acid sub-units are rearranged to make new proteins, which are used to make cells, enzymes, hormones and blood proteins.	meat, fish, eggs, beans, peas, dhal, nuts, milk, yoghurt	
Carbohydrate	Sugar sub-units are our main energy source.	potatoes, bread, pasta, chapattis, corn, yams, rice	
Fat	Sub-units of fats are used to make hormones and cell membranes. Fatty tissues are used as energy stores and to insulate against heat loss.	cheese, eggs, butter, oils, nuts, meat	
Water	Used in blood, tissue fluid and cell cytoplasm.	drinks, fruits and vegetables, milk	
Fibre	Fibre is not a nutrient, but is essential to keep the gut functioning properly.	wholemeal bread and pasta, brown rice, vegetables, pulses, chapattis, some breakfast cereals	constipation bowel cancer
Vitamin A	Used in light receptors in retina. Important for health of skin, mouth and membranes. (Stored in liver.)	milk, cheese, eggs, oily fish, liver, butter, carrots, spinach, apricots, watercress	night blindness, dry eye problems
Vitamin B (actually a mixture of vitamins)	Important in chemical processes involved in respiration. Used in making haemoglobin and blood cells. (Stored in liver.)	milk, meat, eggs, wholegrain cereal and bread	beri-beri, impaired nerves and brain function, pellagra, skin problems, anaemia
Vitamin C	Important for healthy membranes. Helps tissues link together. (Cannot be stored.)	fruits, fresh vegetables (destroyed by cooking and food preparation)	scurvy, bleeding from small blood vessels in gums, wounds heal slowly
Vitamin D	Required for calcium absorption and storage. (Stored in liver.)	milk, cheese, eggs, liver, oily fish, margarine	rickets, weak bones which become deformed, hearing problems
Folic acid	Required for formation of red blood cells, and for correct development of nervous system in fetus.	liver, kidney, dark green vegetables, oranges, bananas (destroyed by cooking)	linked to nervous system problems in infants
Calcium	Required for healthy bone structure, nerve function, blood clotting and muscle contraction. (Stored in bones.)	dairy products, sardines, watercress, bread, cabbage	rickets, soft bones
Iron	Required for formation of haemoglobin, and important for healthy muscles. (Stored in liver.)	liver, kidneys, beef, dried fruit, cocoa	anaemia

1 Why do you think
  a people who are tall and thin
  b small babies
  need more energy per kilogram of body mass than other people?
2 People living in centrally heated houses, who go to work in an office by car, have a lower energy need than their grandparents did at the same age. Explain why.

Everyday activities and work need energy too. The more active a person is, the more energy the person needs (see table 2).

Table 2 *Daily energy requirements of different people.*

Energy requirements (kJ per day)		
Age	Girls and women	Boys and men
Under 1	3 000	3 250
2 years	5 500	5 750
5–6	7 000	7 250
7–8	8 000	8 250
12–14	9 000	11 000
15–17	9 000	12 000
18–34 (moderately active)	9 000	12 000
18–34 (very active)	10 500	14 000
35–64	8 000	11 500
Over 75	7 000	9 000
Pregnant	10 000	–
Breastfeeding	11 500	–

What is a balanced diet?

A balanced diet provides the correct balance of nutrients and the right amount of energy for a person's needs. In a balanced diet, about 60% of the energy should come from foods rich in carbohydrates. Foods containing complex carbohydrates such as starches are more likely to meet other needs at the same time than foods containing refined sugars. For example, boiled sweets and baked potatoes both contain carbohydrate, but potatoes contain fibre, vitamins and minerals as well as an energy source.

Between 20% and 25% of dietary energy should come from fats. It is better for the circulatory system if these are mostly unsaturated fats. Surplus energy-rich food is stored in the body as fat. The fat stores in a healthy adult often serve other functions too, such as heat insulation or cushioning delicate organs like the kidneys. These reserves are used during starvation, or other extreme stresses such as major operations. Women athletes in very hard training and extreme dieters deplete their reserves of fat and their menstrual cycle switches off.

The amount of protein a person needs varies with age and growth phase. A small child needs about twice as much protein per kilogram of body weight as an adult man.

What happens if we do not have a balanced diet?

Healthy weights

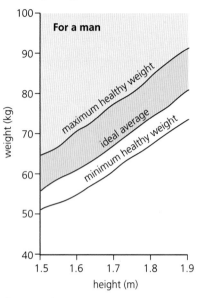

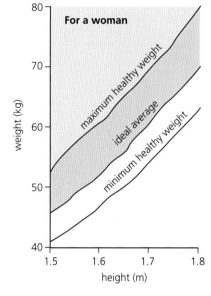

Figure 1 A healthy adult's weight should fall between the limits shown on the graph.

An unbalanced diet contains too much or too little of some nutrients, compared to the person's needs. People who over-eat have an unbalanced diet, because it contains too much of many things. Excess energy is stored as fat around the person's hips and the front of the abdomen. If the person over-eats over a long period, fat is later deposited under the skin all over the body and around the internal organs. The body can cope very well with some excess, but obese adults (who are more than 20 kg overweight) are more likely to suffer from strains on the heart, circulatory system, leg joints and back. A diet that contains more salt than a person needs can also lead to high blood pressure and heart problems.

A diet which does not provide enough of a nutrient leads to **malnutrition**. Shortages of vitamins and minerals lead to deficiency diseases, which can usually be treated by supplying the missing nutrient. Chronically malnourished people often have an imbalance of several nutrients. In industrialised countries, many people are chronically malnourished, although they get enough energy to survive and even grow. They are likely to have diets high in sugar and saturated fat, which provide enough energy (sometimes enough to cause obesity) but are low in vitamins, complex carbohydrates and iron. Malnourished children cope less well in school, and their health is worse in later life.

Many chronically malnourished children in developing countries do not get enough energy-rich or protein-rich foods for satisfactory growth. Repeated bouts of diarrhoea also lead to malnutrition because they prevent nutrients being absorbed in the gut. People who do not have enough energy or nutrients to fulfil their body needs are starving. In the end, starving people lose so much body mass that they die.

Many processed foods have ingredients that are not nutrients but that in some way change the quality of the food. For example, flavourings, preservatives and colourings are all additives (see table 3). Some additives are not 'traditional' food ingredients, and some people are concerned that they might have an adverse effect on health. Even traditional food ingredients are not necessarily good for our health.

Table 3 *Some common food additives.*

Function	Examples	Advantage	Disadvantage
Flavourings	monosodium glutamate (MSG) (an amino acid)	Improves taste.	
	salt	Improves taste.	Contributes to high blood pressure.
	chocolate flavour	Improves taste.	
	sugar	Improves taste.	Rots teeth and is fattening.
Additives to improve nutritional quality	Lysine is added to flours for foods in places where diet is poor.	Enriches poor diets.	Expensive.
Colourings	annatto	Improves appearance, by replacing colour lost in processing.	Some people are allergic to annatto.
Sweeteners	Nutrasweet	Food can taste sweet without being so fattening.	Unsuitable for some people. Gives a bitter aftertaste.
Anti-bacterial additives	vinegar	Reduces bacterial spoilage, on ready-made salads, for example.	Vitamin content of food declines with storage.
Anti-oxidants	sodium ascorbate	Stops fat spoiling and becoming rancid in pre-cooked meats.	
Stabilisers	carragheen	Stops food texture separating.	
Thickeners	guar gum	Gives a thicker consistency and better sensation in the mouth.	

3 The two meals below have approximately the same energy content but a dietician could criticise both meals. Comment on how well these meals form part of a balanced diet.

Meal 1		Meal 2	
Food	Energy content (kJ per portion)	Food	Energy content (kJ per portion)
glass of cola	340	glass of wine	250
fish fingers	749	tomato soup	550
baked beans	270	roast chicken	600
chips	1065	boiled potatoes	339
banana	326	sweetcorn	325
ice cream	698	carrots	98
		apple pie	1100
TOTAL	3448	TOTAL	3262

Summary of balanced diets

- A balanced diet provides nutrients and energy in the right proportions for a person's needs.
- Carbohydrates and fats are energy sources. Protein is used to make new cell materials. Vitamins and minerals are used in cell reactions.
- More energy is needed for growth and for physical activity.
- Malnutrition occurs when a person's diet is not balanced.

7.3 The digestive system

What is the digestive system?

The **digestive system** is a long muscular tube, called the gut, and associated organs that have inputs into the gut (see figure 2). Food is broken down, or **digested**, inside the gut and nutrients pass through its walls into blood vessels running alongside. The nutrients are carried to the liver, where their concentration in the blood is regulated, and some surplus nutrients are stored. Each section of the gut has a specific role in the breakdown of food, and is modified to do its job as efficiently as possible. There are valves, or sphincters, at places along the gut to separate different regions and prevent food passing backwards.

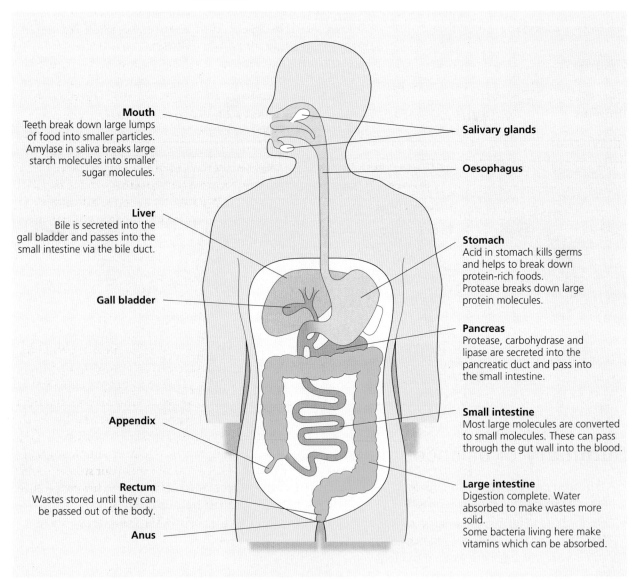

Mouth
Teeth break down large lumps of food into smaller particles. Amylase in saliva breaks large starch molecules into smaller sugar molecules.

Salivary glands

Oesophagus

Liver
Bile is secreted into the gall bladder and passes into the small intestine via the bile duct.

Stomach
Acid in stomach kills germs and helps to break down protein-rich foods.
Protease breaks down large protein molecules.

Gall bladder

Pancreas
Protease, carbohydrase and lipase are secreted into the pancreatic duct and pass into the small intestine.

Appendix

Small intestine
Most large molecules are converted to small molecules. These can pass through the gut wall into the blood.

Rectum
Wastes stored until they can be passed out of the body.

Large intestine
Digestion complete. Water absorbed to make wastes more solid.
Some bacteria living here make vitamins which can be absorbed.

Anus

Figure 2

What is the digestive system for?

Food contains large, insoluble molecules which cannot be absorbed by cells because they are too large to pass through cell membranes. The digestive system digests, or breaks down, large insoluble food molecules into small soluble ones which can be absorbed. Both physical and chemical processes help this breakdown.

Food is physically broken down when it is chewed and churned up in the gut. It ends up as very fine particles. Then chemical breakdown is carried out by **enzymes**, which break large molecules into smaller ones. Grinding food into small particles with a large overall surface area speeds up the action of enzymes because these chemicals can only work at the surface of food particles.

Fats are difficult to break down, because they do not dissolve in the watery mixture in the gut, and tend to join together in globules. Churning the food up helps break up large globules into smaller ones, and disperse them through the food mixture where enzymes can work on them.

Food is pushed along the gut by waves of muscular contraction called **peristalsis**. The gut wall is made up of two layers of muscle. When the walls are stretched by a pellet of food, the circular muscles in the gut wall contract, pushing the food in front, like squeezing toothpaste out of a tube (see figure 3). The tube reopens when the circular muscles relax and the outer muscle fibres contract. The stomach has an extra layer of muscle fibres that help to churn its contents.

Peristalsis

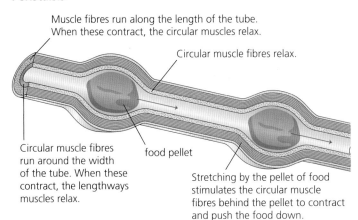

Muscle fibres run along the length of the tube. When these contract, the circular muscles relax.

Circular muscle fibres relax.

Circular muscle fibres run around the width of the tube. When these contract, the lengthways muscles relax.

food pellet

Stretching by the pellet of food stimulates the circular muscle fibres behind the pellet to contract and push the food down.

Figure 3

What happens when we put food in our mouths?

As soon as food enters your mouth digestion begins. It is torn and ground up by your teeth into small pieces. The taste, smell and appearance of food stimulate your salivary glands to release saliva. Saliva is a mixture of water, mucin and an enzyme called **salivary amylase**. It moistens the food, and then the enzyme starts the chemical breakdown. The enzyme needs a slightly alkaline pH to work, which is provided by dissolved salts in the saliva. Salivary amylase is an enzyme that breaks down starch into a simple sugar called maltose. It continues to work until the food reaches your stomach, where conditions become too acidic for it. Once your food is chewed up, it is pushed to the back of the mouth by your tongue which triggers you to swallow. Then pellets of food get pushed down towards your stomach by peristalsis.

4 Why is it possible to stand on your head and drink a glass of water?

Why do we have different types of teeth?

Mammals, unlike other animals, chew their food. They have a soft palate, which separates the nose and mouth so that they can chew food and breathe at the same time.

Different types of teeth do different jobs. Incisors at the front cut and chop food, canine teeth tear food, while molars and premolars at the back grind it up. Figure 4 shows the structure of a human canine tooth.

Figure 4

Section through a human canine tooth

In human teeth, the root constricts as the tooth reaches full size, and the dentine-forming cells stop working. But in herbivore teeth, the root does not constrict so each tooth continues to grow throughout the animal's life.

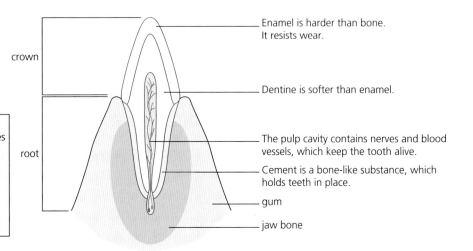

crown

root

Enamel is harder than bone. It resists wear.

Dentine is softer than enamel.

The pulp cavity contains nerves and blood vessels, which keep the tooth alive.

Cement is a bone-like substance, which holds teeth in place.

gum

jaw bone

Why do teeth decay?

Although enamel is the hardest material in any mammal's body, it is vulnerable to attack by acids. Acids are naturally present in fruits and other foods, and they are also made by bacteria living in the spaces between teeth, in crevices on the tooth surface, and at the edges of the gums. Food particles get lodged in these crevices and bacteria feed and grow on them, forming plaque. The acids they produce corrode your tooth enamel, and expose the softer dentine. The enamel on teeth does not extend far below the gum edge, so when plaque forms there the dentine can quickly be attacked. The links between the tooth and its socket can be weakene, and the tooth might fall out. Brushing your teeth regularly, and using an alkaline toothpaste, helps to minimise the harmful activity of bacteria.

Mouthwashes and toothpaste contain anti-bacterial chemicals to reduce the number of bacteria.

5 a Study this graph, which shows children's filling records and the natural fluoride content of water supplies in many areas. Describe what it shows about fluoride and tooth decay.

b In one area, the water naturally contains 0.5 mg/l of fluoride. A content of more than 2.0 mg/l leads to mottled teeth. How much fluoride should the water company add to the supply, to improve the dental health of local children? Give two reasons for your answer.

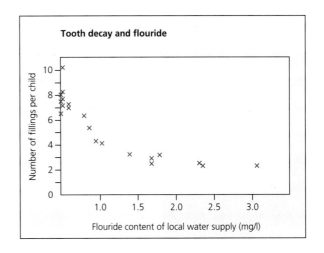

What happens when food reaches the stomach?

Cells in the stomach wall secrete hydrochloric acid. This acid kills some of the microbes in food, and also stops salivary amylase working. Another enzyme called gastric protease is secreted, which works best in acidic conditions. It is mixed with the food and begins breaking down proteins into smaller molecules. The acid and gastric protease could attack the wall of the stomach, but it is protected by a layer of mucus produced by glands in the stomach lining. Babies' stomachs also produce another enzyme called rennin, which coagulates milk proteins to help digest them.

What happens when food reaches the small intestine?

Your small intestine is not small: it is over 6 m long. This long, folded tube is the main site of food digestion and absorption. Several secretions are mixed with the food in the first part of the intestine.

Bile is made in the liver, but concentrated and stored in the gall bladder, and released into the intestine through a short tube (see figure 2 on page 60). Bile contains salts to neutralise the acidity of the food mixture leaving the stomach. Bile also helps fat digestion. Bile salts are emulsifiers, which means that they help prevent small fat globules joining together. Because fats are dispersed as millions of tiny globules, rather than as fewer larger globules, it is much easier for fat-digesting enzymes to work on them. Later, the bile salts help the absorption of digested fat sub-units through the gut wall.

The pancreas, and the glands in the wall of the gut, secrete enzymes which complete the digestion of food in the small intestine. Pancreatic enzymes enter the gut through the pancreatic duct. The enzymes at work in the small intestine include:

- pancreatic amylase, which completes starch breakdown
- lipase, which breaks down fats into fatty acids and glycerol
- proteases, which break down proteins into amino acids.

6 What are protein-digesting enzymes called? How are proteins changed to be absorbed into the blood?

Once these enzymes have finished working on the food, the end product is a mixture of glucose and other simple sugars, amino acids, fatty acids, glycerol and other molecules including vitamins and mineral ions.

How is food absorbed?

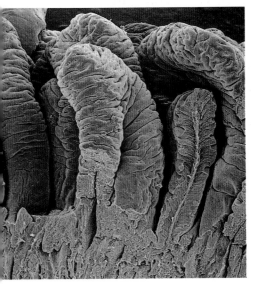

This micrograph shows the lining of the small intestine.

Figure 5 shows how the products of digestion are absorbed into the body from the small intestine. The lining of the intestine is adapted to give a huge surface area for absorption. The inner lining is folded and ridged. The folds in turn carry fine finger-like projections, called villi, all over them. Even the cells covering the villi have projections on their surfaces, to make sure nutrients are absorbed as efficiently as possible.

How nutrients are absorbed

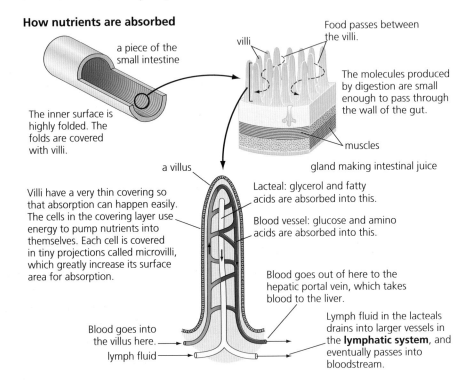

a piece of the small intestine

The inner surface is highly folded. The folds are covered with villi.

villi

Food passes between the villi.

The molecules produced by digestion are small enough to pass through the wall of the gut.

muscles

gland making intestinal juice

a villus

Villi have a very thin covering so that absorption can happen easily. The cells in the covering layer use energy to pump nutrients into themselves. Each cell is covered in tiny projections called microvilli, which greatly increase its surface area for absorption.

Lacteal: glycerol and fatty acids are absorbed into this.

Blood vessel: glucose and amino acids are absorbed into this.

Blood goes out of here to the hepatic portal vein, which takes blood to the liver.

Lymph fluid in the lacteals drains into larger vessels in the **lymphatic system**, and eventually passes into bloodstream.

Blood goes into the villus here.

lymph fluid

Figure 5

What is the large intestine for?

The small intestine joins the large intestine just before the appendix (see figure 2 on page 60).

When food enters the large intestine, most of its useful nutrients have been removed, but it still contains a lot of water. Water and mineral salts are reabsorbed by cells lining the large intestine, before indigestible material such as cellulose is eliminated from the body. The more fibre in the food, the quicker it passes through the gut. Fibre seems to be very important for the health of the large intestine: people with a low fibre diet are more likely to suffer bowel cancer, as well as constipation and backaches. As undigested food passes through the large intestine, it becomes more solid and is formed into faeces, which are expelled through the anus.

Many microbes live in the large intestine. Some useful bacteria make vitamins which are absorbed. They also stop harmful microbes colonising the gut. Other microbes, such as those causing typhoid, cholera and food poisoning, can survive stomach acids and cause infections in the intestines. They damage the cells lining the intestine and affect the way they absorb nutrients and water. The cells may even start to put mineral salts and water back into the intestine from the body, instead of absorbing them. When this happens, the sufferer loses a lot of water and valuable salts in watery faeces called diarrhoea. If the sufferer is very young, old, ill or malnourished these losses can be fatal.

Millions of young children die each year from dehydrating diseases such as cholera. The disease-causing microbes are carried in water and food contaminated with infected faeces. Treatment is very simple – the patient is given drinks to replenish water and salts in the body – but unless the sources of food and water contamination are removed, the disease will recur.

7 What happens to a piece of buttered wholemeal toast, from when it enters your mouth until its nutrients are absorbed?

8 What is fibre? Why is fibre included in a healthy diet?

What happens to nutrients once they are absorbed?

Most of the nutrients absorbed in the small intestine pass straight to the liver. Vitamins A, B and D and iron, are stored in liver cells. If there is enough glucose in the blood, **insulin** from the pancreas stimulates liver cells to take up surplus glucose and store it as glycogen. When blood sugar levels fall below a critical level, another hormone stimulates the liver cells to release glucose back into the blood. If the glucose stores are full, any extra glucose is converted into fat in special fat storage cells round the body. Regulating blood glucose concentration is an example of **homeostasis**. You can read more about this in chapter 10, *Homeostasis*.

Active cells need amino acids to build proteins, but when more are absorbed than are needed, the surplus amino acids cannot be stored. Some kinds of amino acids can be converted into other kinds which *are* needed. The rest are broken down in the liver and parts of the molecule are recycled. The main part of the molecule is converted into glucose or other compounds, but the 'amino' part has to be excreted, because its breakdown product is alkaline and would disturb the pH balance of body fluids. It is converted into a less harmful form called urea, as shown in figure 6. This chemical is carried in the blood to the kidneys, and excreted in urine. You can read more about how the kidneys work in chapter 9, *Water balance*.

The liver also plays an important role in protecting the body against harmful substances absorbed from food. Though our tastebuds and sense of smell give us some warning of poor quality food and drink, there can be small amounts of harmful chemicals that we cannot detect. Sometimes people also eat and drink things that they know are harmful, like alcohol. Liver cells produce enzymes that convert these molecules into less harmful substances that can then be carried to the kidneys and excreted.

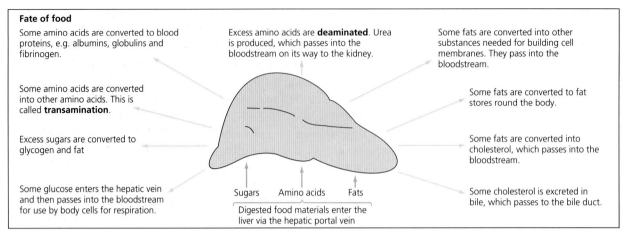

Fate of food

Some amino acids are converted to blood proteins, e.g. albumins, globulins and fibrinogen.

Some amino acids are converted into other amino acids. This is called **transamination**.

Excess sugars are converted to glycogen and fat

Some glucose enters the hepatic vein and then passes into the bloodstream for use by body cells for respiration.

Excess amino acids are **deaminated**. Urea is produced, which passes into the bloodstream on its way to the kidney.

Some fats are converted into other substances needed for building cell membranes. They pass into the bloodstream.

Some fats are converted to fat stores round the body.

Some fats are converted into cholesterol, which passes into the bloodstream.

Some cholesterol is excreted in bile, which passes to the bile duct.

Sugars   Amino acids   Fats

Digested food materials enter the liver via the hepatic portal vein

Figure 6

Summary of the digestive system

- Digestion breaks down large, insoluble food materials into small soluble molecules which can be absorbed.
- Food is broken down physically by the action of teeth and by churning inside the gut.
- Chemical breakdown is carried out by several different enzymes in the mouth, stomach and small intestine. Each enzyme needs particular conditions to work effectively.
- Food is moved along the gut by peristalsis.

- The products of digestion are absorbed in the small intestine.
- The products of carbohydrate and protein digestion are absorbed directly into the bloodstream.
- The products of fat digestion are absorbed into lacteals, and are passed to the bloodstream via the lymphatic system.
- The liver regulates the balance of nutrients in the blood and breaks down harmful materials.

7.4 Digesting specialised diets

How do herbivores cope with their diet?

Herbivores have to eat large amounts of food because most plant materials are largely water and cellulose and contain a low concentration of nutrients. A herbivore's gut has to be large, to cope with the volume of food, and long to give enough time to digest the tough vegetation.

Herbivore mammals have to break open tough cell walls in their plant food to release the more nutritious cytoplasm inside. Their jaws move from side to side, as well as up and down, which produces an effective grinding action between the close-fitting ridged teeth. In order to cope with this constant hard wear, herbivore teeth are open-rooted, and continue to grow throughout the animal's life, replacing the top surface with new dentine and enamel as it wears away. As the teeth wear, layers of dentine wear away slightly faster than the layers of enamel between them, leaving a series of ridges on the top surface which help to crush plant material (see figure 7).

Herbivore teeth

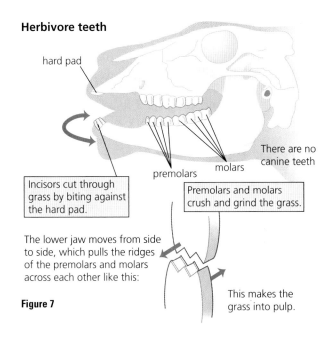

hard pad

premolars

molars

There are no canine teeth

Incisors cut through grass by biting against the hard pad.

Premolars and molars crush and grind the grass.

The lower jaw moves from side to side, which pulls the ridges of the premolars and molars across each other like this:

Figure 7

This makes the grass into pulp.

Birds and reptiles swallow small stones into a gizzard. Here vegetation is ground up as it passes through.

The cellulose in plant cell walls is a potentially valuable energy source because it is made of glucose sub-units. But it is very hard to digest because its sub-units are linked in a way that the starch-digesting enzymes produced by mammals cannot attack. The only way herbivore mammals can digest cellulose is with the help of microbes in their gut which produce a cellulose-digesting enzyme called cellulase. This is a **mutualistic relationship**. The microbes live in extensions of the herbivore's gut, where they digest plant material in exchange for a warm, safe place to live.

Cattle and sheep are **ruminants**: they have an extension of the gut just before the stomach called a rumen (figure 8). As the animal grazes, vegetation passes into the rumen. It stays there fermenting for hours as enzymes produced by the microbes living there digest the plant material. These microbes prefer a low oxygen environment, and release gases like methane as by-products. When food leaves the rumen it goes back to the animal's mouth to be chewed again – this is called chewing the cud – and then passes to the stomach for normal digestion. It can take a day and a half for food to pass through a sheep, which allows it to digest up to 60% of the cellulose in it. Horses and rabbits have an extension to the hind part of the gut, called a caecum, to house microbes. Nutrients can be absorbed directly through the walls of the caecum and rumen.

Figure 8

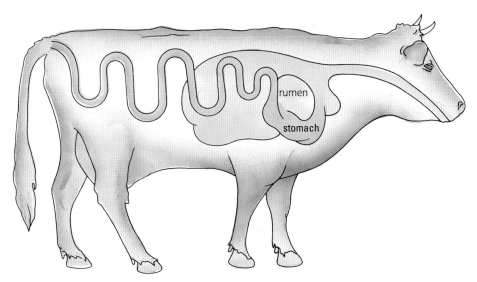

rumen

stomach

How do carnivores cope with their diet?

The jaws of carnivore mammals have powerful muscles and large canine teeth to catch, hold and kill their struggling prey, and then tear up the food into pieces small enough to be swallowed (figure 9). The canine and incisor teeth are very sharp, and even the molars have pointed tops for chopping flesh rather than grinding. The top and bottom teeth do not bite against each other like human teeth – instead the top teeth overlap the bottom ones to slice through meat as the jaws move up and down.

The lion uses her strong, sharp molars and premolars to grasp and slice into her prey.

Carnivore teeth

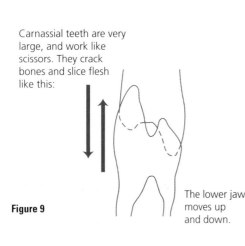

Carnassial teeth are very large, and work like scissors. They crack bones and slice flesh like this:

Figure 9

The lower jaw moves up and down.

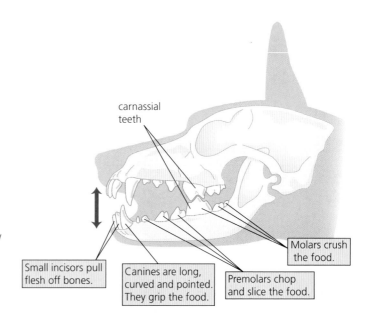

carnassial teeth

Small incisors pull flesh off bones.

Canines are long, curved and pointed. They grip the food.

Premolars chop and slice the food.

Molars crush the food.

Sugar	Rate of absorption (arbitrary units)	
	Living intestine	Poisoned intestine
Arabinose	29	29
Glucose	100	33

9 Give two differences between the teeth and jaws of a carnivore, such as a cat, and a herbivore, such as a cow.

10 The table shows the rate at which two sugars are absorbed into the lining of the small intestine of a mammal. The rates are shown for living intestine and for intestine that has been poisoned with a substance which stops respiration in the cells lining the intestine.

a By what process does arabinose enter the lining of the intestine? Explain your answer.

b What do the data in the table suggest about how glucose enters the lining of the living intestine? Explain your answer fully.

Summary of digesting specialised diets

- Herbivores and carnivores have teeth and jaws which are adapted for the food they eat.

- Herbivores have adaptations of the gut to digest cellulose.

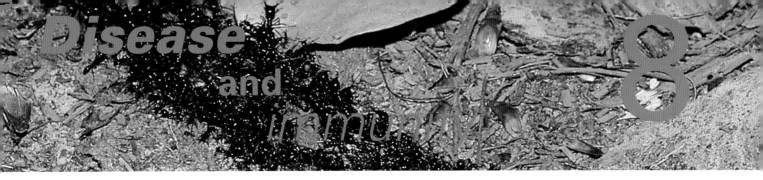

Disease and immunity

Learning objectives

By the end of this chapter you should be able to:

- **list** the causes of disease
- **describe** what is meant by an infectious disease
- **describe** bacteria and viruses
- **list** the ways infectious diseases are transmitted
- **describe** the functions of white blood cells and antibodies

- **explain** why organ transplants sometimes fail
- **describe** how a vaccine works
- **explain** the difference between an antibiotic, a disinfectant and an antiseptic
- **describe** ways to protect the community against infectious diseases

8.1 Disease

What causes diseases

Table 1 *Causes of disease.*

Cause	Examples
Accidents	broken legs, teeth knocked out
Infection by microbes	measles, tuberculosis
Tissues or organs do not work properly	kidney disease, diabetes
Malnutrition	scurvy, obesity
Chemical contamination	lung cancer, asbestosis
Unhealthy life style	coronary heart disease, drug addiction, stress
Genetic disorder	phenylketonuria, sickle-cell anaemia
Allergic responses	hayfever, asthma

To grow into a healthy adult, a child needs:
- the right conditions when developing as a fetus
- clean, warm and safe housing
- a diet that provides the right balance of nutrients
- physical care, emotional support and intellectual stimulation.

But even when you have a healthy life style, things can still go wrong and you can become ill (see table 1).

What is an infectious disease?

Infectious diseases are caused by microbes, mainly bacteria or viruses. Only a few diseases are caused by protozoa, but they are some of the most important in the world. Fungi do not trouble animals much, but they are the main cause of plant diseases.

A microbe that causes disease is called a **pathogen**. Some pathogens are not very infectious, or cause quite mild diseases like the common cold. Others are very infectious, or cause a major illness: these are described as virulent pathogens.

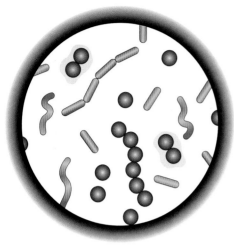

Figure 1 A sample of mouth bacteria is likely to contain coccus (round bacteria), bacillus (longer, rod-shaped bacteria) and spirillum bacteria which are curved into a spiral.

Bacteria are single-celled organisms with a fairly simple structure, as shown in chapter 3, *Cells*. Some have whip-like tails, which enable them to swim from place to place through moisture. Though most bacteria live in soil, water and decaying materials, some are specialised for growing inside animals (see figure 1). Most bacteria are harmless or useful; only a few species cause disease. Pathogenic bacteria damage cells as they grow, and they may release harmful chemicals, or **toxins**. We can see this damage as the symptoms of a disease.

Viruses are not like other living things, because they do not have a cellular structure, or an independent life outside another cell. They are only active inside a host cell. Outside a cell, a virus is an inert particle consisting of a protein coat wrapped around a package of genes on a short nucleic acid molecule. Some viruses contain a few enzyme molecules but most entirely rely on the host cell to produce all the chemicals they need to reproduce themselves (see figure 2).

How do microbes spread to new victims?

Most bacteria and viruses cannot move about on their own. Instead they are carried from one host to another by air or water, or by touch. Disease-causing organisms can be transmitted by:

- droplets in the air
- infections in water
- infected food
- **vectors** (such as insects)
- direct contact.

When an infected person coughs and sneezes, microbe-laden droplets of moisture are ejected from the lungs into the air. Other people become infected when they inhale the droplets. Some droplets stick to walls and furniture and when they dry up the microbes are released. It is very difficult to control the spread of droplet infections, especially when people are crowded together.

The microbes that cause cholera and typhoid leave the victim's body in the faeces or urine, and get carried into rivers. Rivers are often sources of drinking water and if the water is not treated the microbes can infect many other people.

The best control for water-borne diseases is to provide effective sewage and water treatment. Where such treatment is not available, people should sterilise drinking water with chemicals or by boiling, and should not eat foods which could have been in contact with untreated water, such as salads and iced drinks.

Pathogenic microbes can contaminate food and infect those who eat it. Infected catering or food shop workers can get faecal microbes on their hands when visiting the lavatory. If they prepare food without washing their hands thoroughly, the infection could be passed on.

The purple ribbon-like shapes in this light micrograph are the protozoan parasites that cause African sleeping sickness. They are carried by an insect vector called the tsetse fly.

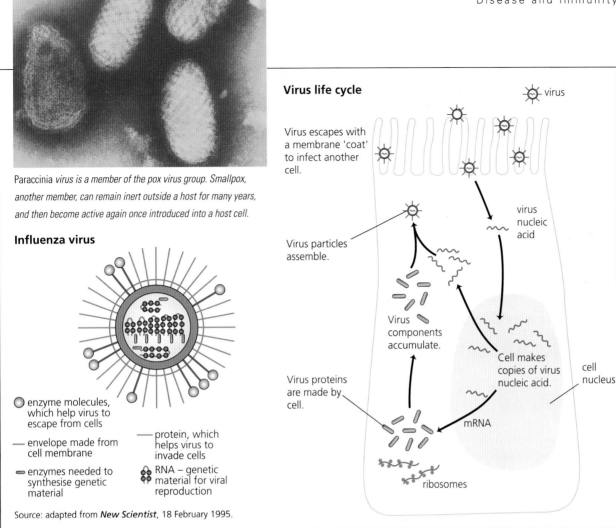

Paraccinia *virus is a member of the pox virus group. Smallpox, another member, can remain inert outside a host for many years, and then become active again once introduced into a host cell.*

Influenza virus

○ enzyme molecules, which help virus to escape from cells

— envelope made from cell membrane

⊖ enzymes needed to synthesise genetic material

— protein, which helps virus to invade cells

RNA – genetic material for viral reproduction

Source: adapted from **New Scientist**, 18 February 1995.

Virus life cycle

virus

Virus escapes with a membrane 'coat' to infect another cell.

virus nucleic acid

Virus particles assemble.

Virus components accumulate.

Cell makes copies of virus nucleic acid.

cell nucleus

Virus proteins are made by cell.

mRNA

ribosomes

Figure 2

One way of controlling the insect vectors that carry disease-causing microbes is to spray the places where they rest and breed with powerful insecticides.

Microbes found in animals' guts, such as *Salmonella* bacteria, can contaminate meat and chicken flesh as the animals are killed and processed. While the meat is chilled the microbes are not very active, but as soon as the meat reaches room temperature they multiply rapidly. *Salmonella* microbes can spread to other foods kept nearby. The microbes are killed when food is properly cooked. Frozen chickens must be fully thawed before they are cooked. If a chicken is still frozen in the middle when cooking starts, this part will be at just the right temperature for bacteria to multiply when the outside is cooked.

Some pathogenic microbes are carried around inside animals, usually insects, which bite or suck human blood. The carrier is called a vector. The microbes are injected into the human host with saliva as the insect feeds, or are deposited in the insect's faeces onto the host's skin. The victim then unknowingly rubs the infected faeces into the irritating bites while scratching. Controlling diseases that are spread in this way, such as malaria and yellow fever, involves controlling the vector as well as the microbe. Although houseflies are not biting or sucking insects they carry bacteria on their bodies and in their mouthparts. They feed on decaying material and can carry microbes from dustbins, toilets and animal faeces to human food left uncovered.

Some disease-causing microbes are passed from one victim to the next during intimate contact such as kissing, breastfeeding, giving birth or sexual intercourse. Often the microbes are in body fluids or blood which pass from a minute cut on one person into a similar wound on another. Diseases that are transmitted in this way can only be controlled by encouraging infected people not to be intimate with others until their infection is cured. A few infections can be passed from one person's skin to another's skin directly (see table 2).

Table 2 Microbes causing infectious diseases.

Type of microbe	Disease caused	Transmitted by
Bacteria	food poisoning (e.g. *Salmonella*)	food
	whooping cough	air-borne droplets
	cholera	water
	bacterial dysentery	houseflies
	tetanus	soil
	diphtheria	water
Viruses	influenza	air-borne droplets
	common cold	air-borne droplets
	chicken pox	direct skin contact
	hepatitis B	body fluids
Protozoa	malaria	Anopheles mosquito bite
	sleeping sickness	tsetse fly bite
Fungi	athlete's foot	spores on the ground
	ringworm	direct skin contact

Some infections can be transmitted in several ways. For example, tuberculosis is usually spread in air-borne droplets as a sufferer coughs. But it can also be caught by drinking milk from infected cows. To prevent it spreading in this way, regulations stop farmers keeping infected cows, and milk must be heat-treated before it is sold.

Over the last century, there has been a huge increase in international travel, which has lead to a far greater movement of pathogens from country to country than ever before. Travellers must be aware of disease in the places they visit, and take appropriate measures, not only to protect themselves, but to prevent infections being carried around the world.

1 Why are people encouraged not to spit, and to use a handkerchief when they sneeze or cough?

2 In hospitals, operating theatre staff wear masks, sterile clothing and gloves.
   a Explain how these measures help to prevent the patient getting infections.
   b Why is the patient at particular risk from infection during an operation?

3 Why do houseflies carry so many diseases?

4 What problems do you think could arise from the method used to control insect disease vectors shown on page 71?

Summary of disease

- Most infectious diseases are caused by bacteria or viruses.
- Microbes can be passed from one person to another directly, in food and drink, by moisture droplets, by vectors and by contact with body fluids such as blood.

- Bacteria are single-celled organisms with a cell wall. They reproduce rapidly by binary fission. A few species cause disease.
- Viruses are made up of a protein coat surrounding a nucleic acid molecule. They can only reproduce inside another cell.

8.2 The immune system

How do our bodies prevent microbial infections?

Some micro-organisms, called commensals, live on skin. They are harmless themselves, but help to prevent other microbes growing by competing with them for space and food. Some commensals release acids as waste products which also help to prevent the growth of pathogens.

For as long as multicellular organisms have existed, they have been prone to infection by microbes. As they have evolved ways to deal with infections, so microbes have evolved to overcome their defences. It is a never-ending race. Humans have several defences to reduce the chances of microbes getting established and colonising our bodies:

- Tough, dry skin with few natural entrances is a barrier against invading microbes.
- Sweat, tears and sebum from sebaceous glands contain chemicals such as lysozyme which inhibit microbial activity.
- Sticky mucus inside the mouth and other passages traps microbes, and prevents them from moving further into the body.
- Stomach acids and fevers kill microbes.
- Vomiting and diarrhoea push microbes out of the body.

What happens if microbes do infect our bodies?

If a microbe does manage to start an infection in your body, your **immune system** becomes active. The immune system consists of organs and glands which produce several sorts of white blood cell (see figure 3 on the next page). Each sort of white cell plays a different part in removing microbes and infected cells from the body. Although they are often called white blood cells, many of them are not in the blood most of the time. Some white cells are lodged in tissues, others circulate round the body.

Your immune system can distinguish between your own healthy cells and other 'foreign' particles. Each molecule in the outer surface of a cell contributes to its shape, making a pattern, in the same way that a combination of features makes a pattern that you recognise as a particular person's face. Some surface molecules are more noticeable to the immune system than others, in the same way that a person's eyes often make more impression than their ears. The molecules that the immune system notices most strongly are called **antigens**. The most important ones on human cells are the MHC antigens. These antigens are determined by genes inherited from your parents and each person has a unique set of MHC antigens.

Your own combination of antigens is recognised by your immune system as 'self'. Microbes are made of quite different chemical components, so the immune system recognises their antigens as foreign, or 'non-self'. Not every chemical you meet is an important antigen, and your body learns to tolerate common antigens in the world around you. Some people's immune systems are less tolerant and they can develop allergic immune reactions to things like pollen, pet hair, strawberries, lactose or even washing powders.

The immune system

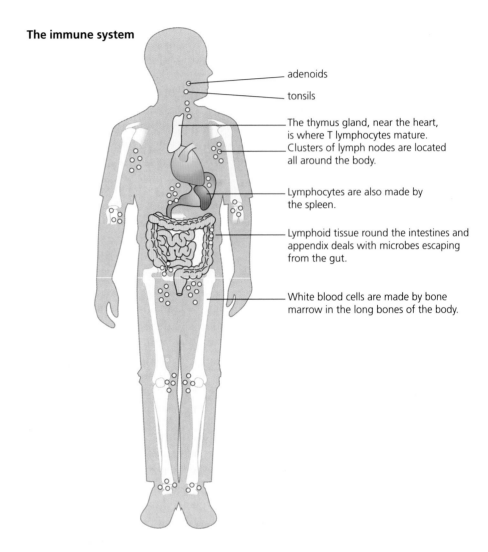

adenoids

tonsils

The thymus gland, near the heart, is where T lymphocytes mature. Clusters of lymph nodes are located all around the body.

Lymphocytes are also made by the spleen.

Lymphoid tissue round the intestines and appendix deals with microbes escaping from the gut.

White blood cells are made by bone marrow in the long bones of the body.

Figure 3

How does the immune system defend the body?

The cells which recognise 'self' and 'non-self' antigens are white cells called T lymphocytes, or T cells, which are made in the **lymph nodes** and circulate in the blood. When a microbe infects the body, T cells detect its antigens. They activate another set of white cells made in the lymph nodes, called B lymphocytes, or B cells. As the B cells multiply, some stay in the lymph nodes making more B cells but most enter the blood. B cells make **antibodies** which match the antigens. Antibody molecules are proteins which coat the microbes and clump them together to stop them moving or harming body cells (see figure 4).

Microbes have several different antigens on their surfaces, and toxins can act as antigens too. Separate groups of B cells make antibodies to match each antigen carried by a microbe. An infection by another sort of microbe activates different sets of B cells, which produce antibodies targeted specifically at its antigens.

The immune response

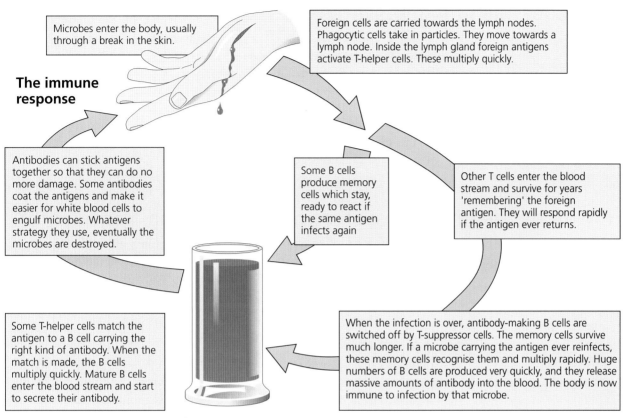

Microbes enter the body, usually through a break in the skin.

Foreign cells are carried towards the lymph nodes. Phagocytic cells take in particles. They move towards a lymph node. Inside the lymph gland foreign antigens activate T-helper cells. These multiply quickly.

Antibodies can stick antigens together so that they can do no more damage. Some antibodies coat the antigens and make it easier for white blood cells to engulf microbes. Whatever strategy they use, eventually the microbes are destroyed.

Some B cells produce memory cells which stay, ready to react if the same antigen infects again

Other T cells enter the blood stream and survive for years 'remembering' the foreign antigen. They will respond rapidly if the antigen ever returns.

Some T-helper cells match the antigen to a B cell carrying the right kind of antibody. When the match is made, the B cells multiply quickly. Mature B cells enter the blood stream and start to secrete their antibody.

When the infection is over, antibody-making B cells are switched off by T-suppressor cells. The memory cells survive much longer. If a microbe carrying the antigen ever reinfects, these memory cells recognise them and multiply rapidly. Huge numbers of B cells are produced very quickly, and they release massive amounts of antibody into the blood. The body is now immune to infection by that microbe.

What is immunity?

Once an infection is over, antibodies circulate in the blood for a long time. The body is protected from another infection by that microbe because T cells and B cells left in the lymph nodes 'remember' the antigens. If the same microbe re-enters the body, the appropriate B cells are generated much more quickly than when the microbe first invaded. The body is now immune to that particular microbe.

What else does the immune system do?

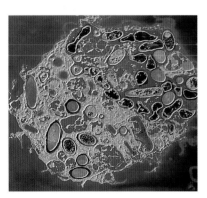

This macrophage has engulfed many bacteria (shown in red and green here).

Different white cells, produced in the bone marrow, get rid of immobilised, antibody-coated microbes, and damaged cell debris. These cells are phagocytic, which means they engulf microbes and destroy them. Phagocytic macrophages stay in tissues where microbes are likely to invade, such as the lungs and around the gut. Polymorphonuclear neutrophils (called polymorphs or phagocytes to save a tongue twister!) circulate in the blood. Wherever cells are damaged by wounds or infection, chemicals are released that attract phagocytes. The phagocytes squeeze through capillary walls to get to the tissue and destroy damaged cells and invading microbes.

Damaged or infected tissues quickly become red, swollen, tender and warm to the touch. A rush of warm blood into the area causes this inflammation, which is triggered by a chemical called histamine.

How does the immune system deal with viruses?

5 What is the difference between an antigen and an antibody?

6 Briefly describe the roles of
   a a B cell
   b a macrophage
   in fighting disease.

Viruses act inside cells, which often makes them difficult to detect and destroy, but their proteins sometimes project through the cell surface. Killer T cells recognise these virus infected cells as being different from 'self', and kill them by enzyme action. Killer T cells also kill rogue cells which develop in the body from time to time. These cells are not necessarily infected, but they do not grow and divide normally. A cancer develops when rogue cells like this manage to avoid stimulating the immune system, and continue to grow and divide unchecked.

How does the immune system deal with organ transplants?

Table 3 *Replacing organs.*

Organs and tissues that have been succesfully transplanted
• Hair
• Cornea
• Skin
• Heart and lungs
• Liver
• Kidneys
• Blood vessels
• Bone marrow
• Fingers and toes
• Muscle

Transplants are used to replace failing organs or tissues, when there is no suitable alternative treatment. In modern hospitals, doctors can now transplant most major organs, as well as smaller body parts (see table 3). Organ transplants pose two major problems:

• finding a donor who no longer needs a particular organ
• getting the transplanted tissue accepted by the new body.

Sometimes it is possible to overcome both problems by transplanting tissues from the patient's own body. For example, blood vessels and skin can be transferred from one part of the body to another, without rejection. Some tissues can be donated by living people, whose own healthy bodies can then replace the lost cells. Blood and bone marrow are provided by living donors. Sometimes, a kidney can be donated to a patient by a living relative who then survives using the remaining healthy one. For all other transplants, the organs must come from people who have died.

When an organ is transplanted, the new body's immune system responds to the foreign antigens on the transplanted cells. Killer T cells enter the transplanted organ and destroy its cells. At the same time, antibodies bind to the transplanted cells and help phagocytes to destroy them.

To minimise the immune response doctors ensure that the transplanted organs have antigens that closely match the patient's. Donated organs have their antigens checked, or '**tissue typed**', and a matching recipient is located. There are not enough organs for transplantation and finding a close enough match is hard. Even when the tissue typing is good, doctors use drugs to suppress the patient's immune system, to give the transplanted tissue time to grow into place.

When bone marrow is to be transplanted, a very close match needs to be found. Bone marrow makes white cells. Since the donated marrow cells will be programmed to recognise the donor's antigens as 'self', and not the recipient's antigens, the marrow could reject the whole of the recipient's body. Close family members can be suitable donors for bone marrow, but the chance of finding a close enough match from the general population is tiny.

7 Why do transplant patients have to be kept away from sources of infection after their transplant operation?

8 Look at table 3. Make two lists, one of organs that can be transferred from one person to another and one of tissues and organs that are moved from one place to another in the same patient.

Can people acquire immunity without getting the disease?

Active immunity

A **vaccine** is a solution of microbial components with important antigens that do *not* cause disease. It could contain dead microbes, or an extract of microbe cells, or even a weakened live strain. Some vaccines are made from genetically modified microbes: harmless bacteria have antigen genes from a pathogen inserted. When someone is given the vaccine, the immune system responds as though it was a real infection, generating B cells and antibodies. A second inoculation a few weeks after the first improves the response. Some diseases need a booster inoculation every few years to keep the B cell 'memory' intact. If the real disease microbes come along later, the body will be able to deal with them before they get established. This is **active immunity**.

Passive immunity

If a person is given antibodies from someone else's body, the person acquires passive immunity. New-born babies are protected by their mothers' antibodies while their own immune systems are maturing. When a baby is breastfed, it receives colostrum at first, which is a secretion produced by the mother's breasts immediately after the birth. Colostrum is particularly rich in antibodies, which protect the baby through its first weeks and months.

Some illnesses are treated with an antibody suspension called **antiserum**. This helps patients through the early stages of the disease until their own immune systems respond. Antiserum is extracted from the blood of humans or animals that have been exposed to the appropriate antigen, and have therefore produced matching antibodies.

9 Explain why the immune response to a microbial infection is faster in someone who has been vaccinated against it than in an unvaccinated person.

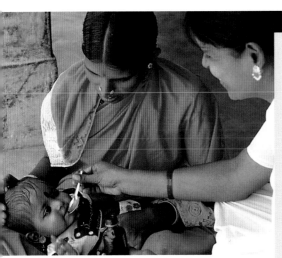

This nurse is giving an infant the oral vaccine for polio. India is one of the few remaining countries where polio is still common.

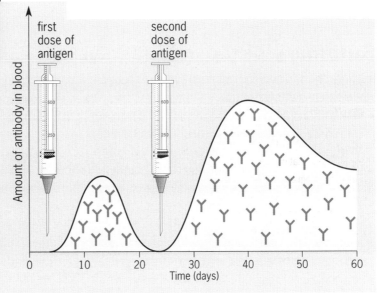

Figure 5

Can we eliminate infectious diseases?

10 Smallpox and polio are suitable diseases for eradication because they do not infect animals. Why is this important?

a Compare the two graphs in figure 6. What does each graph show about the importance of vaccination against whooping cough?

b Why might one graph, on its own, be misleading?

Smallpox was a viral disease which killed millions of people world-wide, until it was eradicated in ten years by treatment and vaccination. It was relatively easy to eradicate smallpox because it did not infect animals, so it could only be transmitted from person to person and there was a very good vaccine. A global programme organised by the World Health Organisation encouraged everyone to be vaccinated.

The next disease that the World Health Organisation aims to eradicate is polio. Immunisation with an oral vaccine has cleared over half the world of polio, including the American continent, but the disease still occurs in Europe. About 90% of children in the world have had the first dose of the vaccine, but fewer complete the course. When all the world's children have been vaccinated, and no new cases have been reported for ten years, this disease will join smallpox on the list of extinct diseases.

Deaths from whooping cough, 1850–1970

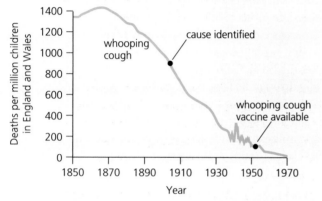

Figure 6

Cases of whooping cough, 1940–90

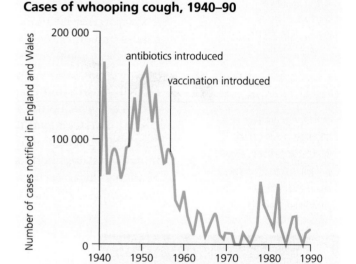

Summary of the immune system

- There are natural defences to prevent microbes starting an infection.
- The immune system is responsible for identifying microbes, disposing of them and 'remembering' them if another infection starts.
- Microbes carry surface chemicals, called antigens. These are recognised as foreign by T cells, which are part of the immune system.
- B cells make antibodies which correspond to antigens. Antibodies combine with antigens on microbes to reduce their ability to infect.
- Phagocytic cells engulf microbes coated with antibodies and destroy them.

- Memory cells in lymph nodes 'remember' antigens.
- A vaccine contains harmless antigens which stimulate the immune system to respond as if a real infection were taking place. The 'memory' is enough to protect against a real infection.
- The immune system treats a transplanted organ as though it were an invading microbe.
- There is a better chance of success if a transplanted organ carries the same antigens as the person receiving the organ. Drugs are used to suppress the immune system while the transplanted organ establishes itself.

8.3 Treating disease

How can we kill disease-causing microbes?

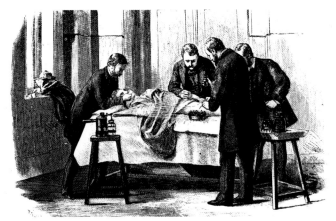

In the 1800s, Joseph Lister used carbolic acid to spray patients' wounds in operations to prevent infections. This was the first antiseptic.

Harmful microbes, or pathogens, can be killed by heating them to high temperatures, by chemical treatment and by drugs.

Chemicals

Disinfectants are strong chemicals such as bleaches (sodium hypochlorite), phenols and carbolic acids. These harm human tissue, so they are only used to kill microbes on surfaces and equipment. Antiseptics are much weaker than disinfectants. They are used to kill microbes on human tissue around a wound or graze. They are also used to disinfect unbroken skin before injections and operations.

Drugs

Antibiotics and other drugs disrupt bacterial activity. For example, penicillin affects microbes that have a particular component in their cell walls. When these bacteria multiply in the presence of penicillin, they cannot make this component because penicillin blocks the necessary enzymes. So the new cell walls are very weak and quickly burst. This gives the immune system time to 'mop up' the infection. The patient must keep taking the drugs for several days to make sure all of the bacteria are wiped out.

Because human cells do not make cell walls, penicillin can act on bacteria without harming the patient's own cells. Viruses are far more difficult to attack with drugs, because viruses use the host cell structures to reproduce. So anything that stops a virus reproducing will almost certainly harm the patient's cells as well.

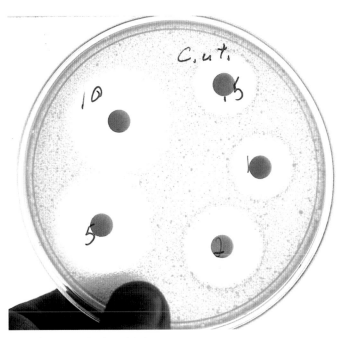

Antibiotics are tested on bacterial plates.

Antibiotics are made by micro-organisms. You can read more about how antibiotics are manufactured in chapter 23, *Microbiology and biotechnology*.

The effectiveness of an antibiotic is measured by testing it on bacteria in a laboratory. A nutrient agar plate is prepared, with bacteria growing all over its surface. Small holes are cut into the agar, and samples of antibiotic are placed in the holes. As the drug diffuses out, it inhibits the growth of susceptible bacteria round the hole, leaving a clear space. The larger the clear area that forms, the more effective the antibiotic is.

11 Why are antibiotics like penicillin most effective against rapidly dividing bacteria?

12 Why are viruses not grown on agar plates?

Why are some bacteria resistant to antibiotics?

Bacteria can evolve ways of resisting antibiotics. For example, they might use an alternative chemical pathway in their cells so they can 'by-pass' the inhibiting effect of the antibiotic, or they might produce an enzyme that breaks down the drug. Some bacteria make enzymes that break down penicillin. When bacteria are exposed to penicillin, vulnerable ones die, but any resistant bacteria that are present multiply in the absence of competition.

Each time someone is prescribed an antibiotic there is a risk that resistant bacteria may survive the drug, and the patient's immune system, and go on to cause infections elsewhere that cannot be treated with this antibiotic. The more times bacterial infections are exposed to antibiotics, the greater is the chance that some bacteria will show a resistance to it.

How can we prevent diseases?

To prevent illnesses, we must try to stop infections becoming established and spreading through a community. We must ensure that food and water are clean and that people are vaccinated against the most common infections.

In the UK, water for washing and drinking is left to stand in reservoirs. Pathogenic microbes need warm, nutrient-rich surroundings, and they quickly die in cold, open water. The water is then filtered to remove particles, and chlorinated to kill any remaining microbes, before it enters the distribution system that delivers it to people's homes. There is usually enough chlorine in the water to eliminate any microbes that leak into the pipes from the surrounding soil.

Dirty water from people's bathrooms, kitchens and washing machines is taken to a treatment works via a system of pipes and sewers. There, a combination of cold and competition for food from soil microbes kills any faecal microbes that could cause disease if they got into the drinking water supplies. Once the water has been treated, it is released into rivers, and some eventually returns to settle in reservoirs. You can read more about how a sewage works cleans up water in chapter 21, *Human effects*.

Microbes can grow in food. Milk, meat, cheese, fruit and vegetables all contain microbes that will eventually spoil them. These microbes make food unappetising, and some are harmful if eaten. By storing and preparing food carefully, we can prevent the spread of food-borne diseases.

Fresh food should be kept in a cool place, like a fridge, to slow down the growth of microbes. Some foods can be preserved for longer by pickling, drying, salting or freezing. Chapter 22, *Food and farming*, shows how some of these processes work.

If food is unwrapped and left in a warm moist place, any microbes it contains will multiply and spoil it, but it can also become further contaminated as it is left exposed. Human hands, plates, cutlery or flies could all deposit additional microbes on the food. When preparing food, people should always make sure their hands and utensils are thoroughly clean, and cover food to prevent flies reaching it.

When catering workers cut themselves, they must wear special dressings to prevent staphylococcal bacteria passing from the wound into the food they are preparing and releasing a food poisoning toxin.

Thorough cooking kills most harmful microbes. Left-over and pre-cooked foods can become contaminated by contact with uncooked foods. They should be stored separately and anything used to prepare uncooked meat should be thoroughly washed before it is used again. Re-heated food must be heated right through to more than 70°C to kill any microbes that have settled in it since it was first cooked.

The potential hazards of food-borne infections are much higher where food is prepared in one place to be eaten by many people. For this reason, Environmental Health Officers and Trading Standards Officers regularly visit meat packing plants, shops, restaurants and markets and enforce regulations concerning the hygienic preparation and handling of food.

Table 4 *Routine vaccinations of children in the UK.*

Age	Vaccine
2 months	first doses of vaccines against polio, tetanus, diphtheria, whooping cough and bacterial meningitis
3 months	second doses of vaccines as above
4 months	third doses of vaccines as above
15 months	MMR (against measles, mumps and rubella)
pre-school	booster against diphtheria, tetanus and polio
14 years	BCG (against tuberculosis)
15 years	booster against tetanus and polio

By taking certain action as a community, people can help protect themselves, and prevent disease spreading to others. For example, in the UK, as soon as a child is born a health visitor encourages the parents to have the baby vaccinated (see table 4). By the time a child has reached 15 months, it is usually protected from many of the major childhood diseases. Vaccination programmes not only protect individuals, but also help to eradicate some diseases once and for all.

Table 5 gives some details about two of the most common infectious diseases in the world, and what can be done to prevent them spreading.

Table 5 *Infectious diseases.*

Disease	Tuberculosis	Measles
Cause	a bacterium *Mycobacterium tuberculosis*	a virus
Transmission	air-borne droplets from coughing of infected people, drinking infected milk	air-borne droplets
Parts affected	Inflamed abscesses in lungs. Spreads to lymph nodes, bone and other organs.	skin and mucous membranes
Symptoms	fever, night sweats, coughing, spitting up blood	Fever, with runny nose and sore throat. Spots in the mouth, blotchy rash on skin.
Treatment	A combination of streptomycin (antibiotic) and non-antibiotic drugs. (Resistant strains are becoming more common.) Stress-free rest and good diet.	Nursing care.
Prevention	Routine vaccination of children and treatment of contacts to prevent spread.	Routine vaccination of children. Very contagious so victims are isolated at home.
Social factors	Some people develop a fairly mild general illness and do not know that they have TB. People are more likely to contract TB if they live with a sufferer, are malnourished, are unwell, live in overcrowded conditions or are homeless. Treatment can be lengthy and homeless people may not be able to complete the drug course. Incidence is increasing in many countries.	Children may develop complications and die.

13 In what ways is the catering worker in the photograph on page 81 reducing the risk of passing pathogens into the food he is preparing? Is there any way he could still pass on microbes?

14 Give reasons why holiday makers to developing countries are advised to brush their teeth with bottled water, refuse ice in drinks and only eat fruit which can be peeled.

15 Give three ways in which the spread of water-borne and food-borne diseases through a population can be prevented.

16 Why are antibiotics not prescribed for a common cold?

17 Why is there a greater risk of dying from a respiratory disease like TB if you:
    a live in crowded conditions
    b work in a quarry?

18 Name two human illnesses caused by viruses.

Summary of treating disease

- The spread of water-borne infections such as cholera is reduced by treating water which is to be used for washing and drinking.
- Food is prepared in ways which reduce the number of microbes in it.

- Antiseptics and disinfectants kill microbes.
- Some bacteria and viruses are killed by drugs which interfere with their growth and reproduction.

Investigations

Anti-bacterial chemicals are widely used to keep people and surfaces clean.

a Devise an investigation to compare the effectiveness of toothpaste, mouthwash, deodorant and antiseptic at killing cultures of the bacterium *B. subtilis*.

b How could you find out the best strength of household disinfectant to use to kill *B. subtilis*?

Water balance

Learning objectives

By the end of this chapter you should be able to:

- **explain** why water is essential to living things
- **describe** how water moves between cells
- **describe** how a plant obtains water and minerals
- **list** the factors that affect water movement through plants

- **describe** how kidneys regulate the water content of blood
- **understand** how organisms are adapted to live in areas of water shortage

9.1 Plants and water

Why do plants need water?

Plants need water for many reasons:

- Water is a raw material for photosynthesis.
- Water in plant cells helps the plant to stand upright and hold its leaves out. Trees and shrubs have special wood fibres for support, but smaller plants rely on the support of **turgid** cells, fully expanded by water, pushing against each other. If plant cells lose water, they become flaccid, and the tissues become soft. The plant wilts.
- Water is used to transport dissolved minerals, amino acids and sugars around the plant.
- Water is used to stretch and enlarge young cells before their cell walls become hardened. A rich sugary solution inside the new cell draws in water by **osmosis**.
- Water is used to open and close guard cells, as described in chapter 6, *Breathing and gas exchange*.

Liverworts and mosses are vulnerable to water loss from their delicate 'leaves', and they cannot take up water efficiently because they have no real roots.

How do plants absorb water?

Most large, land-dwelling plants have roots, which take in water from the soil. The water then passes through special channels in the stem to the leaves and growing tips. This is a one-way system: water enters from the soil and passes through the plant to its surface, where it evaporates out into the atmosphere.

Water is absorbed from the soil by root hairs, which penetrate the spaces between soil particles. They are very fine thread-like structures just behind the growing tip of a root. Water molecules from the surrounding soil moisture move into root hair cells by osmosis (see figure 1).

Figure 1

Water movement through a plant

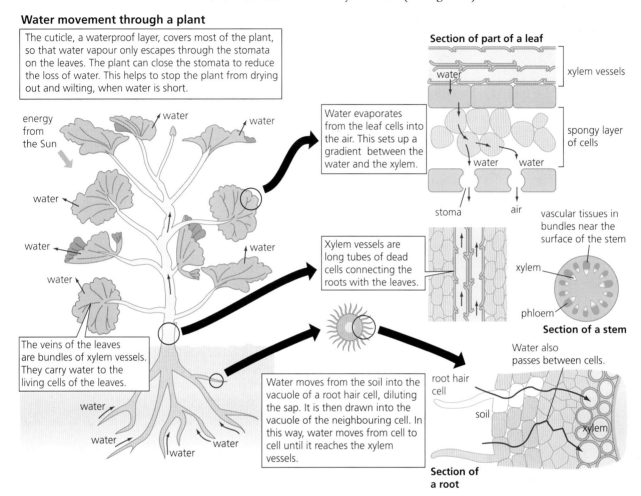

The cuticle, a waterproof layer, covers most of the plant, so that water vapour only escapes through the stomata on the leaves. The plant can close the stomata to reduce the loss of water. This helps to stop the plant from drying out and wilting, when water is short.

energy from the Sun

water

Section of part of a leaf

water

xylem vessels

spongy layer of cells

Water evaporates from the leaf cells into the air. This sets up a gradient between the water and the xylem.

water   water

stoma   air

vascular tissues in bundles near the surface of the stem

xylem

phloem

Section of a stem

Xylem vessels are long tubes of dead cells connecting the roots with the leaves.

The veins of the leaves are bundles of xylem vessels. They carry water to the living cells of the leaves.

Water moves from the soil into the vacuole of a root hair cell, diluting the sap. It is then drawn into the vacuole of the neighbouring cell. In this way, water moves from cell to cell until it reaches the xylem vessels.

Water also passes between cells.

root hair cell

soil

xylem

Section of a root

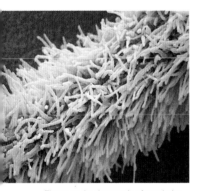

There can be thousands of root hairs like these on one root, which together provide a huge surface area for water to pass through. The rest of the root is waterproofed to reduce water loss when the soil is dry.

Once water has been absorbed, it passes by osmosis from the root hair cell, to the next cell, and then to the next, right across the root until it reaches the **xylem** cells in the centre (see figure 1). These specialised cells are long and wide, with no cytoplasm, and are arranged in columns up the stem of a plant. Their walls are impregnated with waterproofing and reinforcing materials. There are no cross-walls between the cells, so they form long waterproof conducting channels, extending from the roots right up into each leaf and flower, taking water to the cells where it is needed (see figure 2).

In the leaves, water passes out of the xylem vessels by osmosis, and moves into the surrounding cells. It evaporates from the surfaces of cells inside the leaves, and water vapour saturates the air spaces in the spongy layer. From here, water passes out of the leaves when the stomata are open. The movement of water out through the leaves is called **transpiration**.

1 Explain scientifically why a houseplant wilts if you forget to water it.
2 Describe how water enters a plant's roots.

Why does water move up through xylem vessels?

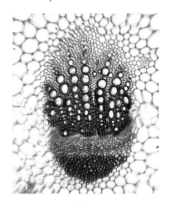

Water molecules in the root, in the stem xylem vessels, and in the leaves are all linked together by intermolecular bonds, making a very long chain. As water molecules evaporate into the leaf air spaces and leave the plant through the stomata, more molecules are pulled up the xylem vessels to replace them. This pull produces a stream of water up through the plant, which is called the transpiration stream. Dissolved materials such as minerals are carried up by the transpiration stream and distributed through the plant.

Because xylem vessels are reinforced, and usually full of water, they not only transport water, but also provide important support. Here, the water carrying cells are the most strongly stained.

What affects the rate of transpiration?

A big tree can draw up to 200 l of water from the soil on a hot sunny day. The water vapour around the leaves makes the air cooler and more moist, and even cools the leaf surfaces.

Plants with access to plenty of water, for example in tropical rain forests, have large xylem vessels which can accommodate large water flows. Conifers which live in colder, drier climates have much smaller xylem vessels and use much less water in transpiration. A number of other factors affect the rate at which water passes through a plant (see table 1).

Sequoia trees (Californian redwoods) grow up to 100 m high. There is a maximum height the water molecule chain can be before links between the molecules break, allow an air bubble to form, and stop water movement. This probably limits how tall trees can grow.

Table 1

Factor	Effect on transpiration
Light intensity	Plants close their stomata and transpiration stops in dim light or darkness.
Air movements and humidity	Water molecules leaving a leaf enter a still layer of air close to the leaf surface. If this layer is already saturated with water, there will not be much difference in water concentration between the leaf interior and the outside air, and the rate of transpiration will be low. This happens when the air is humid, very still or it is raining. Air currents around a leaf blow water molecules away from its surface, so more molecules diffuse out of the leaf down the concentration gradient. The rate of transpiration is greater in dry, windy conditions.
Temperature	Warm air holds more water vapour than cooler air, so an increase in temperature increases the rate of transpiration.

Can plants control water loss?

A layer of fine hairs on a leaf traps moist air over the surface, and reduces the rate of water loss by evaporation.

Source: Adapted from Plant Function and Structure *by Greulach, Collier Macmillan international editions, 1973*

In plants, some water has to be lost to keep the transpiration stream flowing and the plant's distribution system working. In many plants, water loss is limited because the leaves and stems are covered with a waterproof waxy layer called the cuticle. The drier the plant's environment, the thicker the cuticle. Most stomata are in the lower surface of the leaf, where they are sheltered from air currents, and direct heat from the Sun (see table 2). This too helps to reduce the rate of evaporation from the leaves.

Table 2 *The distribution of stomata in different plant species.*

Plant	Average number of stomata per cm^2	
	Upper leaf surface	Lower leaf surface
Apple	0	29 400
Bean	4 000	28 100
Begonia	0	4 000
Tomato	1 200	13 000
Tradescantia	0	1 400
Geranium	1 900	5 900

3 Gardeners recommend planting out young seedlings in the late afternoon, rather than in the morning, with a clump of soil round their roots. Why?

4 Construct a flow chart of the movement of water through a plant.

5 Tomato plants have hairy leaves. Look at the information in table 2 and describe two ways in which tomato plants are adapted for life in their home lands of Central and South America.

What minerals do plants need?

6 Why does a plant need nitrate?

7 How do plants take in the minerals they need?

8 In an investigation into how plants take up ions, two lots of wheat seedlings were set up. One set was grown in a mineral solution from which the seedlings took up the ions they needed. The other set was grown in a similar solution that was oxygen free. These seedlings took up a much smaller amount of ions than the first set. Can you give a scientific explanation for this observation?

Plants need minerals to make cell materials (table 3). They get minerals as dissolved ions from the film of moisture surrounding soil particles.

Table 3 *Minerals and their uses.*

Mineral	Function
Magnesium	Used in chlorophyll. Not usually in short supply.
Calcium	Used to link adjoining cell walls.
Nitrates	Combined with glucose to make amino acids and proteins, and for nucleic acids and ammonium ions. Used in the cytoplasm of new cells. A deficiency limits growth.
Phosphates	Used in energy release and in nucleic acids. A deficiency can limit growth.
Potassium	Activates enzymes. Involved in opening and closing stomata.

Dissolved minerals diffuse into root hair cells down a concentration gradient, but plants need more of some minerals than diffusion can supply. Root hair cells use energy from respiration to pump these ions into their vacuoles and prevent them from diffusing back out again. This is an example of **active** transport. As soon as mineral ions enter the roots, they are carried to the rest of the plant dissolved in water in the transpiration stream. This keeps the mineral ion concentration low in root cells, so the concentration gradient favours the movement of more ions from the soil into the root.

Most soils contain plenty of iron, calcium and magnesium, but other minerals can be in short supply. Farmers and gardeners use fertilisers to increase the quantity of deficient minerals in the soil. Fertilisers are described by their NPK ratio, which is the proportion of compounds they provide that contain nitrogen (N), phosphorus (P) and potassium (K).

How are sugars moved round plants?

Sugar movement through a plant

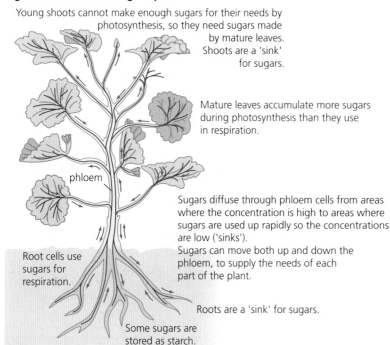

Young shoots cannot make enough sugars for their needs by photosynthesis, so they need sugars made by mature leaves. Shoots are a 'sink' for sugars.

Mature leaves accumulate more sugars during photosynthesis than they use in respiration.

phloem

Sugars diffuse through phloem cells from areas where the concentration is high to areas where sugars are used up rapidly so the concentrations are low ('sinks').

Sugars can move both up and down the phloem, to supply the needs of each part of the plant.

Root cells use sugars for respiration.

Roots are a 'sink' for sugars.

Some sugars are stored as starch.

Figure 2

Sugars are moved around a plant through a network of cells called sieve tubes, in **phloem** tissue. This transport is called **translocation**. Sugars move from the 'source' of the sugar, usually a photosynthesising leaf, to a 'sink', which is a site where the sugar is being used. Sinks include growing tips in shoots and roots, fruits, young expanding leaves that have not yet become self sufficient, as well as storage organs such as developing potatoes. Sugars move from cell to cell through cytoplasmic threads and in the film of moisture between cells. Figure 2 explains how sugars are transported through phloem vessels.

Summary of plants and water

- Plants take in water by osmosis through root hair cells, which are adapted to give a large surface area for absorption.
- Minerals enter root hair cells by diffusion, or by active transport which requires energy from respiration.
- Water evaporates from a plant's leaves, mostly through the stomata. This is transpiration. Stomata are arranged to prevent excessive water loss.

- The rate of transpiration is affected by light levels, air movement and humidity, temperature and water availability.
- Water containing dissolved minerals is distributed through the plant by xylem vessels. The water flow, or transpiration stream, is one-way: from the roots to the leaves.
- Sugars are carried around the plant through phloem vessels. This is a two-way transport system.

9.3 Animals and water

How do animals control water balance?

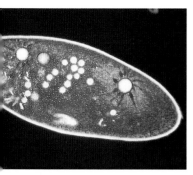

As fast as water enters this protozoan by osmosis, vacuoles form to expel it. The two large white dots with dark lines radiating from them are contractile vacuoles.

Animals evolved in sea water where the concentration of salts is similar to the concentration of solutes in cell cytoplasm. So for marine animals, water movement should not be a great problem. But some marine animals take in more salt than they need and have to excrete any excess. Some have salt glands, while others excrete salt from various parts of the body.

Single-celled animals in fresh water have problems with water balance. Their cytoplasm is a more concentrated solution than the pond water or soil moisture around them, so water moves into their cytoplasm by osmosis and the cells get bigger. Their cell membranes are not strong enough to withstand stretching and they may burst. These animals collect excess water in their cytoplasm in a small bubble, or contractile vacuole. They push this bubble to the cell surface and squirt the water out of the cell.

Land animals need to conserve water in their bodies, to be able to live in dry places, so they have waterproof outer layers to reduce water loss by evaporation.

Inside a multicellular animal's body, cells are surrounded by tissue fluid. Water and dissolved materials are freely exchanged between cells and the fluid. It is important for cells that their surroundings stay constant, because an increase in the concentrations of dissolved materials in the tissue fluid would draw water out of cells by osmosis and dehydrate them. If the tissue fluid became too dilute, cells would take in more water and could be damaged by the extra volume. Animals use several different mechanisms to keep their tissue fluid concentration constant. Keeping the internal environment constant is part of homeostasis, which is described in chapter 10, *Homeostasis*. The kidneys are the organs that regulate the concentrations of water and salts in mammalian tissue fluids.

9 How does *Amoeba*, a fresh water protozoan, control its water content?

How do humans control water balance?

Your body's water intake and losses must balance, to keep your tissue fluid concentration stable, and your cells healthy (see figure 3 on the next page). Your kidneys play a very important part in maintaining this water balance.

The kidneys are part of the urinary system (see figure 4 on the next page), and carry out several functions. Healthy kidneys:

- regulate the water content of body fluids
- regulate the concentration of salts in blood
- help to keep blood at the correct pH by excreting acid ions
- excrete urea made in the liver by the breakdown of excess amino acids.

The kidneys process blood very quickly: in humans, on average, 20% of the total blood volume of the body passes through the kidneys each minute. There are about a million fine kidney tubules, or **nephrons**, which make urine (see figure 5 on page 91). The nephrons are interwoven with dense networks of blood capillaries.

Average adult water intake and loss (per day)

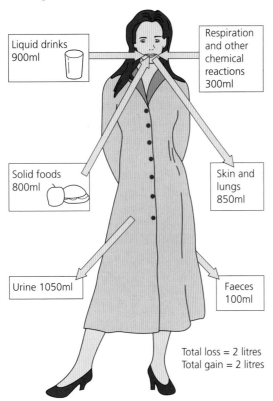

Liquid drinks
900ml

Respiration and other chemical reactions
300ml

Solid foods
800ml

Skin and lungs
850ml

Urine 1050ml

Faeces
100ml

Total loss = 2 litres
Total gain = 2 litres

Figure 3

The kidneys and linked structures

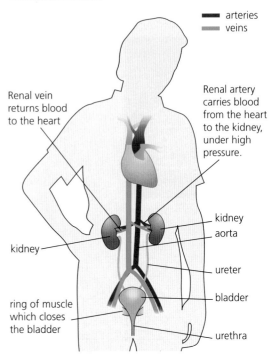

■ arteries
■ veins

Renal vein returns blood to the heart

Renal artery carries blood from the heart to the kidney, under high pressure.

kidney

kidney
aorta

ureter

bladder

ring of muscle which closes the bladder

urethra

Figure 4

How is urine formed?

Blood pumped from the heart passes, at high pressure, through the renal artery, and into smaller vessels. At the start of each kidney tubule there is a small capillary network called a **glomerulus**. As the blood enters the glomerulus, pressure forces some water and dissolved materials from the plasma through the thin capillary walls, into the start of the kidney tubule. Large blood proteins and antibodies cannot pass through: neither can blood cells or platelets. This process is called ultra-filtration. The glomerulus blood then passes through a network of capillaries wound around the kidney tubules. It is more concentrated now, because it has lost a lot of water, so water in the more dilute solution in the kidney tubule is drawn back into the blood by osmosis.

The liquid that enters the kidney tubule during ultra-filtration contains some useful materials. Most of them diffuse out of the filtrate in the first part of the kidney tubule, and back into the blood. Glucose is actively transported back into the blood by kidney tubule cells. If someone has an unusually high blood glucose concentration because of diabetes some remains in the filtrate and escapes in the urine. Antibiotics and other drugs, as well as waste substances like urea, are not reclaimed in the kidney tubules so they remain in the filtrate and are lost in the urine.

Figure 5

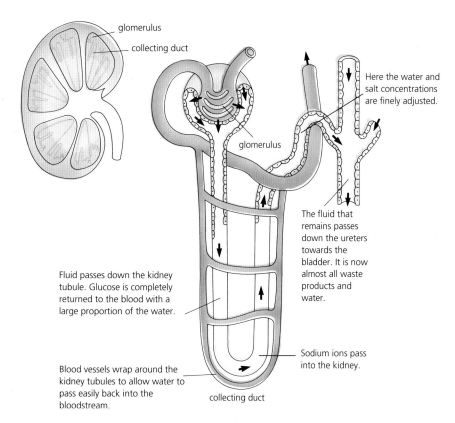

glomerulus

collecting duct

glomerulus

Here the water and salt concentrations are finely adjusted.

The fluid that remains passes down the ureters towards the bladder. It is now almost all waste products and water.

Fluid passes down the kidney tubule. Glucose is completely returned to the blood with a large proportion of the water.

Sodium ions pass into the kidney.

Blood vessels wrap around the kidney tubules to allow water to pass easily back into the bloodstream.

collecting duct

How do the kidneys control water balance?

The amount of salt in the blood determines how much water is reclaimed in the kidney tubules. The salt concentration in blood is detected by receptors in a part of the brain called the **hypothalamus**. If there is too much salt, and not enough water, the hypothalamus stimulates the pituitary gland to release **anti-diuretic hormone (ADH)** into the blood. When ADH reaches the kidneys, it changes the permeability of the last part of each tubule and the collecting ducts, to let water pass through the walls. Water then leaves the filtrate in the tubules and ducts, and eventually re-enters the blood. Less water is left in the filtrate, so there is a small amount of concentrated urine.

At the same time, cells in the hypothalamus trigger the feeling of thirst, so the person drinks more. As more water enters the blood, the water concentration increases, and the salt concentration drops. Once the concentrations are back within acceptable limits, the pituitary gland stops producing ADH. Less water is reclaimed from the kidney filtrate, so there is more, dilute urine.

10 **a** What nitrogen-containing compound is excreted in urine?

b What makes fluid leave the blood and enter the kidney tubule?

c Name one useful substance returned to the blood by kidney tubules.

d Look at figure 3. Explain why your own values for each amount may be different from the averages.

11 During a long match on a hot day, a tennis player sweats large amounts. Give one change you might expect to see in the tennis player's blood as a result of sweating. Explain how this would affect the rate of urine production.

What happens if people's kidneys do not work properly?

Fortunately, kidneys have a large spare capacity so even if they are damaged they can still control water balance and excrete waste substances fairly well. Nevertheless, failing kidneys affect many people each year. When they fail, much less blood passes through them than normal and fewer toxins are removed. Kidney failure happens when:

- a person loses a large amount of blood and does not have high enough blood pressure to keep the kidneys functioning properly
- a person's kidneys are damaged by high blood pressure, infections or other traumas
- a baby's kidneys do not develop fully.

People with failing kidneys have to change their diet. They eat less protein and salt to reduce the amount of wastes in the blood. Eventually sufferers may need treatment by a **dialysis** machine, which mimics the kidneys. Some people can have a kidney transplant if a suitable donor can be found.

What is a dialysis machine?

Inside a dialysis machine, the patient's blood flows across a sterile cellophane membrane. Like the walls of the glomerulus, the membrane acts as a filter and allows water, salts and other small molecules to diffuse through. On the other side of the membrane is a dialysis solution. Its composition ensures that water and wastes move down a concentration gradient through the membrane into the dialysis fluid. Valuable molecules do not diffuse through, but stay in the patient's blood, because their concentration in the dialysis fluid is similar to that in the blood.

Other parts of the dialysis machine monitor the blood and fluid concentrations, pump the fluids through, and prepare the blood to be returned to the patient. The blood is treated with an anti-clotting agent, warmed to body temperature, and cleared of air bubbles. Many kidney failure patients spend several hours every few days linked to a dialysis machine. Fortunately, modern machines can be small enough to be installed in a patient's home.

12 How do dialysis machines make sure valuable molecules, such as glucose, are not lost from a patient's blood?

Kidney patients must stay connected to a dialysis machine for several hours, three times a week.

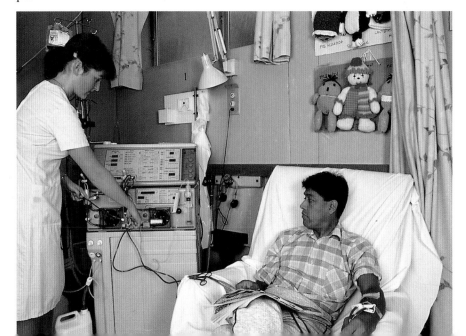

What happens in a kidney transplant?

Some kidney failure patients can have a healthy kidney transplanted into the body to take over from the failing organs. The third kidney is inserted into the groin and linked to blood vessels serving the legs, and to the ureter.

The main problem with transplants like this is obtaining a suitable kidney. A patient's immune system will only accept a kidney that has the same, or very similar, tissue type antigens to its own cells (see chapter 8, *Disease and immunity*). Sometimes a relative of the patient has a close enough match to be able to donate a kidney. Most donated organs come from people who have just died.

Surgeons have only a few hours after a death to get permission from relatives to use the kidneys, identify the tissue type and locate a matching recipient. Once the kidney has been removed it is cooled in ice and rushed to the hospital where the recipient and transplant team is standing by.

There are not enough kidneys for all those who need them. It is very difficult for doctors to ask the relatives of those who have just died about donating organs. Often, the relatives are too grief stricken to think about it. Some people carry donor cards which show that they are willing for their organs to be used after death. Relatives still need to give permission, but at least they can then be sure of the dead person's wishes. Unfortunately, people die without their cards. To help overcome this problem, there is a national register of donors in the UK: people can inform the National Health Service that they wish their organs to be used, and the information is kept centrally so it is always available.

Summary of animals and water

- Multicellular animals regulate the concentration of their body fluids in order to use the effects of osmosis to maintain water balance.
- Water regulation in humans is carried out by the kidneys under the influence of a hormone (ADH). Blood is filtered, useful materials are re-absorbed, and wastes pass out in the urine.

- Failing kidneys can be supplemented by a dialysis machine which simulates kidney activity. Kidney transplants are available under certain circumstances.

9.4 Desert conditions

How do organisms control water balance in deserts?

Life in areas where water is short is very difficult. Most organisms faced with a water shortage either move, go into a form of hibernation, or die. Some animals and plants have adaptations for exploiting the more favourable spots in arid regions.

The tenebrionid beetle from the Namib desert in Africa gets just enough water from the droplets of mist that condense on its body.

Deserts can be hot and dry, cold and dry, or salty and dry. In hot, dry deserts the air can reach 45 °C and the ground get up to 60 °C during the day, but temperatures drop to near freezing at night. In burrows, crevices, and holes in rocks, the temperature is slightly cooler and the air is more moist than in the open. Animals and plants that can squeeze into these sheltered spaces face a slightly less harsh environment.

Many desert animals can manage without drinking water: they get just enough moisture from their food and from respiration. Some plants and animals can harvest water from the air. At night, moisture in the desert winds condenses to a thin mist or dew which these plants and animals take in. Desert plants have a deep and widespread root system to exploit any water sources over a large area.

In dry coastal habitats, animals and plants have to resist being dried out by strong winds. They must also cope with high salt concentrations in the sandy soil.

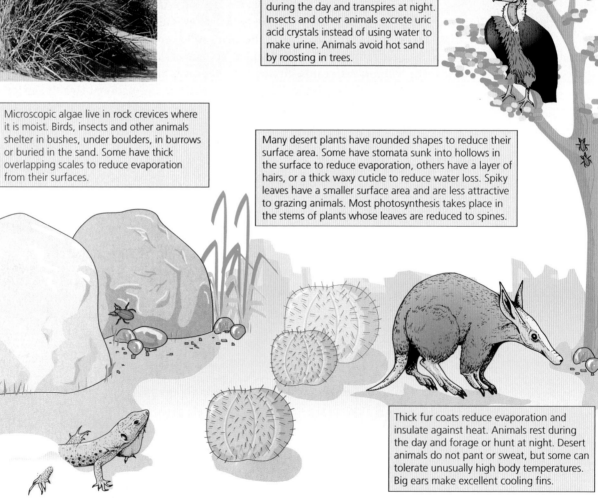

The desert acacia closes its stomata during the day and transpires at night. Insects and other animals excrete uric acid crystals instead of using water to make urine. Animals avoid hot sand by roosting in trees.

Microscopic algae live in rock crevices where it is moist. Birds, insects and other animals shelter in bushes, under boulders, in burrows or buried in the sand. Some have thick overlapping scales to reduce evaporation from their surfaces.

Many desert plants have rounded shapes to reduce their surface area. Some have stomata sunk into hollows in the surface to reduce evaporation, others have a layer of hairs, or a thick waxy cuticle to reduce water loss. Spiky leaves have a smaller surface area and are less attractive to grazing animals. Most photosynthesis takes place in the stems of plants whose leaves are reduced to spines.

Thick fur coats reduce evaporation and insulate against heat. Animals rest during the day and forage or hunt at night. Desert animals do not pant or sweat, but some can tolerate unusually high body temperatures. Big ears make excellent cooling fins.

Figure 6 Desert organisms have adaptations to reduce water loss, and can withstand losing a lot of water without permanent damage.

Section of a marram grass leaf

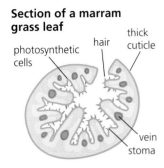

photosynthetic cells · hair · thick cuticle · vein · stoma

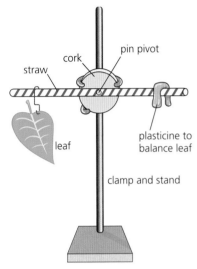

straw · cork · pin pivot · leaf · plasticine to balance leaf · clamp and stand

13 Marram grass colonises sand dunes at the edge of a beach. Look at the cross-section of a marram grass leaf in the diagram.

a What problems does marram grass face living on sand dunes?

b List three adaptations which would help marram grass survive in its habitat.

14 Surinder and Andrew set up a counterpoise balance as seen in the diagram. After a while the balance started to tip like a see-saw and Andrew had to move the plasticine towards the pivot to get it back in balance. Surinder recorded the distance they had to move the plasticine to keep it in balance. They then repeated the exercise using the same leaves but this time they held a hair drier, set on the lowest setting, near to the leaves. The table shows their results.

Time (minutes)	Distance of plasticine from pivot (mm)			
	Holly leaf		Silver birch leaf	
	Still air	Windy	Still air	Windy
0	87	83	76	66
5	85	82	73	63
10	85	81	72	62
15	84	81	71	60
20	84	80	69	58
25	84	79	68	56

a Why did the balance tip?

b Why did the silver birch leaves make the balance tip more than the holly leaves?

c Explain scientifically the difference between the results in still air and in 'windy' conditions.

d Can you think of any alternative explanations for these results?

e This is not a fair investigation. What could Andrew and Surinder do to obtain:

　i more reliable results

　ii more valid results?

Summary of desert conditions

- Organisms living in desert conditions have adaptations that allow them to survive extreme water shortages.

Investigations

1 Transpiration is the movement of water through a plant and out of its leaves.

a List the factors which affect the rate of transpiration.

b Devise an investigation into the effect of either air temperature or wind speed on the rate of transpiration.

Learning objectives

By the end of this chapter you should be able to:

- **list** the endocrine glands in the human body
- **list** the effects of four hormones in human beings
- **explain** how the body maintains a safe blood sugar level and why this is important
- **explain** the term 'homeostasis'

- **explain** the term 'basal metabolic rate'
- **explain** how the body maintains a constant internal temperature and why this is important
- **list** the differences between nervous and hormonal co-ordination

10.1 Adrenaline

Why do your palms sweat when you get nervous?

Makers of 'thriller' films use music, special lighting effects and a range of other tricks to frighten us. The tension builds, and when the hero loses his grip and seems about to fall hundreds of metres to his death, our bodies react exactly as the director intended. We *know* the film is just a pattern of lights on a screen, but we *feel* as if it was real. The director has used a simple, automatic reaction in our bodies that produces this tension. This reaction depends on **adrenaline**.

Endocrine glands

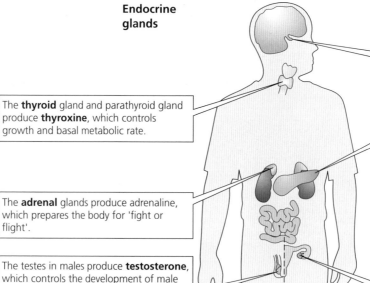

The **thyroid** gland and parathyroid gland produce **thyroxine**, which controls growth and basal metabolic rate.

The **adrenal** glands produce adrenaline, which prepares the body for 'fight or flight'.

The testes in males produce **testosterone**, which controls the development of male secondary sexual characteristics.

The **pituitary** gland produces many hormones, including LH, FSH and ADH which control other endocrine glands.

The islets of Langerhans in the pancreas produce **insulin** and **glucagon**, which together control blood sugar.

The ovaries in females produce **oestrogen** and **progesterone**, which control the development of female secondary sexual characteristics.

Figure 1

Effects of adrenaline

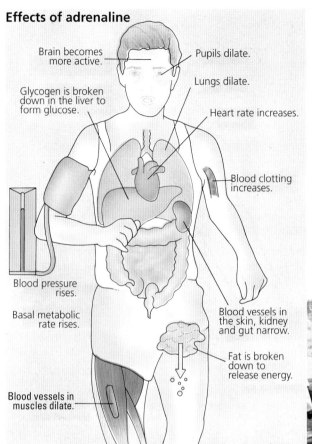

Brain becomes more active.

Pupils dilate.

Lungs dilate.

Glycogen is broken down in the liver to form glucose.

Heart rate increases.

Blood clotting increases.

Blood pressure rises.

Basal metabolic rate rises.

Blood vessels in the skin, kidney and gut narrow.

Fat is broken down to release energy.

Blood vessels in muscles dilate.

Figure 2

2 Explain how each of the reactions shown in figure 2 helps to prepare the body for action.

Adrenaline is an example of a chemical called a **hormone**. A hormone circulates in the blood and changes the way other parts of the body work (figure 1). Hormones are produced by glands called **endocrine glands**. The parts of the body that the hormone affects are called the **target organs**.

Adrenaline is secreted by cells in the adrenal glands, and causes target organs across the body to prepare for extra activity (figure 2). The changes it causes are part of the fight–flight response. You notice the effects of adrenaline as nervousness, fear or excitement.

1 Draw a table to show the endocrine glands, the hormones they produce and their target organs.

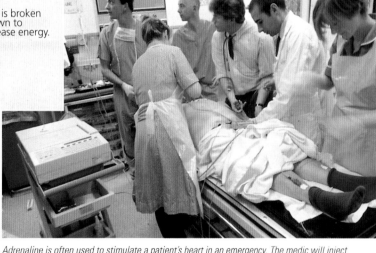

Adrenaline is often used to stimulate a patient's heart in an emergency. The medic will inject adrenaline directly into the heart to encourage it to start beating.

Summary of adrenaline

- Endocrine glands release hormones directly into the bloodstream.
- Hormones change the way different parts of the body, called target organs, work.

- Adrenaline prepares the body for strenuous activity.

10.2 Controlling blood sugar

How is the blood sugar level kept constant?

Adrenaline is also involved in everyday reactions. **Insulin** is a hormone that encourages body cells to take up glucose and store it as glycogen. (You can read about glycogen in chapter 2, *Chemicals of life*.) Adrenaline has exactly the opposite effect – it acts antagonistically to insulin. The balance between these hormones helps to maintain the blood sugar concentration at safe levels.

Figure 3

Blood sugar level control

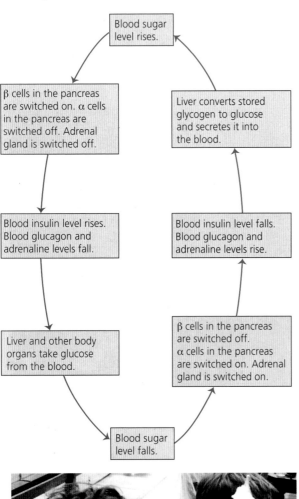

The concentration of glucose in blood plasma is normally about 90 mg/100 cm^3. This glucose provides cells throughout the body with an instant supply of energy. It is particularly important for cells in the brain and nerves, which cannot respire fat stores to release energy in an emergency. A higher level of glucose than this raises blood pressure, stops the kidneys working properly and can cause eye damage. However, glucose is constantly being taken from, and added to, the blood by tissues throughout the body. The glucose level needs to be kept within safe limits.

The liver can take glucose from the blood and convert it to glycogen for storage in the liver cells. It can also make glucose from a variety of other food chemicals, including fats and amino acids. The liver is the only organ that can secrete glucose directly into the bloodstream and so provide a rush of energy-giving glucose in an emergency.

Two sets of hormones control how the liver treats glucose. Insulin, made by the pancreas, encourages the liver to take up glucose and convert it to glycogen. A number of hormones do the opposite, but the most important are probably glucagon and adrenaline.

Small groups of cells called **islets of Langerhans** in the pancreas secrete the hormones that control blood sugar. The islets take up only one per cent of the pancreas and contain two types of cells – α cells which secrete glucagon and β cells which secrete insulin; see figure 3 for the details of blood sugar control.

3 Look at the photo of a child eating candyfloss. Draw a flow chart to show how the child's body will respond to the rise in blood sugar the candyfloss will cause.

What is diabetes?

The blood sugar control system works well in most people. However, some people cannot produce enough insulin to control their blood sugar levels. These people suffer from a disease called **diabetes**.

If the child with the candyfloss in the photograph was a diabetic, the sugar from the sweet would rush into his blood and push the level above the upper safe limit. The liver would not control the extra sugar because the pancreas could not produce enough insulin.

After a while, the blood sugar level would fall as body cells used up the glucose and some passed out of the body in urine. If the level fell too far, it might dip below the lower safe level. This is even more serious for the child. At this level, the blood will not provide enough glucose for all the body tissues. Muscle cells switch to using fat reserves for energy instead of glucose so that the brain can mop up all the available blood sugar. However, using fat for respiration produces chemicals called ketones which can make the blood too acidic. This can cause other problems. In the worst situations, this can lead to the child losing consciousness and going into a very deep sleep called a coma. If the sugar level continues to fall, cells in the brain may die as they run out of glucose completely.

4 a Diabetics need to inject carefully measured doses of insulin to control their blood sugar levels. What would be the effects if they used a dose that was:
  i too high
  ii too low?
b Which do you think is the most dangerous mistake, and why?

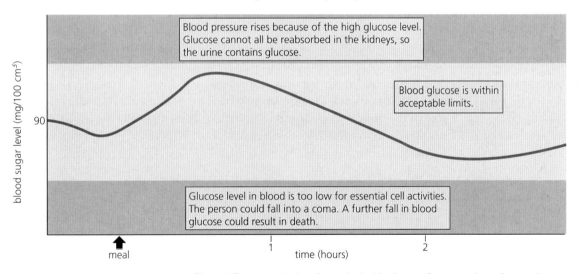

Figure 4 The concentration of sugar in the bloodstream fluctuates, depending on when a person last ate.

Summary of controlling blood sugar

- Insulin encourages cells to take up glucose and so reduces blood sugar levels.
- Glucagon and adrenaline encourage the liver to release glucose into the blood.
- The islets of Langerhans in the pancreas secrete insulin and glucagon.

- High blood glucose levels cause high blood pressure, excretion of glucose in urine and can lead to eye damage.
- When the blood sugar level falls too low, the body starts to respire fats. This produces ketones which can cause damage to cells. Very low blood sugar levels lead to a coma and possible death.

10.3 Homeostatic control

The blood sugar control system is a good example of homeostatic control. **Homeostasis** describes the way living things try to keep conditions inside their bodies within certain limits. The conditions inside are sometimes called the **internal environment**. To stay alive, every cell in the body must have a healthy environment, in the same way that the whole organism needs a safe external environment. The blood sugar level is only one aspect of the internal environment. The body does not try to keep it constant – it just makes sure that the level does not go beyond certain, safe limits.

The body also controls its internal temperature. This varies a certain amount every day but homeostatic mechanisms make sure that it cannot go beyond safe limits. In humans, body temperature is about 37 °C. This is much higher than most environments, and takes a great deal of energy to maintain. The advantage to the body is that chemical reactions work faster at this high, stable temperature so that our body chemistry is not controlled by the external temperature.

5 'Homeostasis means keeping everything the same inside the body'.
Why is this definition wrong? Write down an improved version.

In cold climates humans need extra insulation to maintain their body temperature. Fish are 'cold blooded' which means they do not control body temperature within a narrow range, as we do.

The temperature of the body depends on the balance between heat loss and heat gain. The body takes actions which affect both heat gain and heat loss so that any change in temperature slows down and is reversed (figure 5). These actions keep pushing the temperature back towards the normal value. The part of the body that organises these actions is the **hypothalamus**. This is a very small area at the base of the brain, which is involved in many important homeostatic mechanisms.

What is the basal metabolic rate?

The main internal source of heat is respiration. This chemical reaction takes place in all living cells and produces some waste energy as heat. This heat energy is used to keep the body temperature constant. The amount of energy needed to stay alive is called the **basal metabolic rate** (BMR), measured in kilojoules per hour (kJ/h). It is the amount of energy used by a resting person in a comfortably warm room 12 hours after the last meal. The figures are adjusted to take the person's body mass into account. An average man has a BMR of about 287 kJ/h, while an average woman needs about 229 kJ/h. Women usually have a lower BMR than men because they have a higher proportion of body fat. Fat-storing tissue needs less energy than metabolically active tissue like muscle. People with a rounder shape are also more efficient at conserving heat than very thin people.

The BMR is often used as a measure of how fast all the reactions in the body are working. It is a bit like the volume on a stereo. At a particular volume

6 Study figure 5 and explain how each of the actions in the blue box will help to warm up a cold body.

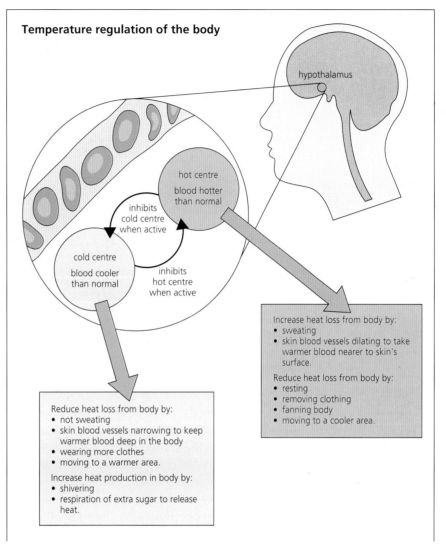

Temperature regulation of the body

hypothalamus

hot centre

blood hotter than normal

inhibits cold centre when active

cold centre

blood cooler than normal

inhibits hot centre when active

Increase heat loss from body by:
• sweating
• skin blood vessels dilating to take warmer blood nearer to skin's surface.

Reduce heat loss from body by:
• resting
• removing clothing
• fanning body
• moving to a cooler area.

Reduce heat loss from body by:
• not sweating
• skin blood vessels narrowing to keep warmer blood deep in the body
• wearing more clothes
• moving to a warmer area.

Increase heat production in body by:
• shivering
• respiration of extra sugar to release heat.

Figure 5

7 a What factors do you think will affect a person's BMR?
b If someone starts exercising, the BMR will fall as a proportion of the total energy needs. Explain why.

setting, the music will contain sounds that are louder, or quieter, but if you turn up the volume all the sounds will become louder. In a similar way, as the BMR increases, all body reactions speed up. The hormone thyroxine, produced by the thyroid gland, helps control the BMR.

Doctors use the heat given out by a naked, resting person as a measure of the BMR. The BMR is not the same as the energy a normal person will need during a typical day, because any movement will increase the need for energy. The BMR for a typically active person is usually about two-thirds of their normal energy needs.

Summary of homeostatic control

• Blood sugar level is controlled by a homeostatic control mechanism.
• The basal metabolic rate is a measure of the reactions going on in the body.

• Thyroxine controls the basal metabolic rate.
• Respiration produces a lot of waste energy as heat. The body uses this to maintain a body temperature that is higher than the environment.

10.4 The action of some endocrine glands

What are steroids?

The outer layer of each adrenal gland secretes a group of hormones called **steroids**. The adrenal glands secrete a steroid hormone called cortisol during periods of physical and emotional stress. Cortisol encourages cells to break down proteins to amino acids. These amino acids pass into the blood and are taken to the liver. The liver converts the amino acids to glucose to provide an energy supply for the brain and heart.

Other types of steroids have different effects. The drugs that officials test for in sporting events are **anabolic steroids**. This name gives you a clue about their use in the body – they control the growth of muscles and bones. Anabolic steroids encourage body cells to take up amino acids and convert them to protein.

8 Explain how anabolic steroids might help athletes to build muscles.

What are sex hormones?

Many animals have **breeding seasons** that are timed to make sure any young born have the best chance of surviving. So, deer will breed only in the spring so that young are born in summer when there is plenty of food available. Many birds will only build nests, court, mate and lay eggs during a particular period of the spring. Again, this ensures that the eggs hatch during the warmer summer months when food is plentifulThe mechanisms that switch on the breeding season involve hormones.

Humans can breed at any time of the year. However, a female only releases eggs from her ovaries for part of her life, and then only at particular times. Girls do not start to release eggs until a package of sex hormones speeds up their development at **puberty**. Women then release eggs regularly until the **menopause**. At the menopause the pituitary gland stops producing many of the important sex hormones and eggs no longer develop in the ovaries. Males cannot produce sperm until they start to produce sex hormones at puberty and the amount of sperm produced decreases as they get older. However, there does not seem to be an equivalent of the menopause for males and the fall off in fertility takes longer than in females.

How do hormones control the menstrual cycle?

Although humans do not have a breeding season, women do not produce fertile eggs continuously. A typical woman will release a fertile egg once every month or so. This monthly cycle is called the **menstrual cycle**, and is controlled by a set of hormones (figure 6). There is considerable variation in the length of cycles and some women produce eggs, or ovulate, irregularly. In the past, poor diets meant women would ovulate much less frequently and often without a clear cycle.

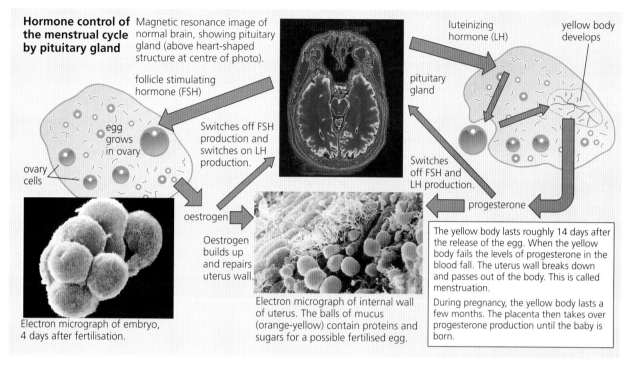

Hormone control of the menstrual cycle by pituitary gland Magnetic resonance image of normal brain, showing pituitary gland (above heart-shaped structure at centre of photo).

follicle stimulating hormone (FSH)

egg grows in ovary

ovary cells

Switches off FSH production and switches on LH production.

oestrogen

Oestrogen builds up and repairs uterus wall.

luteinizing hormone (LH)

yellow body develops

pituitary gland

Switches off FSH and LH production.

progesterone

The yellow body lasts roughly 14 days after the release of the egg. When the yellow body fails the levels of progesterone in the blood fall. The uterus wall breaks down and passes out of the body. This is called menstruation.

During pregnancy, the yellow body lasts a few months. The placenta then takes over progesterone production until the baby is born.

Electron micrograph of internal wall of uterus. The balls of mucus (orange-yellow) contain proteins and sugars for a possible fertilised egg.

Electron micrograph of embryo, 4 days after fertilisation.

Figure 6

9 **a** Look at figure 6. Draw up a table to show the effects of each pituitary hormone on the ovary.

b Draw a flow chart to show the way pituitary and ovarian hormones interact to produce a regular menstrual cycle.

10 The contraceptive pill is a package of hormones that prevents egg release. The fertility pill is a package of hormones that stimulates egg production and release.

a Suggest suitable hormones for: **i** a contraceptive pill,   **ii** a fertility pill.
Explain your choices.

b Explain why doctors find it much easier to decide on a dose for a contraceptive pill than for a fertility pill.

How do the nervous and hormonal systems interact?

Both nerves and hormones control the body, but they work in different ways. Table 1 summarises the differences.

Table 1 *Differences in the ways nerves and hormones control the body.*

	Nerves	Hormones
Speed of response	usually very fast	relatively slow
Scale of response	can be very focused	spread over a wide area
Duration of response	over and done with quickly	can last for hours or days
Mode of action	nerves usually stimulate an organ	different hormones can stimulate or inhibit

11 Explain how the nervous and hormonal systems interact to build tension slowly and then produce a sudden shock.

Think back to the tension generated by thriller films. Is it nervous or hormonal mechanisms that make us feel scared? In fact, both systems play a part, but each has slightly different effects. In the film *Alien* there are lots of sequences where the heroine walks quietly and slowly down the corridors of a spaceship. Nothing seems to happen but the tension gradually builds. At other times the alien creature leaps out and kills a crew member. The viewer might jump with fright. This is a sudden reaction.

Which hormones are useful in medicine?

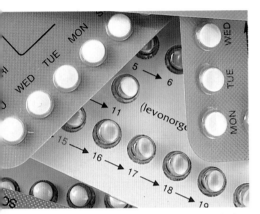

Contraceptive pills contain synthetic hormones that act on the reproductive organs, mimicking the action of natural sex hormones.

Since hormones are chemicals, they can be extracted and purified to form useful drugs. Doctors use hormones to control some of the most important processes in the body (table 2). Drug companies can make artificial hormones which are often much more powerful than their natural equivalents.

Table 2 *Medical uses for hormones.*

Hormone	Use
Adrenaline	Stimulates the body in times of crisis, e.g. after a heart attack.
Insulin	Controls levels of blood sugar.
ADH	Linked to control of diabetes.
Thyroxine	Treats a range of metabolic illnesses.
Growth hormone	Treats growth disorders.
Sex hormones	Control fertility.
Anabolic steroids	Encourage the body to repair itself and build new tissues.

Summary of the effects of some endocrine glands

- Hormones can have an effect on growth across the body. Pituitary hormones control the growth and functioning of sex organs.

- The contraceptive pill is a package of artificial hormones that prevent the release of eggs by the ovaries. Fertility pills are a different package that encourage egg production and release.

Investigations

1 a Why does a rise in body temperature increase the BMR?

b A slight fall in body temperature also tends to raise the BMR. Why?

c A large fall in body temperature reduces the BMR. Why?

d Plan an investigation to find out how temperature affects the activity of a typical human enzyme. You could use salivary amylase which breaks down starch to sugar, and is easily collected from the mouth in saliva.

e Carry out your investigation making sure you gather enough evidence to check your predictions.

f Write up your investigation including all your results. You may need to process your results to make them easier to interpret – perhaps draw a graph or chart. Use the reults from your investigation to decide if your original prediction was correct or not. You may decide you need more evidence before you make a conclusion. If this is the case suggest further work or ways to improve your existing method.

Behaviour

Learning objectives

By the end of this chapter you should be able to:

- **explain** why animals behave
- **recognise** stimuli and responses
- **use** reflex arcs to explain how animals respond
- **list** a number of reflexes

- **explain** the difference between reflexes and learned behaviour
- **explain** how courtship and parental behaviour improve an animal's chances of survival

11.1 Explaining behaviour

It is easy to see that animals are alive because they move and react to their surroundings. Small children often find it difficult to imagine that plants are alive, because they do not seem to do anything. However, all living things, including plants and microscopic bacteria, do respond to their environment. We call the way an organism responds to the environment its **behaviour**.

An organism's behaviour changes the way it interacts with its environment. The change usually means that the organism has a better chance of survival and growth. In order to behave sensibly, an organism needs to:

- gather information about its environment
- process this information and decide on a suitable response
- change the way it interacts with its environment

These three actions are common to all living organisms. In animals, the sense organs gather the information, the brain processes it and the muscles respond (see chapter 12, *Sense organs*). In plants, there is no brain, and the responses are usually concerned with growth rather than movement.

Why do organisms behave?

1 Study the list on the next page and give examples that illustrate each reason for behaviour. The photographs will help.

Animals respond to their environment to:

- search for food
- escape from predators
- move
- find a mate
- mate
- provide a safe environment for offspring
- avoid unfavourable conditions
- maintain a territory.

Plants respond to their environment to:

- avoid poor growing conditions
- collect water
- conserve water
- reproduce at the best time.

These pictures show living organisms responding to their environment in order to find food, build a safe home, and reproduce at the best time.

What is a reflex?

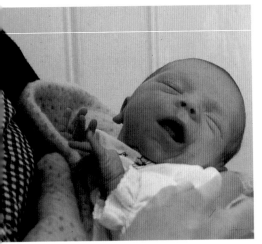

*Human babies show a **rooting reflex**. If you brush its cheek, the baby will turn its head and try to suck on whatever is touching its face.*

The pupil of your eye always gets smaller in bright light. This is a good example of a simple cause and effect, based on a **stimulus–response pair**. The rise in light level is the **stimulus** and the change in the size of the pupil is the **response**.

Many stimuli are internal – they are to do with the condition of our bodies. For example, you might prepare a sandwich because chemical stimuli in your blood tells your brain that you are hungry.

However, the simplest stimulus–response pairs seem to be inborn, automatic responses which protect even the youngest and most inexperienced organisms from danger. These stimulus–response pairs are called **reflexes**.

A reflex is a simple stimulus–response pair that an animal inherits from its parents. It does not need to be learned and is usually to do with protecting the animal from harm. Reflexes are very fast responses, because they do not need conscious thought. Indeed, some reflexes cannot be controlled by the conscious brain. You can read more about the way the nerves control reflexes in chapter 13, *Nervous systems*.

2 What are the advantages of the rooting reflex shown in the photograph to the parent and the child?

What is a sign stimulus?

Organisms live in a complex, confusing world. Animals can detect a wide range of different stimuli – how do they know which ones are important and which can be ignored? Stimuli that produce responses are called **sign stimuli**. Herring gulls use a sequence of sign stimuli to feed their young. Sign stimuli that act between members of the same species are called **releasers**.

Herring gulls

Young herring gulls use a series of reflexes to get food from their parents. The parents begin the sequence by calling a long drawn-out note. This alerts the gull chick. The parent then approaches the chick with food in its beak. The chick pecks at the parent and opens its mouth. The parent then puts the food in the chick's mouth and the chick swallows.

Herring gulls live in noisy colonies of many hundreds of nesting pairs. The noise and movement around newly hatched chicks must be very confusing. How do the chicks know which stimuli in their confused environment are important for feeding behaviour and which can be ignored?

Two researchers called Tinbergen and Perdeck investigated the sign stimuli for chick feeding in the late 1940s. They collected newly hatched chicks and approached them with models of gull heads, and noted how the chicks responded. They used a variety of head models to see which ones produced the strongest response.

Tinbergen and Perdeck could alter a single factor at a time to see the effect on the feeding behaviour of the chicks. They decided that feeding was most successful when the model beak had a collection of features. The most successful head:

- had a moving shape
- had a long shape
- was low down near the chick's head
- pointed down towards the chick
- had something sticking out from the beak
- had a red spot.

3 Draw a flow chart to show the stimulus–response pairs in herring gull chick feeding.

Spot colour	Reactions compared with reactions to red spot
Red	100
Black	105
Blue	85
White	71
No spot	30

4 The table on the left shows some results from Tinbergen and Perdeck's experiments, in which they varied the colour of the spot on a model gull head used to elicit feeding behaviour in gull chicks. The total number of chick reactions was 938.

   a There were 240 chick reactions to the red spot. How many reactions did the white spot produce?
   b What is the releaser for the parent to release its food?
   c Do you think Tinbergen and Perdeck could assume that the responses of the chicks were instinctive and not learned by watching other birds feeding? How could they check this idea?

Robins

The robin is a bird that shows very strong territorial behaviour. A male robin will adopt a territory and will display against other robins that fly into its area. The display involves loud singing and puffing up of the breast to show off the robin's red feathers. The birds will fight if the display does not frighten the intruder away. However, if the brave defending robin flies into the ex-intruder's territory, the situation will be reversed. Here, the original defender becomes much more submissive and less likely to display. The original intruder finds his courage and displays with vigour. Robins are most aggressive in their home territory and will display against anything with red feathers – even stuffed models of birds!

5 a What is the releaser for the robin's display?
b Explain how territorial behaviour is an evolutionary advantage for robins.

Summary of explaining behaviour

- All living things behave in some way.
- Behaviour requires systems that gather and process information and produce a response.
- The information gathered by organisms includes many stimuli. The ones that cause a response are called sign stimuli.

- Many types of behaviour are sets of linked reflexes where behaviour in one organism can release behaviour in another.

11.2 Learned and unlearned behaviour

Can animals learn new reflexes?

An animal is born with reflexes that are appropriate for many situations. It is because these inbuilt reflexes are appropriate that the animal has survived and produced young who will also have the same set of reflexes. However, not every situation is covered by these inbuilt reflexes. Animals can learn to produce new reflex responses to new situations. These learned responses are called **conditioned reflexes**. The first scientist to work with conditioned reflexes was the Russian, Ivan Pavlov (1849–1936).

When a dog smells food, it starts to produce saliva. The dog has no control over this reaction. The reaction is a simple reflex which prepares the digestive system to receive food. Pavlov used to forget to feed his dogs sometimes and so fixed up a simple alarm to remind him when the dogs' food was due. One day the alarm bell rang but Pavlov was too busy to feed the dogs. However, the dogs still began to salivate even though no food was ready. Pavlov suggested the dogs had learned that when the bell rang, food was on the way.

The following day, he rang the bell without providing any food and, again, the dogs salivated. The dogs linked the two stimuli (bell and food) and produced the same response to both (salivating). This linking of stimuli is called **association**.

Pavlov suggested that there were two types of reflex. Innate reflexes are reflexes that animals are born with and which do not need to be learned. For example, the muscles in the iris of the eyes increase the size of the pupil in dim light. Conditioned reflexes are reflexes that an animal learns by associating two events. For example, Pavlov's dogs associated the alarm bell with food and responded to the bell or the food in the same way.

Pavlov found that after a few days of feeding the dogs and ringing the bell at a different times, the conditioned reflex was destroyed. This meant the conditioned reflex had been unlearned or extinguished. However, the reflex had not been forgotten because he found it was much easier to train the dog with the bell in the future. It was as if the reflex was already present, but needed to be reawakened.

6 a Explain how conditioned reflexes are useful to animals.
  b Why is it useful for an animal to be able to relearn a reflex more quickly than it was learned in the first place?

Why do animals show courtship and parental behaviour?

Before animals can produce offspring, they need to mate. Sometimes this means they have to find each other, and that may not be easy. A blue whale looking for a mate may have to search through many cubic miles of ocean. Some whales give out low-frequency sounds called whale songs to help to find a suitable partner.

Female insects often release smells called **pheromones** to attract males, sometimes over many miles. Males of the Chinese Saturnid moth *Arctias selene* can find a receptive female at distances of up to 11 kilometres.

After the animals have found each other, they may need to go through special behaviour to prepare for mating. This special behaviour is called **courtship**. For example, the male garden spider is smaller than the female. When he approaches to breed with her he shakes the web in a particular way to make sure the female recognises him as a mate, and not a trapped fly which is destined to be her next meal. Despite this behaviour the life of a male spider is not happy – females tend to eat the males after mating anyway!

Some of the most complex mating rituals are found in birds and fish. These probably help to make sure the offspring have the best possible chance of survival. Even these complex behaviours are controlled by simple stimulus–response pairs, with one individual providing a stimulus which brings a response from the potential mate. The mate's response then acts as a stimulus for the next part of the courtship pattern.

After mating, the animals may have complicated behaviours which help the young through the first, most dangerous stages of life. This behaviour is called **parental behaviour.**

Again, fish and birds tend to have the most complex parental behaviour patterns. For example, the first ten days of life for *Tilapia* fish pass entirely inside their mother's mouth. After that they are allowed to venture outside but return if there is any sign of danger. Crocodiles also care for their offspring by keeping them inside their mouths while they are very young. Many birds build complex nests in which to lay their eggs. This behaviour is stimulated by an increase in the levels of the hormone oestrogen in their blood.

7 Explain why courtship and parental behaviour is useful to animals.

Summary of learned and unlearned behaviour

- Complex behaviour patterns, like courtship, have a survival value for the organism.
- Complex behaviour patterns can be explained at a number of different levels.

- Animals can learn to produce new reflexes by associating two events.

Investigations

1 Woodlice are simple crustaceans that lose water very quickly to their environment. In order to survive they must find areas that are cool and moist. Woodlice have very simple nervous systems that use a few simple reflexes to make sure they find, and stay, in cool, damp areas.

  a Woodlice tend to cluster under stones and rocks. List the advantages of this behaviour to the woodlice.

  b Woodlice cannot chose where to live – they respond to a selection of environmental factors which force them to stay in safe areas. List the parts of the environment the woodlouse could respond to.

  c Which of these do you think are likely to have the largest effect? Why?

  d Plan an investigation to explore the effects of these factors on woodlice behaviour.

  e Carry out your investigation making sure you gather enough evidence to check your predictions.

  f Write up your investigation including all your results. You may need to process your results to make them easier to interpret – perhaps draw a graph or a chart. Use the results from your investigation to decide if your original prediction was correct or not. You may decide you need more evidence before you can make a conclusion. If this is the case suggest further work or ways to improve your existing method.

Sense organs

Learning objectives

By the end of this chapter you should be able to:

- **describe** the parts of the mammalian eye and ear
- **list** the function of each part of the mammalian eye and ear
- **explain** how the eye focuses images on to the retina
- **explain** how eye defects can be compensated for
- **explain** the advantages of stereoscopic vision
- **list** the adaptations of an animal's eyes to its way of life

- **explain** the meanings of the terms frequency, amplitude and wavelength
- **list** the adaptations of an animal's ears to its way of life
- **describe** the structure of the human skin
- **explain** why the body needs sense organs inside its body
- **list** some things plants can detect

12.1 Sensing changes

Animals use their **external senses** to detect changes in their environment. An animal's senses provide the information that is most useful for that animal's survival. There are five external senses:

- sight
- hearing
- smell.
- taste
- touch

The male gypsy moth can detect a female many miles away by smell.

Rabbits have very sensitive hearing, to help detect approaching danger.

Internal sensors detect changes inside the body. For example, we feel hungry or thirsty when cells in the brain detect changes in the chemical balance of the blood.

Each sense depends on **sense organs**, which collect information and convert it into nerve impulses. The eye converts light into nerve impulses which pass along the optic nerve to the brain. A part of the brain, called the optic lobe, uses the pattern of nerve impulses to create an image of what the eye originally saw. So, senses depend on three components:

- sense organs to convert external signals into nerve impulses
- sensory nerves to carry signals to the brain
- brain cells to interpret the nerve impulses.

12.2 Sight

How do eyes work?

1 List the parts of the eye labelled in figure 1. For each part, explain what it does to help the eye work properly.

Eyes are the most useful sense organs for many mammals. They can gather information from great distances and also work very close up. The eye:

- focuses light from different distances
- converts the light into nerve impulses.

The eye

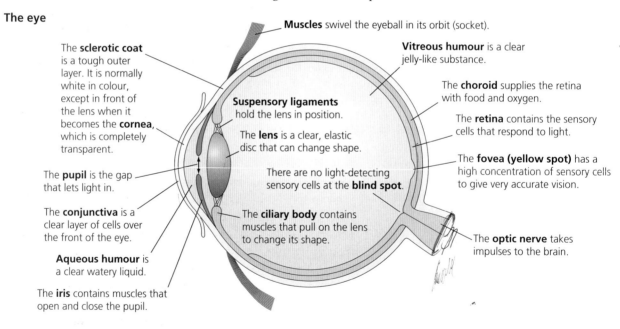

The **sclerotic coat** is a tough outer layer. It is normally white in colour, except in front of the lens when it becomes the **cornea**, which is completely transparent.

The **pupil** is the gap that lets light in.

The **conjunctiva** is a clear layer of cells over the front of the eye.

Aqueous humour is a clear watery liquid.

The **iris** contains muscles that open and close the pupil.

Muscles swivel the eyeball in its orbit (socket).

Vitreous humour is a clear jelly-like substance.

The **choroid** supplies the retina with food and oxygen.

The **retina** contains the sensory cells that respond to light.

The **fovea (yellow spot)** has a high concentration of sensory cells to give very accurate vision.

The **optic nerve** takes impulses to the brain.

Suspensory ligaments hold the lens in position.

The **lens** is a clear, elastic disc that can change shape.

There are no light-detecting sensory cells at the **blind spot**.

The **ciliary body** contains muscles that pull on the lens to change its shape.

Figure 1

Light rays from an object go into the eye and are bent so that they come together at a point on the **retina** (see figure 1). Most of the bending of the light is done by the cornea, but a small amount of fine focusing is needed, particularly for objects close to the eye. The lens does this fine tuning.

When a light ray enters a lens, it bends slightly. When the light ray leaves the lens, it bends again. The amount of bending depends on:

- the material the lens is made from
- the angle at which the light beam hits the lens
- the shape of the lens.

The eye adjusts its focusing automatically, so that the image formed on the retina is always sharp. We call this focusing **accommodation**. The eye cannot change the material the lens is made from, or the angle at which the light hits the lens, so it controls the shape of the lens.

The lens is normally shaped to focus light rays from objects near the eye. Objects far away are out of focus and look blurred. When muscles in the ciliary body contract, they pull the lens into a much thinner shape. This brings the light rays from distant objects to a sharp focus on the retina.

The eye's focusing mechanism uses muscles to pull on the lens, but relies on the natural elasticity of the lens to return it to its resting, more convex shape, when the muscles relax.

What can go wrong with eyes?

The most common sight defect in humans is caused by a failure in focusing. As a person gets older, the lens in each eye gets less elastic and so is less able to return to its normal fat shape when the muscles of the ciliary body relax. Many people find that after the age of about 40, near objects are permanently blurred even though distant objects are perfectly clear. This condition is called **long-sightedness**.

The opposite problem occurs if the lens is too strong. Objects close to the eye are clearly focused but the lens cannot be stretched far enough and so distant objects are blurred. This is called **short-sightedness** or myopia.

Opticians compensate for defects in the eye's focusing mechanism by using an extra lens (see figure 2). The bending power of the extra lens measured in dioptres has to be carefully matched to the person's needs.

Even if the lens does not have any effect, parallel rays of light entering the eye are focused on the retina by the cornea, which has a power of about 40 dioptres. The lens is only needed for focusing on objects near the eye, when reading, for example.

The best way for an optician to decide just how strong the extra lens needs to be is to test the patient with a variety of different extra lenses and find the least powerful extra lens that will give clear vision. This is the lens the optician will prescribe. It can then be mounted in a variety of frames to produce a pair of spectacles. People normally have their eyesight checked regularly as they get older so that their lens prescription can be swapped for a more powerful one if necessary.

Using lenses to correct sight defects

long-sighted eye

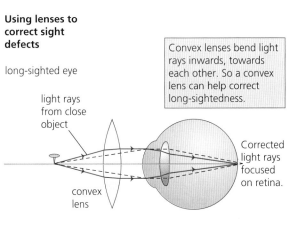

Convex lenses bend light rays inwards, towards each other. So a convex lens can help correct long-sightedness.

light rays from close object

convex lens

Corrected light rays focused on retina.

short-sighted eye

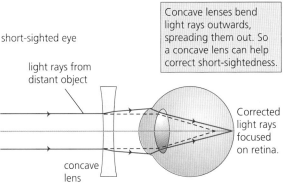

Concave lenses bend light rays outwards, spreading them out. So a concave lens can help correct short-sightedness.

light rays from distant object

concave lens

Corrected light rays focused on retina.

Figure 2

2 a What type of lens would help someone with short sight? Explain why.

b People who are short-sighted often find their eyesight improves as they get older. Explain how this might happen.

Sometimes the cornea becomes scratched or damaged so that its shape is permanently changed. This interferes with the focusing mechanism. The best way to treat this is to replace the damaged cornea with a transplant.

Cataracts are areas where the lens becomes opaque. A person suffering from cataracts seems to be looking through a thick milky film and cannot see individual objects. As for a damaged cornea, the best cure for a cataract is a lens transplant.

How are light images transmitted to the brain?

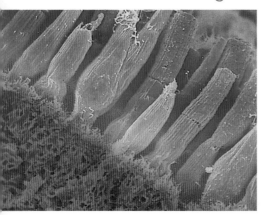

The retina is a complex mat of nerve cells lining the inside of the back of the eyeball. It contains two types of light-sensitive cells, rods and cones, and a number of different nerve cells to transmit impulses to the brain (figure 3). The **rods** are very sensitive and work well in low light conditions. However, they do not give very good resolution. The **cones** are less sensitive but give better resolution and are sensitive to a particular colour of light (figure 4). The brain interprets the pattern of impulses from all the cones to produce a full colour image of the environment.

The **fovea**, or yellow spot, is a part of the retina where there are more cones and fewer rods than usual. This means it is particularly useful for looking at something in very close detail, but needs plenty of light to work properly.

In this electron micrograph of the retina, rod cells are shown in blue, and cone cells are green-blue.

Figure 3 The retina contains light-sensitive rod and cone cells, which trigger impulses to the brain.

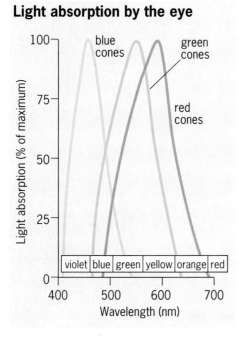

Light absorption by the eye

Figure 4 Different cones in the retina absorb different wavelengths of light.

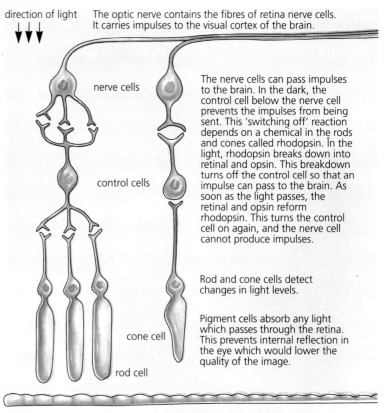

direction of light   The optic nerve contains the fibres of retina nerve cells. It carries impulses to the visual cortex of the brain.

nerve cells

The nerve cells can pass impulses to the brain. In the dark, the control cell below the nerve cell prevents the impulses from being sent. This 'switching off' reaction depends on a chemical in the rods and cones called rhodopsin. In the light, rhodopsin breaks down into retinal and opsin. This breakdown turns off the control cell so that an impulse can pass to the brain. As soon as the light passes, the retinal and opsin reform rhodopsin. This turns the control cell on again, and the nerve cell cannot produce impulses.

control cells

Rod and cone cells detect changes in light levels.

Pigment cells absorb any light which passes through the retina. This prevents internal reflection in the eye which would lower the quality of the image.

cone cell

rod cell

3 An eye that has rods and cones is better than one with only cones. Explain why.

The part of the brain that interprets nerve impulses from the eye is called the optic lobe or optic cortex. The optic nerves connect the lobe with the eyeballs. When you look at an object immediately in front of you, both eyes see it. Each eye sends information to the brain along its own optic nerve. The nerves intermingle at one point, so that information about the left and right halves of the field of view cross over halfway between the optic lobe and the eyes. The optic lobe uses information from both eyes to reconstruct each side of the field of view.

Which animal has the best eyesight?

Falcons have very large eyes in comparison with their body size. The eyeball is like a tube with the retina against the flat back wall giving a clearer image.

Chameleon eyes normally move independently to scan a wide field of view.

Animals have eyes designed to help them survive in their natural environment. Carnivores, like lions or tigers, have eyes at the front of their heads to give good **stereoscopic vision**. Animals with stereoscopic vision can judge distances very well. Each eye sees the same object, but has a very slightly different view because the eyes are a short distance apart. The brain interprets the slightly different signals from each eye to build a three-dimensional image of the world. It also uses clues from other senses like hearing and information from previous experience. This complex calculation is done instantly to help the animal make sense of the world around it.

One disadvantage of stereoscopic vision is that both eyes must be facing in the same direction. This limits the field of view. A herbivore like a rabbit needs to keep a constant lookout for danger and needs a field of vision that extends all around the animal. So rabbits' eyes are placed on the sides of their heads to give a wider field of view.

A horse can focus on the grass close to its eyes and still keep the distant field in focus to look out for predators. Since the lens cannot be more than one shape at any one time, the eyeball is shaped to allow light from close objects more space for focusing than light from distant objects.

4 List five different animals and explain how their eyes are adapted to help them survive.

Summary of sight

- Eyes convert light energy in the environment into nerve impulses. The brain interprets these impulses to create a picture of the outside world.
- The eye focuses images on to the retina using the cornea and the lens.
- People with long sight cannot focus images of near objects on to the retina. A convex lens can cure this problem.

- People with short sight have a lens that is too strong and focuses images in front of the retina. A concave lens can cure this problem.
- Colour vision depends on cone cells in the retina. Rod cells can detect lower levels of light, but cannot tell the difference between different colours.
- The pigment rhodopsin in the light sensitive cells of the retina converts light into nerve impulses.

12.3 Hearing

The other sense that gives animals information about distant objects is hearing. In some animals, the sense of hearing is better developed than the sense of sight. Bats, in particular, have very good hearing and can find their way through dark areas by emitting high-pitched squeaks and listening to the echoes. The bat builds up a picture of its environment from these echoes.

What are sounds?

Sounds are patterns of vibrations (see figure 5). Sounds can travel through gases, liquids and solids, usually travelling fastest through solids. Something that makes a sound is setting up a series of pressure vibrations in the air. These pass through the air in every direction, and can be detected as sound. To describe a sound we need to know:

- the **frequency** – this affects the pitch of the sound
- the **amplitude** – this controls the volume of the sound
- the quality or **timbre** – this allows us, for example, to tell the difference between two sounds with the same pitch and volume but made by two different instruments.

Graph to represent a sound wave

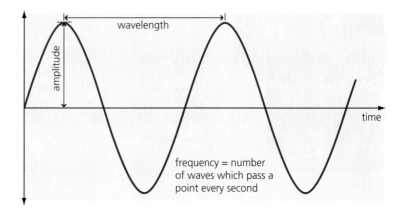

Figure 5

How do we detect sounds?

Microphones convert sound waves into electrical signals that vibrate in the same way as the original sound. Loudspeakers do the opposite – they convert vibrating electrical signals into sound waves with the same frequency, amplitude and quality. If these three factors do not change, the sound can be converted and reconverted many times. The ear converts sound waves in the air into vibrations in bones, then pressure vibrations in a liquid, and finally into nerve impulses (see figure 6). The brain interprets the pattern of impulses to recreate the original sound.

Figure 6 From the ear to the brain.

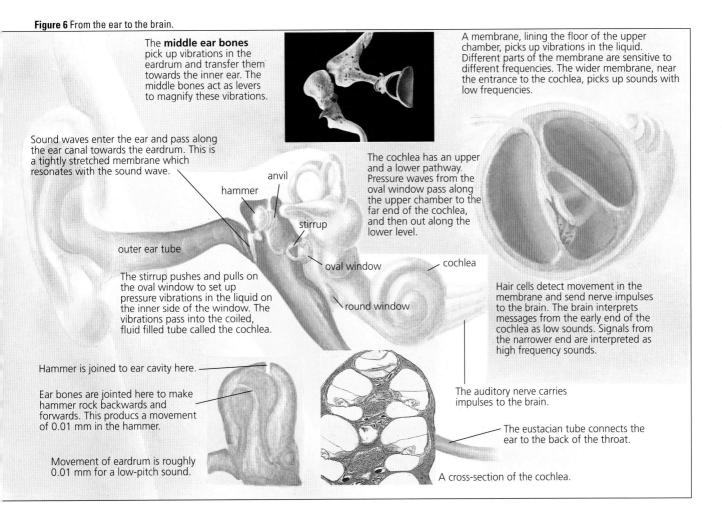

The **middle ear bones** pick up vibrations in the eardrum and transfer them towards the inner ear. The middle bones act as levers to magnify these vibrations.

A membrane, lining the floor of the upper chamber, picks up vibrations in the liquid. Different parts of the membrane are sensitive to different frequencies. The wider membrane, near the entrance to the cochlea, picks up sounds with low frequencies.

Sound waves enter the ear and pass along the ear canal towards the eardrum. This is a tightly stretched membrane which resonates with the sound wave.

The cochlea has an upper and a lower pathway. Pressure waves from the oval window pass along the upper chamber to the far end of the cochlea, and then out along the lower level.

hammer

anvil

stirrup

outer ear tube

oval window

round window

cochlea

The stirrup pushes and pulls on the oval window to set up pressure vibrations in the liquid on the inner side of the window. The vibrations pass into the coiled, fluid filled tube called the cochlea.

Hair cells detect movement in the membrane and send nerve impulses to the brain. The brain interprets messages from the early end of the cochlea as low sounds. Signals from the narrower end are interpreted as high frequency sounds.

Hammer is joined to ear cavity here.

Ear bones are jointed here to make hammer rock backwards and forwards. This produs a movement of 0.01 mm in the hammer.

Movement of eardrum is roughly 0.01 mm for a low-pitch sound.

The auditory nerve carries impulses to the brain.

The eustacian tube connects the ear to the back of the throat.

A cross-section of the cochlea.

5 **a** Draw a flow chart to show how the ear converts a sound in the air into a nerve impulse.

b What happens to the stirrup when the hammer moves in and out?

c The hammer moves 0.01 mm for a low-pitched sound. How far would the stirrup move for the same sound?

d As people grow older, the joints between their ear bones stiffen. How will this affect their hearing?

What happens in the inner ear?

The inner ear has two functions: balance and hearing. The balance organs are the swollen ends of the semicircular canals. These contain small nerve cells that detect movement of the liquid in the canals. The cells are attached to structures shaped like paddles. When the liquid moves, it pushes against the paddles and these stimulate the nerve cells. Any movement of the head will make the liquid move and the nerves will send impulses to the brain. The brain interprets these signals.

Hearing depends on an organ called the **cochlea**. The cochlea is a long, liquid-filled tube which converts pressure waves in the liquid into nerve impulses. A high-pitched, quiet sound will stimulate the sense cells at the narrow end of the cochlea. The louder the sound, the more signals will be sent. A quiet, low-pitched sound will stimulate different cells at the opposite end of the cochlea. Since the brain knows which sense cells are stimulated and how often they are sending signals, it can distinguish between low and high notes and quiet and loud sounds. The quality, or timbre, of the sound depends on the pattern of cells stimulated – different instruments have a different pattern of frequencies.

Which animal has the best hearing?

Ears detect sounds that are important for the animal's survival. A prey animal like a rabbit has very sensitive ears which receive sound from all around. A fox has ears which are more directional and better suited to an animal that hunts. The differences depend on the outer ear. This acts as an ear trumpet and funnels sounds towards the eardrum.

Summary of hearing

- The ear converts sound waves in the air into nerve impulses which the brain interprets as sound.
- The eardrum converts sound waves in the air into movements of the ear bones in the middle ear. The ear bones pass on these movements to the cochlea in the inner ear.
- The frequency of a sound wave controls the pitch of the sound.

- The amplitude of a sound wave controls the loudness of the sound.
- The pattern of frequencies in a sound wave controls the quality of the sound.
- The inner ear is also responsible for the sense of balance and movement.
- Animals have ears that are adapted to their particular lifestyle.

12.4 Other senses

How do we detect taste and smell?

Smell and taste are chemical senses – they detect particular chemicals in food or in the air. Air taken in through the nose passes over a layer of mucus in the spaces behind the nose. The mucus covers millions of sensory nerve endings which can respond to chemicals in the air. The brain interprets an impulse from one of these sensory cells as a particular smell. The many thousands of odours you can recognise depend on many thousands of different receptors.

One group of odours called **pheromones** are thought to stimulate instinctive behaviours. So, certain smells are believed to increase sexual activity and some perfume manufacturers have claimed that people

wearing pheromone-containing perfumes will be more attractive to the opposite sex. This has never been conclusively proven in human beings although in other animals it is known that smell is an important part of the signals that pass between males and females during the **breeding season**.

This pig is smelling out underground mushrooms called truffles. These truffles sell for high prices in restaurants, and specially trained pigs can make their owners a lot of money in the truffle-hunting season.

How do we detect things by touch?

The sense of touch depends on sense organs in the skin. Obviously, it can only provide information about things very close to the animal.

Skin structure

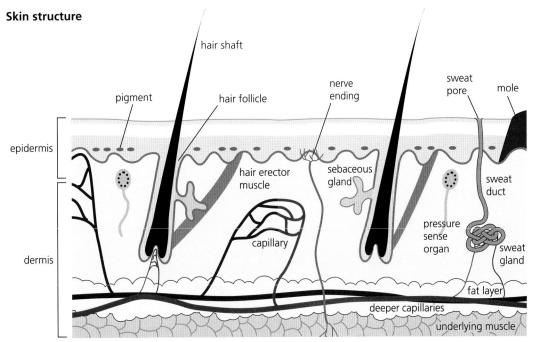

Figure 7 The skin contains a collection of different sense organs and some free nerve endings (figure 7). The sense organs are specialised to detect particular types of touch. Sense organs near the surface of the skin detect gentle pressure. A heavy pressure will stimulate different sense organs deeper in the skin. Some of the free nerve endings detect heat, others detect cold and another set seem to detect pain. It is up to the brain to work out what is happening to the skin by interpreting the signals coming from a variety of sense organs.

How do we detect changes inside the body?

The detectors that cause the pain in earache are examples of **interoceptors**. Interoceptors are part of the sensory systems that monitor the inside of the body. Other interoceptors monitor:

- the blood – temperature and dissolved carbon dioxide and sugar
- the muscles – whether the muscle is tense or relaxed
- the stomach – the amount of food in the gut
- the whole body – any unexpected changes in the tissues.

Interoceptors allow the body to monitor the internal environment and check nothing is going wrong. If the interoceptors detect unexpected changes the body will try to do something to correct the change. You can read more about the changes that interoceptors detect in chapter 10, *Homeostasis*.

How can plants detect changes in the environment?

Cacti seem to thrive on lack of care. Some are only stimulated to flower if you forget to water them!

Plants respond to changes in their environment more slowly than animals, but they still respond. To respond, they first need a system to detect changes in the environment.

Since plants cannot move, they do not need senses that respond as rapidly as animal senses. Plant senses are concerned with monitoring the levels of chemicals or light. Most plant responses are growth responses. You can read more about these in chapter 15, *Growing and developing*.

6 Why do you think cacti flower if conditions begin to get worse? Think about the chances of survival of a seed compared with a fully grown cactus.

7 Plants detect changes in:

- water supply • light levels • length of daylight • temperature • the effect of gravity.

Explain why each of these factors may be important to a plant.

Summary of other senses

- Taste and smell are chemical senses. They tend to detect things near to the organism.
- Touch gives an organism information about its immediate environment.

- Interoceptors detect conditions within the body. We are not usually aware of signals from interoceptors unless something goes wrong.

Investigations

1 Anglers use maggots as bait. They keep the maggots in tins and jars mixed in with sawdust. When the anglers open the bait tins the maggots bury themselves in the sawdust.

a Which sense organ might the maggots need to behave in this way? Think of at least three explanations for this behaviour.

b Plan and carry out an investigation to find out which of your explanations is most likely to be correct.

Learning objectives

By the end of this chapter you should be able to:

- **recognise** information transfers in living organisms
- **explain** why animals need nerves
- **describe** the parts of a mammalian nerve
- **explain** how nerves control reflexes
- **explain** why animals need brains

- **describe** the functions of different parts of the human brain
- **explain** how the brain remembers things
- **explain** the need for a responsible attitude to drugs

13.1 Nerves

Why do animals have nerves?

Plants respond slowly to changes in their environment. Usually their responses involve growth. Animals respond much more quickly. Animal responses usually involve movement towards food or away from danger.

1 Describe the ways each of the animals in the photographs are responding to their environment.

In order to respond, an animal must have information about its environment and be able to make decisions based on this information. Sense organs or sensory **nerve** endings (**receptors**) gather this information and nerves carry it to the brain. For example, a rabbit may see a fox stalking it from the bushes. Its brain interprets this information and decides how to respond. In the case of the rabbit the response would probably be to bolt down its burrow as quickly as possible!

These animals have complex nervous systems that allow them to sense changes in their environments and to react to them.

The nervous system

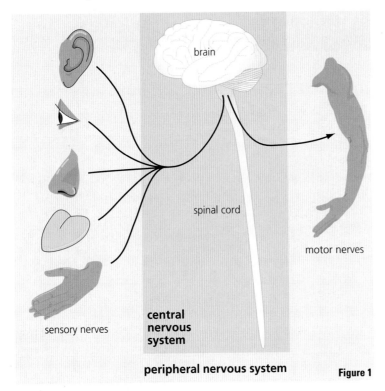

Figure 1

Even very simple movements involve lots of muscles acting in a co-ordinated way at the appropriate time. In mammals, the brain organises the action of the muscles. Since the brain is protected inside the bony skull, its instructions need to be carried quickly to muscles all over the body. Nerves act as these information carriers (see figure 1).

A nerve is a bundle of fibres linked together rather like a telephone cable. One nerve might have thousands of fibres, for example a nerve connecting cells in the brain to cells in the muscles of the legs. An individual nerve cell is called a neurone (figure 2). Neurones are some of the largest cells in the human body. A single sensory neurone can link a sense organ in the skin of your foot with a neurone in your brain.

Neurones

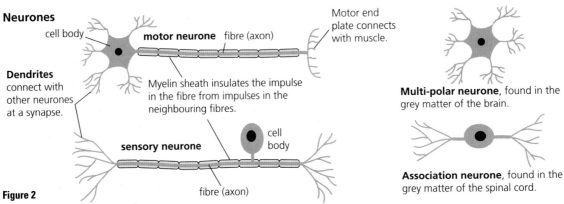

cell body

motor neurone fibre (axon)

Motor end plate connects with muscle.

Dendrites connect with other neurones at a synapse.

Myelin sheath insulates the impulse in the fibre from impulses in the neighbouring fibres.

sensory neurone

cell body

fibre (axon)

Multi-polar neurone, found in the grey matter of the brain.

Association neurone, found in the grey matter of the spinal cord.

Figure 2

Nerves and neurones

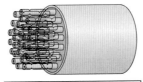

Each nerve is like a telephone cable, with lots of different 'lines'. Each 'line' is a single neurone, and is insulated from all the others by its own myelin sheath.

Figure 3

2 a Explain the difference between a nerve and a neurone.
b List the differences you can see between the motor, sensory and multipolar neurones.
c Multipolar neurones are usually found in the brain, not in the nerves. Explain how their structure reflects this fact.

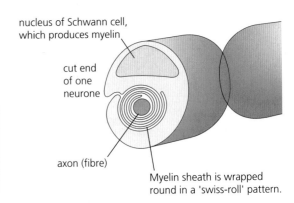

nucleus of Schwann cell, which produces myelin

cut end of one neurone

axon (fibre)

Myelin sheath is wrapped round in a 'swiss-roll' pattern.

What is a nerve impulse?

Note

Parkinson's disease is an illness caused by the level of a neurotransmitter in the brain, called dopamine, falling below a certain level. People with Parkinson's disease often cannot control their muscles properly and suffer from very shaky hands.

A **nerve impulse** is an electrical signal that passes along a neurone. A neurone carries this impulse quickly, and passes it on to another neurone. The impulse must not leak out and start impulses in nearby neurones in the nerve, or the brain could receive a confusing mixture of signals instead of one clear one. This explains why neurones must be insulated from each other (see figure 3).

Impulses pass along neurones and between neurones. The place where two neurones meet is called a **synapse**. Neurones do not actually touch at a synapse, but the gap between them is very small (roughly 20 nm). **Dendrites** also help to make the transfer of the impulse easier.

The end of a dendrite is flattened to increase the surface area exposed to the next neurone. When a signal arrives at the end of a neurone, a chemical is released which drifts across the small space to the next neurone. This chemical is called a **neurotransmitter**.

How do nerves control reflexes?

An example of a reflex in humans is dropping something that is hot. If you pick up something very hot, like a saucepan lid, you quickly put it down before it burns your fingers. The nerves provide the fastest possible reaction to stop your fingers from being damaged.

Figure 4 A reflex arc.

3 a Look at the reflex arc in figure 4. Write down the parts in the reflex arc that do the different jobs in a stimulus–response reaction.
b How is the impulse passed to the brain?
c The interconnecting neurone slows down the signal. Why is this useful to the body?
d Draw a flow chart to show what happens when you step on a nail.

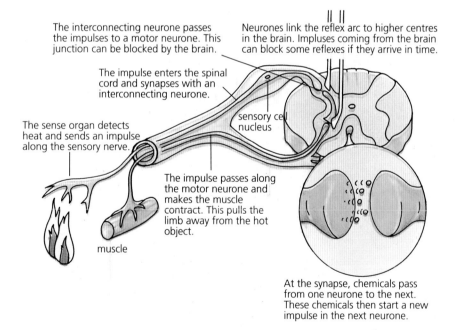

The interconnecting neurone passes the impulses to a motor neurone. This junction can be blocked by the brain.

Neurones link the reflex arc to higher centres in the brain. Impulses coming from the brain can block some reflexes if they arrive in time.

The impulse enters the spinal cord and synapses with an interconnecting neurone.

The sense organ detects heat and sends an impulse along the sensory nerve.

sensory cell nucleus

The impulse passes along the motor neurone and makes the muscle contract. This pulls the limb away from the hot object.

muscle

At the synapse, chemicals pass from one neurone to the next. These chemicals then start a new impulse in the next neurone.

Summary of nerves

- Sensory nerves carry impulses from receptors to the central nervous system. Motor nerves carry impulses from the central nervous system to muscles.
- Nerves are bundles of neurones a bit like telephone wires in a cable.

- Myelin is a chemical which insulates neurones from each other.
- A nerve impulse is an electrical signal that passes down an axon.
- Reflexes depend on simple neurone circuits and do not need to involve the brain.

13.2 The brain

Why do animals have a brain?

4 Some parts of the body have a large amount of brain controlling them, while other parts have very little. Explain the pattern you can see in the brain distribution in figure 5.

Figure 5 In the human brain, different areas tend to carry out different functions.

Nerves can control reflexes by themselves, but animals also have a large mass of nervous tissue called a brain. Most animals have a front and a back end. The front end is the one that tends to lead the way as the animal moves through its environment. Sense organs gather information about the threats and opportunities of the environment, and so most of the sense organs tend to be at the front, or head end, of the animal.

During the course of evolution, the front end of the spinal cord swelled to provide the processing power for the sensory inputs and a simple brain developed. Over time, the brain has become larger and more complex to handle more and more information from sense organs. The extra information also means more complex behaviour becomes possible. This needs better and better thinking skills and more nerves to control the muscles. All these factors tend to lead to increased brain size and complexity (figure 5).

The human brain

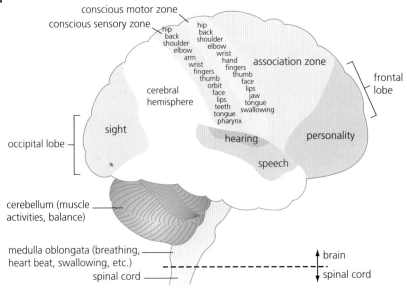

What is a stroke?

A small blockage in one of the blood vessels that supply the brain can be very serious. Without a fresh supply of food and oxygen brain cells die very quickly. Once a cell has died, it cannot be replaced. If enough cells die, the body can be paralysed, often down one side. The sudden damage to the brain caused by a blocked blood vessel is a called a **stroke**. Strokes are one of the major causes of death in the UK and seem to be linked to smoking, eating a fat-rich diet and having high blood pressure.

Stroke victims can recover even though the dead cells are not replaced. It seems that the brain may be able to re-route signals through undamaged neurones to reconnect the brain and muscles.

How do we remember things?

When someone tells you their name, certain neurones in your brain pass impulses to each other in a complex pattern of connections. The connections act as a code for the name so that you can remember it even after the sound has died away. This **short-term memory** is useful, but fades after a few seconds when the impulses stop flowing. Without a constant flow of impulses the code, and the memory, disappears.

Some names are more important and you transfer these to **long-term memory**. Here the synapses that connect the neurones are changed in some way to preserve the pattern of impulses. Now the memory is fixed because there have been chemical changes to the connections between the cells. The code is to do with the connections rather than the impulses.

Summary of the brain

- The brain is a large lump of nerve tissue that developed to deal with complex sensory data.
- Brains have two main tissue types – grey matter which is the cell bodies, and white matter which contains the long connections surrounded by myelin.
- Different parts of the brain have different functions.

- The right half of the brain controls the left side of the body. The left side of the brain controls the right side of the body.
- A stroke is damage to the brain caused by a blood clot. Strokes can lead to paralysis, often to one side of the body, or death.
- Neurone circuits in the brain code short- and long-term memory.

13.3 Drugs

What are drugs?

Drugs are chemicals that change the way cells in our bodies work. Some drugs act directly on the brain. These can change the way we feel and behave.

We do not understand how the chemical machinery of our brains produces the thoughts and emotions that we call our mind. However, we can use some chemicals to change some of our feelings. These chemicals include painkillers like aspirin, medically prescribed drugs like phenobarbitone which controls epilepsy, and a range of recreational drugs like alcohol and marijuana. It is this last group of drugs that causes increasing concern. People sometimes take recreational drugs to try to find a 'happiness chemical'. The drugs are taken without medical supervision, and this is called **drug abuse**.

What types of drugs are abused?

There are four basic types of so-called recreational drugs (see table 1). Some are legal, others are illegal. They can also be divided into 'hard' drugs, which are generally the most dangerous illegal ones, and 'soft' drugs which, although still illegal, are thought to be less damaging. However, it is very difficult to decide exactly how dangerous a drug might be because the eventual effect of the chemical depends on the circumstances in which it is used. For example, alcohol abuse kills many more people in the UK every year than heroin addiction, but there are millions of people who use alcohol safely. It is more difficult to find heroin users who can manage their drug use safely.

Table 1 *The main drug groups and their effects.*

Group	Examples	Effects	Dangers
Hypnotics	tranquillisers and sleeping pills	calming, relaxing	addiction
Stimulants	ecstasy, speed, caffeine	increase mental activity, seen to provide energy and keep people going	addiction
Inebriants	alcohol, solvents	disorientation, giving a feeling of well-being and confidence	addiction, specific organ damage, e.g. solvents can cause severe liver and lung damage
Hallucinogens	LSD 'acid'	produces hallucinations	addiction, potential brain damage

Almost all drugs are controlled in some way by laws. Drugs like heroin and ecstasy are illegal although heroin can be prescribed by a doctor in certain circumstances. A number of other drugs are not illegal but are discouraged through taxation, for example cigarettes and alcohol. Other drugs are available over the counter without any restriction, for example aspirin or paracetamol. Even these often have detailed instructions for safe use on the packet. The status of drugs can change from country to country and time to time. For example, heroin was legal in the UK in Victorian times and marijuana is available through certain legally licensed bars in Holland.

What is addiction?

When people start to use alcohol, they find they feel the effects of it quite easily. Over time they find that they can take more drink before they begin to feel the same effects. This need to increase the dose shows they are developing **tolerance**. Some people find they need to drink more and more to stop feeling depressed or upset. They have become **psychologically addicted** to alcohol.

5 Explain the difference between tolerance, psychological addiction and physical addiction.

A drug like heroin also causes **physical addiction**. Here the person needs to increase the dose over time to feel the effect they had at first, and also to prevent physical symptoms like sweating, shaking, muscle pains and diarrhoea from developing. The body has adapted so that it needs the drug to maintain a normal state, and if the drug is not given the person suffers from **withdrawal sickness**.

How are solvents abused?

Solvents are a mixed group of chemicals used in glues, paints, varnishes, cleaning fluids and as lighter fuels. Glue-sniffers inhale the vapours from these substances and the chemicals pass very quickly into the blood vessels lining the mouth, nose and lungs. This means they have a very rapid effect, and it also means that damage can be done very quickly. Many of these chemicals are poisonous and cause brain and liver damage.

Compressed liquids such as lighter fluids expand when they are inhaled, and take energy as heat from the larynx to do this. This freezes the tissues and can make the lungs fill with liquid. Butane, a common lighter fluid, also causes the heart to be more sensitive to adrenaline making it race, which could lead to a heart attack.

Why do people abuse drugs?

6 a Alcohol is a legal drug that causes, directly and indirectly, thousands of deaths every year in the UK. List the biological and social arguments for and against banning the sale of alcohol.
b Would *you* ban the sale of alcohol? Explain the reasons for your answer.

Many drugs have perceived links with particular groups of people. Ecstasy is often associated with rave music in the same way that heroin used to be linked to rock music. Tranquilliser addicts are thought of as people who were prescribed the drug over many years by a less than careful doctor. Cocaine is often thought to be popular with high-achieving yuppies working in the financial markets. As with all stereotypes, there is a degree of truth in these images but also a large amount of nonsense. Doctors and psychologists find it very difficult to predict which sorts of people will become drug abusers and even the abusers themselves may not be able to explain the reasons for their habit. It is true to say that the use of recreational drugs is increasing in the UK and is causing concern to health workers. The involvement of organised crime with the supply of illegal drugs is also a problem for the police.

Summary of drugs

- Drugs are chemicals which change the chemistry of the body.
- Drugs can have medical uses or be used for enjoyment (recreational drugs).
- Addiction occurs when the body's chemistry alters so that it needs continual doses of the drug.
- Attitudes to drug use vary between countries and from time to time.

Learning objectives

By the end of this chapter you should be able to:

- **explain** why animals move
- **explain** how muscles bend and straighten the arm
- **list** the factors that affect muscle strength
- **explain** how chemical reactions produce a pulling force in muscles

- **describe** the layout of the human skeleton
- **explain** how the body heals broken bones
- **explain** how joints combine mobility and safety
- **list** some of the things that can go wrong with joints

14.1 Movement

Why do animals move?

1 Study the photographs here and list the advantages of movement for each animal.

Movement costs energy, so animals will move only as much as they need. Faster movement tends to cost more energy than slower movement, so an animal like the cheetah will run at its top speed of 90 km/h for the shortest possible time. If the cheetah decides it is unlikely to catch its prey, or the prey is not worth the effort of catching it, it will stop running and look for an easier kill.

All animals rely on movement at some stage in their life cycle. Most animals move every day.

Animals move to:

- find food
- escape from predators
- find a mate.

What do we need for movement?

Movement in animals depends on muscles, bones and nerves. The muscles contract and the bones give them something to pull against. Nerves control the muscles so that they work in co-ordinated patterns. Joints between the bones allow the limbs to bend to make the movements smooth and efficient. Damage to any of these components – muscles, bones, joints or nerves – will lead to a failure of movement.

Summary of movement

- Animals move to find food, to escape from predators and to find a mate.

- Movement depends on muscles, bones and nerves.

14.2 Muscles

How do bones move?

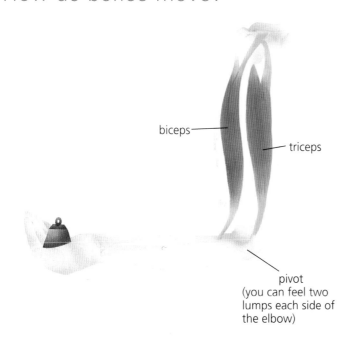

biceps

triceps

pivot
(you can feel two
lumps each side of
the elbow)

Muscles are protein-rich tissues that are able to contract by up to 10% of their resting length. A 10% movement is quite small, so bones act as levers to magnify this movement.

Each bone has at least two muscles attached to it – one to pull it in one direction and another to pull it the opposite way. This is because muscles can only pull, they cannot push. A contracted muscle can relax, but it cannot push itself back to its original length – it needs another muscle to do that. Pairs of muscles acting in opposite directions are called **antagonistic pairs**. All muscles must be paired with other muscles to act as antagonists, as shown in figure 1.

Figure 1 The biceps and triceps muscles in the upper arm act as as antagonistic pair.

2 a In figure 1 which muscle will bend the arm at the elbow?
 b Which muscle acts as an antagonist to the biceps?

How do muscles contract?

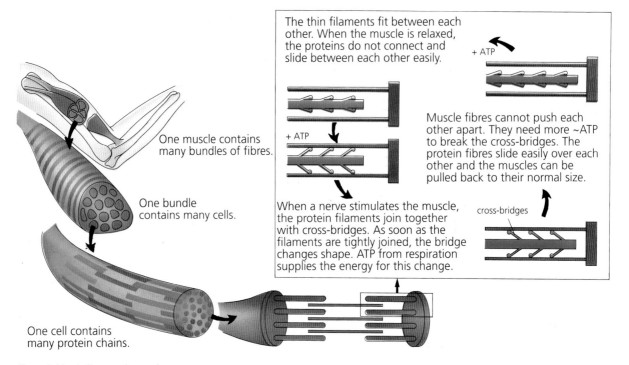

The thin filaments fit between each other. When the muscle is relaxed, the proteins do not connect and slide between each other easily.

+ ATP

+ ATP

Muscle fibres cannot push each other apart. They need more ~ATP to break the cross-bridges. The protein fibres slide easily over each other and the muscles can be pulled back to their normal size.

When a nerve stimulates the muscle, the protein filaments join together with cross-bridges. As soon as the filaments are tightly joined, the bridge changes shape. ATP from respiration supplies the energy for this change.

cross-bridges

One muscle contains many bundles of fibres.

One bundle contains many cells.

One cell contains many protein chains.

Figure 2 Muscle fibres need energy in the form of ATP to contract. You can read more about ATP in chapter 4, *Energy transfers.*

3 Draw a flow chart to show how muscles contract.

A muscle is made up of many elongated cells, each of which contains many muscle fibres. These fibres contain chemicals that produce the force that shortens the muscle (figure 2). So the strength of a muscle depends on the number of contractile fibres it has. The easiest way to estimate the number of fibres in a muscle is to measure its width – thicker muscles contain more fibres and so are stronger. Body-builders and fitness fanatics are quite right – the larger the biceps the stronger the pull.

How are muscles specialised?

The muscles we have described so far are **skeletal muscles**. These are muscles that are attached to bones and are used to move the body. Skeletal muscles can contract powerfully, but get tired easily. They are also controlled by the conscious brain, so you have to decide to run to catch a bus or pick up a cup of coffee.

Another group of muscles are the **smooth muscles** of the gut. These muscles cannot contract very powerfully, but do not tire easily and can stay contracted for long periods of time. They are not attached to bones and are not under conscious control. Rings of smooth muscles contract and relax to push food along your gut without you having to think about it. This is called **peristalsis**. Peristalsis depends on two sets of antagonistic muscle fibres – one ringing the gut and the other running lengthways along it (see chapter 7, *Feeding*).

4 Draw up a table or chart to show the differences between the three types of muscle.

A third kind of muscle is only found in the heart and is called **cardiac muscle**. This muscle can contract powerfully and rhythmically and does not get tired. Your heart will beat billions of times during your life without, hopefully, ever needing a rest!

What effects does training have on muscles?

Training can increase the amount of muscle in the body, and can help to make muscles work more effectively. Training usually improves the heart and lungs as well as individual muscles. This will ensure that a good supply of blood reaches the muscles during exercise. However, training does strain the body and an inappropriate exercise programme can do damage to muscles and joints.

Summary of muscles

• Muscles can only contract or relax. They are arranged in antagonistic pairs which pull in opposite directions.

• Training increases the strength of muscles by increasing the number of individual muscle fibres in a muscle.

14.3 Bones

How do bones form?

All bones start as **cartilage**. Cartilage is a softer, more flexible tissue that forms the 'bones' of the human fetus. As the fetus grows, more and more calcium-containing minerals are added to the cartilage to stiffen it. By the time the baby is born, much of its skeleton has been converted to bone.

The evolution of the internal skeleton seemed to follow a similar path. The earliest, most primitive fish had cartilage to stiffen their bodies. Sharks and dogfish, some of the oldest types of fish, still have cartilage. The next stage was to develop tougher bones and, by the time land animals evolved, strong bone was available to support the heavy bodies out of water. Dinosaurs, for example, had some of the largest bones ever developed by living organisms.

Bones were linked together by joints into complex skeletons. Different animals had different skeletons which matched their lifestyle (see figure 3). All mammals share a common pattern for the bones in their limbs, and this supports the idea that they evolved from a common ancestor.

The animal group with the largest number of different species has used a completely different strategy for body support. Insects have their skeleton on the outside of the body. These **exoskeletons** are made of chitin, a completely different substance from the cartilage or bone found in fish, birds, reptiles and mammals (figure 4).

Skeletons

Typical bird

Bird bones are hollow, to cut down on weight. The wing bones are arranged in a specific way to allow the bird to fly.

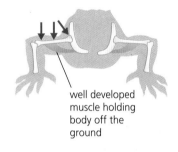

tendon goes behind bone

powerful downstroke muscle

section through hollow bone to show strengthening bars

large bone for muscle attachment

Typical reptile

Reptiles have a slightly different skeleton arrangement from mammals. A crocodile's legs are attached to the side of its body, rather than underneath. This creates a strain on the thigh muscles, and limits the speed with which a crocodile can move.

well developed muscle holding body off the ground

Insect limb

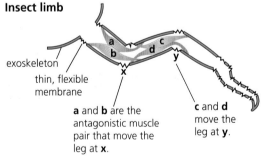

exoskeleton

thin, flexible membrane

a and **b** are the antagonistic muscle pair that move the leg at **x**.

c and **d** move the leg at **y**.

Figure 4 Insects have exoskeletons.

Typical jumping mammal

large pelvis allows room for muscle attachment

powerful muscles

pelvis links with spine to have something to push against

Typical tetrapod mammal (e.g. horse)

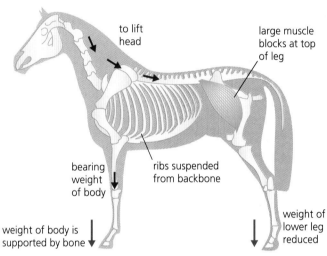

to lift head

large muscle blocks at top of leg

bearing weight of body

ribs suspended from backbone

weight of body is supported by bone

weight of lower leg reduced

Figure 3 The arrangement of bones in an animal's skeleton reflects its lifestyle.

5 Compare the insect limb in figure 4 with the human upper arm in figure 1. List the similarities and differences and explain how these affect the way each limb works.

What happens when bones break?

Bone is a living tissue which grows and can repair itself (see figure 5). It also acts as a store for calcium, which can be released into the blood when necessary. Bone needs a constant supply of food and oxygen and produces waste products which must be cleared away.

Bone tissues

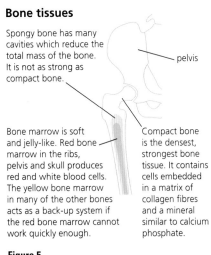

Spongy bone has many cavities which reduce the total mass of the bone. It is not as strong as compact bone.

Bone marrow is soft and jelly-like. Red bone marrow in the ribs, pelvis and skull produces red and white blood cells. The yellow bone marrow in many of the other bones acts as a back-up system if the red bone marrow cannot work quickly enough.

— pelvis

Compact bone is the densest, strongest bone tissue. It contains cells embedded in a matrix of collagen fibres and a mineral similar to calcium phosphate.

Figure 5

When a bone breaks, the body quickly grows a cartilage plug to cover the broken ends. This fixes the bones in place. Cells then lay down extra calcium minerals to convert the cartilage into bone. Finally, a different set of cells dissolve away any spare bone and remodel the plug to match the original bone.

The rate of bone healing depends on age – the younger you are, the quicker the bone heals. People with low calcium or low protein diets also need longer to heal bone breaks.

Osteoporosis is a condition that causes weakness in bones. It seems to be linked to sex hormones and is most common in older women. Calcium withdraws from the compact bone to convert it to softer spongy bone. This causes weakness and makes fractures more likely.

Summary of bones

- Bones are living structures made of mineral and protein components. Large bones have bone marrow in the middle which makes blood cells.
- Since bones are living structures they can repair themselves if they break.
- A skeleton is an organised structure of jointed bones. Skeletons support the body, protect internal organs and provide a site to attach muscles.

14.4 Joints

What are joints like?

A joint is any connection between two bones. There are three types of joint, **fibrous**, **cartilaginous** and **synovial** – as shown in figure 6.

Joints

Fibrous joints can't move at all. Skull sutures are a good example.

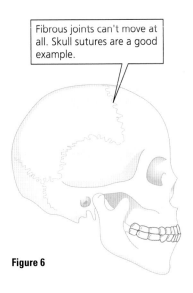

In cartilaginous joints, a little movement is possible. An example is the pubic symphysis, which holds the two halves of the pelvis together.

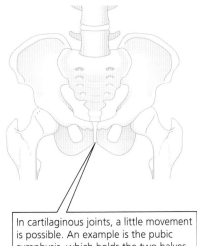

The ball-and-socket joint of the hip is a good example of a synovial joint. It allows plenty of movement. There are other types of synovial joints, such as the hinge joint of the elbow and finger joints.

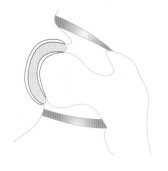

Figure 6

133

Synovial joints are the only type that allow much movement. Look back at the diagram of the upper arm in figure 1 to see two synovial joints – the elbow and the shoulder.

The elbow joint is a **hinge joint**. It only allows movement in a single plane, rather like the hinge on a door. This may seem to be a disadvantage, but hinge joints are very stable and are not easily damaged or dislocated.

The shoulder joint is a **ball-and-socket joint**, and allows a much wider range of movements. Unfortunately, the ball can pop out of the socket, for example, during a gymnastics exercise. This dislocation can be very painful and a doctor will need to push the ball back into the socket – which is also painful!

Ligaments join bones to other bones. Ligaments are flexible and can stretch slightly so that there is some give at the joint. **Tendons** join muscles to bones. They do not stretch.

6 List the features of the synovial joint and explain how each one helps it to function effectively.

7 Explain why it is important that ligaments have some stretchiness, but tendons have none.

What is arthritis?

Joints suffer from a range of problems. They have to fit perfectly together or they can dislocate easily. However, if the joints swell the bone ends may grind against each other. This causes pain and damage to the bones. Doctors use the term 'arthritis' to describe inflammation of the joints. Arthritis can have many different causes but the result is always the same – swollen and painful joints.

Arthritis tends to affect older people and can be made worse by cold or damp weather. Some people find particular kinds of food can make the condition worse. At the moment there is no cure for arthritis other than powerful painkillers which deal with the symptom (the pain) rather than the cause (which could be one of many, or unknown).

Summary of joints

- The connection between bones is called a joint. Different types of joint allow different amounts of movement.

- Synovial joints allow the greatest range of movement.

14.5 Movement in plants

Do plants move?

Individual parts of some plants can move quite quickly, but most large plants do not move around. This is mainly because the roots they need to absorb water and minerals keep them fixed firmly in one place. However, microscopic plants like the phytoplankton floating in the sea move with the water currents, and a number of organisms like *Euglena* are able to move themselves using flagella and **cilia**.

Water lily flowers open wide in sunlight but close at night. The opening and closing is linked to the time of day when the insects that pollinate the flowers are active. Flowers like honeysuckle, which are pollinated by night-flying insects, open at dusk.

The sundew is a carnivorous plant native to the UK. It grows in wetland areas where the soil is lacking in nitrates. When a small fly lands on the leaf, hair-like projections bend to enclose the insect. A sticky fluid on the leaf surface helps to trap the fly and also contains protein-digesting enzymes which break down the insect body. The sundew absorbs the nitrogen-containing compounds and the indigestible residue blows away in the wind. The plant itself is capable of photosynthesis and obtains most of its organic carbon in this way, rather than by its carnivorous activities.

Insectivorous plants, like this Venus fly trap, have parts that move. The trap shuts in less than a second when a fly touches two sensitive hairs on the modified leaves.

Mimosa pudica *folds up its leaves at dusk, in roughly one second. It is not clear why the plant should benefit from this very rapid movement.*

8 Explain how plants benefit from movements.

Summary of movement in plants

- Most large plants do not move around, though individual parts of some plants can move relatively quickly.

- Plant movements do not involve organs like muscles.

Investigations

1 Weight lifters train to produce the largest possible muscle mass. A common sense idea is that people with the largest muscles are the strongest – but is this always true?

a What factors may affect a weight lifter's performance? Plan and carry out an investigation to find out which of these were the most important.

b How could your results be useful to a trainer for a weight lifter?

2 Some trainers use a technique called visualisation to help their team's performance. Visualisation means imagining that the kick you are about to make will go into the goal. It is about imagining a succesful result and is to help build confidence.

Plan an investigation to see if visualisation will help with a task like throwing a ball into a bucket. In your plan you will need to explain how you can overcome the problem that people get better at a task after some practise anyway.

15 Growing and developing

Learning objectives

By the end of this chapter you should be able to:

- **choose** a suitable way to measure growth rates in a range of organisms
- **interpret** statistics on growth of animals
- **explain** how animals control their growth and development

- **describe** a range of growth responses in plants
- **explain** how these responses help the plant to survive
- **explain** how plants control their growth and development

15.1 Growth in animals

How can we measure growth in animals?

All living things grow and develop during their lifetime. Simple organisms like bacteria and protozoa grow to a maximum size and then split into two smaller individuals. This is called **binary fission** (see chapter 3, *Cells*). The offspring repeat the cycle, sometimes as often as once every 20 minutes, so that enormous numbers of cells can be produced in a very short time.

More complex organisms usually have more complex growth cycles. Human adults are not simply a larger version of a baby. Different parts of the body grow at different rates and some parts change the way they work over a lifetime.

Medical staff monitor babies very closely in the first few months of life for any strange growth patterns.

Although doctors can recognise when a baby is not growing properly, or 'failing to thrive', they need a way to record exact changes. The usual method is to monitor change in mass and increase in length. Table 1 shows important data on the growth of babies over the first few years of life.

Table 1 *Data on baby growth.*

Age	Average weight (kg)		Average height (cm)		Average skull circumference (cm)	
	Boys	**Girls**	**Boys**	**Girls**	**Boys**	**Girls**
Birth (term)	3.5	3.4	50	50	35	35
3 months	5.7	5.2	60	58	41	40
6 months	7.8	7.3	66	65	44	43
9 months	9.3	8.7	71	70	46	44
12 months	10.3	9.6	75	74	47	46
18 months	11.7	10.9	81	80	49	47
2 years	12.7	12.0	87	85	50	48
3 years	14.7	14.1	95	93	50	49
4 years	15	16	101	100		
5 years	19	18	108	107	51	50
6 years	21	20	114	114		
7 years	23	23	120	120		
8 years	25	25	126	125	52	52

What is 'normal' growth?

No two babies are the same, and what may be healthy growth for one might be slow growth for another. This variation in growth means it is sometimes difficult to decide what is normal. Doctors use charts that show the average height at different ages and the spread of heights which covers a specified percentage of people. This means that graphs for height and mass have broad bands that describe the range for normal, instead of narrow lines. The change in weight with time, for a growing child, is more important than the distance from the average weight. So, a baby which is below average weight and grows slowly, maintaining its position below average for its age is much less worrying than a child who starts at average weight and then grows slowly to fall below average.

1   **a**   Adam weighed 3.7 kg at birth. Does that mean he was above or below average birth weight?
    b   Draw a graph to show changes in average height for girls from birth to 8 years.
    c   Compare the growth in the skull circumferences with the growth in height for boys from birth to 8 years.

Do all parts of the body grow at the same rate?

Different parts of the body grow at different rates. This means that the balance of organs in the body changes as we get older. For example, babies tend to have larger eyes compared with the size of their heads than adults.

Human babies and adults are obviously the same species when you look at them, but some animals grow so that the adults look completely different from the young. For example, the cabbage white butterfly seen in the summer looks nothing like the pale green caterpillar that devastated the gardener's vegetables in the spring. Tadpoles swimming in the pond in spring seem completely different from the frogs that overwinter under stones at the bottom of the garden. This large change in body pattern during growth is called **metamorphosis**.

2   What is the advantage to an insect of having two completely different body forms during its life cycle?

137

What controls growth?

Growth is not usually steady. In humans, growth is very rapid before birth and during the early years. It slows down around 10 years of age, but then speeds up again during puberty. By the age of 20, growth in height has almost finished. In other animals growth occurs in bursts in a similar way. Metamorphosis is the most extreme example of growth spurts, when a completely new body might be formed in a relatively short time.

In almost all animals these growth spurts and changes are controlled by hormones. For example, in humans, the pituitary gland (see chapter 10, *Homeostasis*) secretes human growth factor (HGF), which works with other hormones to encourage cell division and growth. Some children fail to grow because they cannot produce HGF, but if they take the hormone as a drug, they may grow normally.

Growth is affected by:

- genetics – tall parents tend to produce tall offspring
- food availability – poor diet can reduce growth
- illness – certain illnesses can reduce growth as a secondary effect
- growth disorders – these are illnesses whose main effect is on growth.

With so many factors affecting growth, it is not surprising that things can go wrong quite easily. However, the normal range includes the vast majority of people and very few are classed as having a particular growth problem.

3 Explain why human growth factor is not used if failure to grow is due to poor diet.

What happens as we get older?

Ageing and growth are part of the same process. Younger bodies grow more quickly and can repair themselves more easily than older bodies. Scientists do not know exactly why this happens. It may be something to do with the way cells divide. At every cell division, the genetic material of the cell is copied. It seems likely that the cell makes some mistakes in this copying and, when the cell divides again, more mistakes are added. This build up of mistakes may lead to cells which cannot work properly. We call this ageing. Some scientists have suggested that an adult body allows itself to die after a certain time to make way for its offspring with younger, more efficient cells.

Summary of growth in animals

- Growth is the increase in size of an organism. Different parts of an organism may grow at different rates.
- Since different parts of an organism may grow at different rates the adult may look and behave very differently from the young.
- Some organisms undergo a major developmental change, for example from caterpillar to butterfly. This is called metamorphosis.
- Growth in animals is affected by a range of environmental factors and is controlled by hormones produced by endocrine glands.

15.2 Growth in plants

How can we measure growth in plants?

Plants grow in height and width. They get heavier and can change shape and appearance dramatically. How can we measure growth changes?

The mass of plant material is a good measure of plant growth. However, the same plant will have a different mass before and after a good watering. For this reason botanists often use dry weight as a measure of the total plant material. The dry weight is the mass of a plant when all the water has been removed by drying the plant in an oven at 110 °C for 24 hours.

4 What is the only disadvantage of recording growth using dry weight?

Plants grow and change during their life cycle in the same way as animals (see figure 1). In oaks the complete life cycle can be 300 years, while some desert plants can germinate from seed, flower, set seeds and die in a matter of two weeks.

Modern apple trees are often small to reduce the material wasted in the trunk and branches, but still carry as many apples as older varieties.

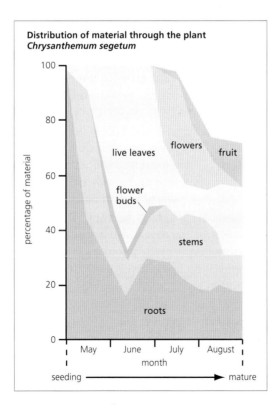

Distribution of material through the plant
Chrysanthemum segetum

live leaves
flowers
fruit
flower buds
stems
roots

percentage of material

May June July August
month
seeding ——————————→ mature

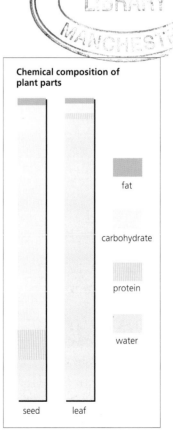

Chemical composition of plant parts

fat
carbohydrate
protein
water

seed leaf

Figure 1

LORETO COLLEGE LIBRARY MANCHESTER

How do plants grow?

Cambium growth

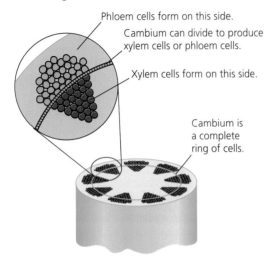

Phloem cells form on this side.

Cambium can divide to produce xylem cells or phloem cells.

Xylem cells form on this side.

Cambium is a complete ring of cells.

Figure 2

A plant gets bigger when it increases the number and size of its cells. Cell division increases the number of cells and occurs in regions called **meristems**. Meristems are named after the part of the plant where they are found. For example, the apical meristem is found at the tip or apex of a growing shoot. An axillary meristem is found in the joint between the side branches and the main stalk – the axil. A special meristem exists as a single layer of cells in the root and stem. This is called the **cambium**. The apical meristem controls growth in length and the axillary meristems growth in bushiness. The cambium controls the growth in width (figure 2).

Meristems also produce a range of hormones which control the development of cells in other parts of the plant. These hormones control how large an individual cell becomes. So meristems control growth by both cell division and cell size.

New **xylem** vessels produced in the wet spring are much larger than those produced in the dryer autumn. This change gives a tree trunk a pattern of rings with one ring for each growing season. It is possible to date the tree by counting the number of rings, and to work out which seasons were the best for growth by comparing the width of the rings.

How can plants respond to environmental changes?

Dandelion plants have flowers which respond to light levels. They only stay open during the daylight. At night the buds close up.

Plants respond to changes in their environment more slowly than animals, but they still respond. Any response needs a system to detect changes in the environment. Plants respond by growing in particular ways.

A growth response in a plant is known as a **tropism**. Plant seeds do not know which way up they are when they hit the ground. As soon as the root starts to grow, it must find the soil and a supply of moisture.
The shoot needs to find a source of light if the plant is to photosynthesise. The different parts of a plant need to be able to tell which way to grow.

The root is positively geotropic. This means it grows towards gravity, – in effect downwards. The root is also negatively phototropic – it grows away from light. The shoot is positively phototropic because it grows towards light. So, tropic responses can be positive (towards) or negative (away from).

5 Roots are hydrotropic. 'Hydro' means water. Are roots positively or negatively hydrotropic? Explain your answer.

Tropic responses are controlled by a group of chemicals called **plant growth hormones**. The most famous group of these are the **auxins**. The most well known auxin is indole acetic acid or IAA, sometimes just called auxin.

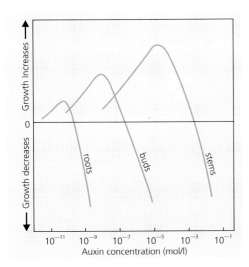

Figure 3 This graph shows the effect of the concentration of auxin on root, bud and stem growth.

Auxin controls the rate of expansion of plant cells. When plant cells divide at a meristem, the new cells are quite small. The cells then absorb water by osmosis and swell up to their final size. As they swell, they push against their rigid cell walls. Auxin seems to be able to make the cell wall softer so that it is easier for the newly formed cells to increase in size. However, auxin's effects depend on the type of cells involved and the concentration of the auxin (figure 3).

6 Describe the effect of cell type and auxin concentration on plant growth as shown in figure 3.

IAA is a small molecule, which is made in any actively growing cells in the tip of a root or shoot. The plant passes this auxin from cell to cell actively. Its movement is not controlled by diffusion, and requires an energy input by the plant. The movement is sensitive to gravity, and auxin tends to collect on the lower side of roots or shoots.

How does auxin bring about geotropism?

In vertical roots, auxin is moved back from the growing tip evenly and causes equal elongation of cells on both sides of the root. However, if the root is growing horizontally the auxin is moved to the lower side of the root. It reaches a concentration which will inhibit cell elongation so the upper surface grows more quickly. This bends the root downwards into the soil.

In vertical shoots, auxin moves downwards evenly to produce vertical growth. In a horizontal shoot, auxin moves to the lower surface and reaches a concentration that encourages cell elongation. The shoot grows upwards.

How does auxin bring about phototropism?

Shoots grow away from gravity, but also grow towards the light. Again, auxin controls this growth. Auxin is made from an amino acid called tryptophan by a reaction which is inhibited by light. As a result, plants with light on one side only will produce more auxin on the shaded side of the shoot. This means the shoot will bend towards the light, as the side with the higher auxin concentration grows more quickly.

What controls seed germination?

Many plants produce flowers in the summer and seeds and fruits in the autumn. If the seeds germinated straight away they would have to grow through the cold winter. To improve the chances of survival the seeds wait until spring to germinate. The seeds become **dormant** to survive the winter. A seed is dormant if it has all the right conditions to grow, but will not germinate. Before germination can occur the dormancy must be broken.

Dormancy can be produced by several features:

- Tough outer seed coats can prevent water absorption, for example in rose seeds. As the seed coats rot in the ground, they split and let water in. The seeds can then germinate.
- Citrus fruits contain acids which inhibit germination of the pips. Once the fruit flesh has decayed, the seeds can germinate.
- The seeds of mistletoe plants need to pass through a bird's gut to break their dormancy.
- Many seeds need a period of rising temperature before they can germinate. In this way they can detect the spring and so start growing at the best possible time.
- Some seeds contain a germination inhibitor. In wet conditions this inhibitor slowly leaches out. The seed can germinate when the concentration of inhibitor falls below a certain level.

---

7 Draw up a table to summarise the types of dormancy, and how they can be broken. Give some examples of plants that show each type of dormancy.

What controls fruit development?

Very few flowers release their seeds without some adaptation to make survival more likely. These adaptations of seeds usually develop from the wall of the ovary and are called **fruits**. For example, the blackberries that many people gather in the autumn are there to attract birds. The birds eat the fruit and then pass the undigested seed out through the gut in its own little package of fertiliser! Fruits are an essential part of a plant's survival strategy.

The development of flowers and of fruits need to be carefully controlled. A flower is adapted to produce seeds and this must be done before the fruit forms. Once the flower's task is over the petals wither and the ovary wall swells to produce a fruit. The seed secretes hormones which control fruit development (figure 4).

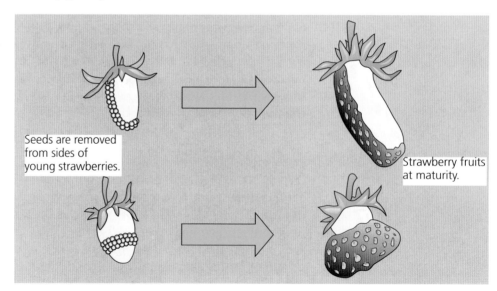

Seeds are removed from sides of young strawberries.

Strawberry fruits at maturity.

Figure 4 The seeds control the development of strawberry fruits. If the seeds are removed, no fruit develops.

Tomato fruits show the usual stages of development:

- Flowers are fertilised to produce seeds.
- Petals wither.
- Seeds secrete hormones and make the ovary wall swell.
- Food reserves are diverted from the rest of the plant to feed the swelling fruit.
- The fruit builds large energy storage compounds.
- Chemical changes convert large carbohydrate molecules into sugars.
- The fruit skin colour changes from green to red.

8 Explain how each of the stages in the development of a tomato fruit helps to ensure successful germination of the seeds and survival of the plant's offspring.

Some seedless grapes miss out the fertilisation stage altogether. Growers spray the vines with a mixture of hormones which stimulate fruit production. This produces fruits without seeds – useless from the plant's point of view, but perfect for the supermarket!

Summary of growth in plants

- Since plants contain such a high proportion of water, dry mass is used as a measure of growth.
- Plants grow from regions of cell division called meristems. Growth depends on an increase in cell number at the meristem and an expansion in individual cell size near the meristem.

- Plants respond to changes in the environment by changing their growth patterns. These growth responses are called tropisms.
- Plant tropisms are controlled by hormones.
- Flowering and fruit development are controlled by hormones.

Investigations

1 When seeds germinate they start to break down food stores to provide energy and materials for growth. Eventually the plant needs to start producing its own food by photosynthesis.

a What does the plant need before photosynthesis can start?

b As the seed grows it produces a small shoot which grows towards light sources and a small root which grows towards water. Why are these growth responses essential for the plant?

c Plan an investigation to find out if the colour or the intensity of the light has any effect on the growth of the seedlings shoot. Does bright light control the growth of the shoot more strongly than dim light? Is there an optimum light level that produces the best response?

d Carry out your investigation making sure you gather enough evidence to check your predictions.

Learning objectives

By the end of this chapter you should be able to:

- **explain** the differences between sexual and asexual reproduction
- **list** the advantages of sexual reproduction
- **list** the stages in sexual reproduction in flowering plants
- **describe** how flowering plants produce gametes

- **explain** how flowers are adapted to wind or insect pollination
- **describe** the process of fertilisation in flowering plants
- **describe** the adaptations of fruits and seeds to dispersal

16.1 Types of reproduction

Why do organisms reproduce themselves?

All organisms produce offspring which will eventually compete with their parents for food, drink and living space. For example, a single oak tree produces thousands of acorns over its life span. If all these grew to maturity, the offspring would outnumber the original parent. For an animal, even producing a single youngster uses up a great deal of energy as the animal prepares to reproduce, finds a mate and cares for the youngster until it is independent. If generating offspring is such a strain, why do living organisms do it?

As an organism grows, it ages. Damage to its cells accumulates through every division so that older organisms are less efficient than younger ones. In order to ensure that its genetic characteristics are passed on to the younger, more efficient individuals in the next generation, an adult organism must reproduce before it dies.

Asexual reproduction only needs a single parent and produces exact copies of that parent. Asexual reproduction wastes no energy finding a mate and can produce many offspring very rapidly. This allows organisms to exploit favourable circumstances very efficiently.

But, sex seems to be biologically important. Almost all organisms can reproduce sexually – even those that also reproduce asexually. **Sexual reproduction** depends on specialised cells called **gametes**. Two gametes, usually one from each parent, join together to form a **zygote**. The zygote is the first cell of the new individual.

Some animals, and many plants, are **hermaphrodite** which means that a single individual can produce male and female gametes. Sexual reproduction depends on two gametes, rather than two individuals.

Does reproduction need sex?

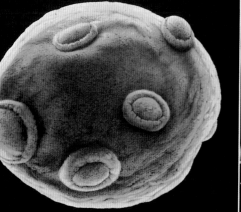

Yeast cells carry out the simplest form of reproduction. When a yeast cell reaches a certain size, it produces an outgrowth which separates from the original cell and grows into a new individual. This is called budding.

A sea anemone can bud off a complete new organism from its body.

Seed potatoes are survival structures which can grow into new potato plants. A single potato plant can produce many potatoes each of which will grow into a new individual.

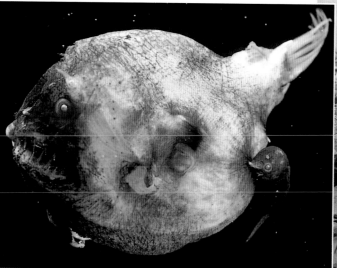

The male angler fish stays close to its mate at all times. It is attached by a sucker and cannot survive away from the larger female.

The male humpback whale may need to search through hundreds of cubic kilometres to find a female to mate.

The flower on a potato plant relies on insects to pollinate it so that it can produce seeds.

Sexual reproduction is usually more complex than asexual reproduction to organise, it requires specialised gametes and generally produces fewer offspring. However, the advantage is that sexual reproduction produces individuals that are slightly different from their parents and from the other offspring produced at the same time. So some of these offspring will be better suited to the environment than others, or than their parents. They could exploit new resources and spread into new areas. Over many generations these slight differences can lead to populations which are quite different from each other. Chapter 20, *Evolution*, explains how this can lead to completely new types of plants and animals developing.

Sometimes the pressure of numbers of a species in an area forces certain individuals to spread into new areas. If this happens successfully, the species will have colonised a new area. This increases the chances of new types of organisms developing, as the populations split into two or more separate groups.

Reproduction leads to an increase in:

- numbers
- distribution (linked to colonisation)
- variation (only in sexual reproduction).

1 a List the similarities and differences between sexual and asexual reproduction.
b What advantage does each of the organisms shown in the photographs on page 145 have from its chosen method of reproduction?

Summary of types of reproduction

- Asexual reproduction produces large numbers of identical offspring very quickly.

- Sexual reproduction produces a variety of offspring and usually requires more energy than asexual reproduction.

16.2 Reproduction in flowering plants

What are flowering plants?

The most successful group of plants is the flowering plants. These are the only plants to have true flowers and produce seeds with a tough protective coat. These adaptations allow flowering plants to reproduce sexually without a watery environment. When a flowering plant reproduces sexually it is able to:

- produce male and female gametes
- transfer the gametes between flowers
- fuse the gametes to produce a zygote
- produce seeds to protect the embryo from drying out and provide the new plant with food stores
- distribute seeds to new areas.

What is a flower?

Flower structure

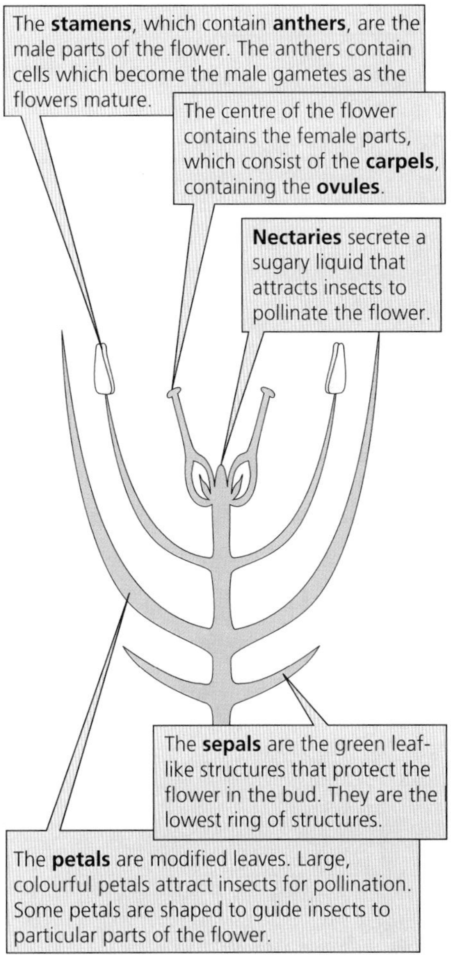

The **stamens**, which contain **anthers**, are the male parts of the flower. The anthers contain cells which become the male gametes as the flowers mature.

The centre of the flower contains the female parts, which consist of the **carpels**, containing the **ovules**.

Nectaries secrete a sugary liquid that attracts insects to pollinate the flower.

The **sepals** are the green leaf-like structures that protect the flower in the bud. They are the lowest ring of structures.

The **petals** are modified leaves. Large, colourful petals attract insects for pollination. Some petals are shaped to guide insects to particular parts of the flower.

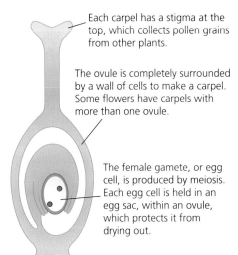

Figure 1

All flowers have a similar basic arrangement (figure 1). They have structures stacked one on top of each other along a short stem, arranged either in a spiral or in separate rings.

The male part of a flower is the ring of stamens. There may be up to 100 stamens, or fewer than a dozen. Each stamen consists of two parts – the anther at the top and a stalk called the filament.

The **pollen grains** contain the male gametes in flowering plants. Pollen develops in the pollen sacs of the anthers. Cells lining the inside of the pollen sacs divide by **meiosis** to give four cells. Each of these cells develops into a pollen grain (figure 2). As the grains mature, they develop a thick outer wall to protect the delicate nuclei inside. When all the pollen grains in the anther are mature, the anther splits open to release them.

Pollen grain formation

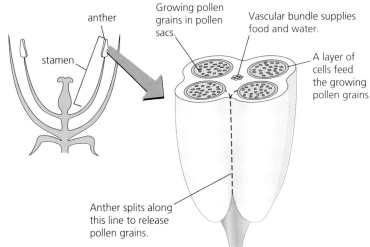

stamen

anther

Growing pollen grains in pollen sacs.

Vascular bundle supplies food and water.

A layer of cells feed the growing pollen grains

Anther splits along this line to release pollen grains.

Figure 2

Each carpel has a stigma at the top, which collects pollen grains from other plants.

The ovule is completely surrounded by a wall of cells to make a carpel. Some flowers have carpels with more than one ovule.

The female gamete, or egg cell, is produced by meiosis. Each egg cell is held in an egg sac, within an ovule, which protects it from drying out.

Figure 3

The female part of the flower is the carpel which produces the female gametes. A flower can contain more than one carpel, each with its own style and stigma. The stigma is the part of the carpel that collects the pollen.

The carpel is a bit like a hollow sac which protects the female gamete from the dry air outside. The carpel contains one or more ovules and each ovule produces a single gamete by meiosis (figure 3). The egg sac contains the nucleus which will fuse with the pollen grain nucleus to form the zygote – the first nucleus of the new individual.

2 **a** List the differences between stamens and carpels.
   b Explain how each difference is linked to the functions of pollen and ovules.
   c List the similarities in the way stamens and carpels produce gametes.

How does the pollen get to the stigma?

Plantain flowers (top) and tulip flowers (bottom) are adapted to use different methods of pollination.

Different plants adapt the basic pattern to produce very different looking flowers. The adaptations are to do with the method of pollination. Pollination is the transfer of pollen from the stamen of one plant to the stigma of another. Most plants use either insect or wind pollination.

Table 1 *Typical features of insect and wind pollinated plants.*

Wind-pollinated plants	Insect-pollinated plants
Have no scent.	Are often scented.
Have no nectaries.	Nectaries are present at the base of the flower. Nectaries produce a sugary liquid.
Have many anthers which are often large and hang outside the flower.	Have a few small anthers which are usually held inside the flower.
Pollen grains have smooth outer walls.	Pollen grains have patterned outer walls.
Stigmas are large and feathery, often hanging outside the flower.	Stigmas are small and held inside the flower.
Have few ovules.	Have many ovules.
Plants tend to grow in clumps.	Plants tend to grow singly.

3 **a** Look at the photographs. Decide which flower is wind pollinated and which is insect pollinated. Give reasons for your choice.

b Explain how each of the adaptations in the insect-pollinated column of table 1 makes pollination more likely.

c Nectaries will not prevent a wind-pollinated flower from being pollinated. So why don't wind-pollinated flowers have nectaries?

Cross-pollination occurs when the pollen from one plant transfers to the stigma of a different plant. However, plants can produce both male and female gametes and it is possible for the pollen from one plant to pollinate its own stigma. This is called **self-pollination**. Most flowering plants try to prevent self-pollination by using **self-incompatibility systems**.

Some plants produce only flowers of a single sex, which obviously makes self-pollination impossible. For example, holly bushes are either male or female. People growing holly bushes for Christmas decorations need to know that the plant they have bears female flowers or there will be no berries, only green leaves.

Some plants have flowers that contain male and female parts, but the different parts mature at different times. For example, white deadnettle stamens mature and release their pollen before the stigma is mature. When all the deadnettle's pollen has gone, the female parts mature and can receive pollen from other flowers. Bluebells use a similar system but the female parts mature before the male parts.

Even if pollen from one flower manages to reach its own stigma, the pollen grain will tend to grow more slowly than a foreign grain. This means that nuclei from foreign pollen grains are more likely to fertilise the egg cell in the ovule.

4 Why is it an advantage to a plant to prevent self-pollination?

How do the gametes fuse?

5 Draw a flow chart to show the sequence of events from pollination to seed formation.

Pollination transfers pollen from anther to stigma. Fertilisation occurs when the nucleus from the pollen grain fuses with the nucleus in the egg sac. To get from the tip of the stigma to the egg sac, the grain produces a thin tube called the **pollen tube** (see figure 4).

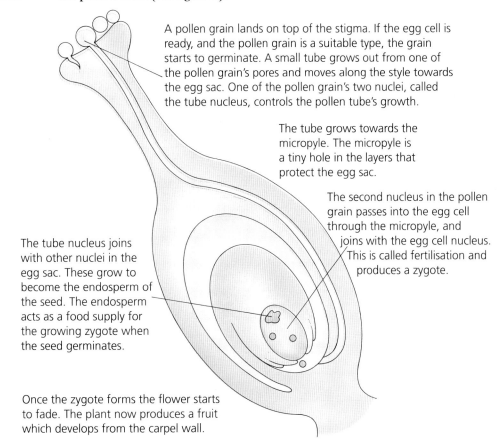

A pollen grain lands on top of the stigma. If the egg cell is ready, and the pollen grain is a suitable type, the grain starts to germinate. A small tube grows out from one of the pollen grain's pores and moves along the style towards the egg sac. One of the pollen grain's two nuclei, called the tube nucleus, controls the pollen tube's growth.

The tube grows towards the micropyle. The micropyle is a tiny hole in the layers that protect the egg sac.

The second nucleus in the pollen grain passes into the egg cell through the micropyle, and joins with the egg cell nucleus. This is called fertilisation and produces a zygote.

The tube nucleus joins with other nuclei in the egg sac. These grow to become the endosperm of the seed. The endosperm acts as a food supply for the growing zygote when the seed germinates.

Once the zygote forms the flower starts to fade. The plant now produces a fruit which develops from the carpel wall.

Figure 4 Pollination and fertilisation.

Why do flowering plants produce seeds?

The zygote develops quickly to form an embryo plant, which needs to be protected from drying out. This embryo plant contains tissues which will become roots, stem and leaves when it starts to grow or germinate. **Germination** does not usually occur while the embryo is still attached to the parent plant. The embryo is said to be **dormant**. You can read more about dormancy in chapter 15, *Growing and developing*. Flowering plants develop **seeds** to protect these embryo plants. Seeds often contain food storage compounds called **endosperm**.

Seeds develop from the ovules. The wall of the carpel also develops to form a fruit. A pea pod shows the difference well – the peas are the seeds which contain the embryo plants, and the pod is the fruit.

How do plants distribute their seeds?

6 Summarise in a table the seed dispersal strategies in figure 5.

Seeds that fall from a plant onto the ground below could germinate. They would produce new individuals that would compete with the parent plant and possibly reduce the success of both. For this reason plants tend to distribute their seeds into new areas (see figure 5).

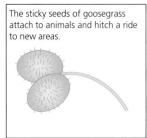

The sticky seeds of goosegrass attach to animals and hitch a ride to new areas.

Poppy heads dry out as the seeds mature. The heads scatter seeds through small openings when the wind shakes the stalk.

Each seed in a dandelion clock has a parachute of fine hairs attached. The seeds fly well in dry air. As a seed flies into damp air, the hairs clump together and the seed sinks slowly to the ground.

Lupins have pods that split open as they dry out. This splitting can catapult seeds away from the parent.

Seed dispersal

Sycamore seeds have wings which make them spin as they fall. This keeps them in the air longer and so lets them spread further from their parent.

Birds eat hawthorn berries and then pass the hard seed out in their faeces elsewhere. The seeds are dispersed, and get a dose of fertiliser!

Squirrels help to distribute nuts by collecting them and burying them in the ground. Often the buried seeds germinate before the squirrel finds them again.

The fibrous outer husk of a coconut allows it to float in sea currents to new areas. Many tropical islands have a line of coconut palms along the top of the beach.

Figure 5 Plants use all kinds of strategies to disperse their seeds.

What happens at germination?

7 a Draw a flow chart to show the changes that occur during the germination of a pea.
b Explain how each step in your chart increases the chance of the pea seedling growing into an adult plant.

Germination is a time when seeds use up their food reserves and grow rapidly to produce a new plant. If germination is too slow, other seedlings may grow and block out the light or use up all the available space, so each seed germinates as quickly as possible. This rush to develop means that the germinating seeds need a great deal of energy in a hurry – they need to **mobilise** their food reserves. This mobilisation uses enzymes which break down large carbohydrate molecules into smaller sugars. These sugars are respired to provide energy until the seedling is able to produce its own supply by photosynthesis.

The changes that occur at germination are to do with mobilising and respiring food reserves. Germination begins when the seed absorbs large amounts of water. The water helps to provide the right environment for the enzymes to work and to inflate the cells. As insoluble starch is broken down to soluble sugar, the water potential of the seed drops so even more water is drawn in by osmosis. The rate of respiration rises, needing a good supply of oxygen. This respiration tends to transfer some waste energy as heat, so germinating seeds warm up slightly.

Germination does not need light, and may be inhibited by light, but the new seedling will grow rapidly towards a light source. In fact, one of the characteristics of plants grown in low light conditions is that they become taller than usual and are often very thin and yellowish rather than their normal green. Gardeners use this reaction to 'force' plants like celery which grow rapidly in the dark and produce white leaves suitable for salads.

The changes at germination are controlled by hormones. Chapter 15, *Growing and developing*, explains more about how hormones control the time at which seeds germinate, and how they develop into adult plants.

Summary of reproduction in flowering plants

- Flowering plants reproduce sexually using flowers. A flower is a specialised collection of structures arranged in rings or in a spiral.
- The stamens are the male parts of flowers which produce the male gametes called pollen grains.
- The carpels are the female parts of the flower which produce the female gametes called egg cells.
- Pollination is the transfer of pollen from anther to stigma. Fertilisation is the fusion of male and female gametes to form a zygote.
- Fruits and seeds are adapted to disperse the zygote from the original parent.

- Germination is the first stage of the development of a seed to produce an adult plant.
- Germination requires oxygen, a suitable temperature and moisture. Light is not needed until leaves have been formed.
- Germination uses up stores of food materials until photosynthesis can start to build organic matter.
- The process of germination is controlled by a series of plant hormones.

Investigations

1 Insect pollinated flowers must attract insects or they will not be able to produce seeds.
   a List the things that these flowers use to attract insects.
   b Which factor is most important?
   c Different flowers attract different insects. What differences can the insects see and respond to?
   d List the factors that will help the insect to recognise a suitable flower and plan and carry out an investigation to see which one has the greatest effect.

Learning objectives

By the end of this chapter you should be able to:

- **describe** the structure and function of the male and female sex organs in humans
- **explain** how egg and sperm cells are adapted to their functions
- **describe** the changes that occur during the growth of a fertilised egg in human beings
- **describe** the stages of labour and birth
- **describe** how humans try to increase or decrease fertility
- **describe** patterns of behaviours in parents that increase the chances of survival for their offspring

17.1 Human reproduction

How do males and females differ?

Changes at puberty

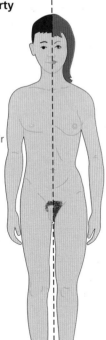

In males:
- Skin can become slightly greasy, which can lead to acne.

- Voice breaks and deepens.

- Body and facial hair start to grow.

- Juvenile fat decreases.

- Penis grows.

- Testes start to produce sperm.

In females:
- Skin can become slightly greasy, which can lead to acne.

- Breasts develop.

- Body hair starts to grow.

- Ovaries start to produce mature eggs.

- Menstrual cycle begins.

- Body shape changes.

Figure 1

Men have testes which produce sperm and secrete a range of sex hormones. These hormones control the development of many other characteristics that make an individual male rather than female, such as facial hair, a deeper voice, a body with a slightly higher muscle to fat ratio than females, a different shape to the pelvis and a greater chance of going bald and dying young. Having testes is the **primary sexual characteristic**, while other aspects of a male are the **secondary sexual characteristics**.

In females, the ovaries produce the **eggs** and a package of hormones that control the development of the female secondary sexual characteristics. These characteristics include the growth of breasts and a lack of facial hair.

Many of the differences between males and females that we take for granted depend on cultural rather than biological factors. However, the most obvious physical differences between males and females depend on hormones, and these differences do not appear until **puberty**. Puberty is a time of sudden changes caused by hormones released into the bloodstream by glands in the brain and the sex organs. It is a time when the body grows rapidly for the last time before settling down to its adult size (see figure 1).

Generally, females enter puberty slightly earlier than males. In the UK girls will typically start having periods at the age of 13, although the ovaries may not release eggs until slightly later. Many boys will not notice the effects of puberty until they are 14 years old. These times of change can be confusing and no one fits the norm exactly. For example, girls often do not develop a consistent **menstrual cycle** (one period about every 28 days) until they are much older. Many will never have such a regular pattern – the figure of 28 days is an average value for a wide range of variation. Similarly, some boys will develop body hair much more slowly than others.

1 a Almost all plants have male and female parts in a single individual. Almost all animals have individuals of only one sex. List at least three advantages of this separation of sexes for animals.
b Why is it an advantage for a mammal to have a gap between the birth of an individual and the time when the new individual is sexually mature and can reproduce?

How do human beings produce gametes?

2 a What distance does the sperm swim as a proportion of its own length?
b Work out the distance an adult human male, 180 cm tall, would swim in the same time if he could swim as far as his sperm compared with his own height.

Special cells in the testes called sperm mother cells divide by a special type of cell division called **meiosis** to produce sperm (see chapter 18, *Genetics*, for more about meiosis). Each newly formed spermatid (immature sperm) contains a single set of chromosomes, instead of the double set present in all other body cells. Other cells in the testes feed the growing spermatids as they develop into mature sperm.

A single sperm is really just a nucleus with a tail attached at one end and a small package of enzymes at the other. The tail has plenty of mitochondria to supply **ATP** for movement. A human sperm is roughly 14×10^{-3} mm long and can travel the 15 cm from the vagina to the neck of the cervix in about three hours. The production of sperm is highest in the early twenties and declines from middle age until old age when the testes can no longer produce sperm.

Women have a store of immature eggs in their ovaries at birth. From puberty onwards, hormones control a cycle which produces a single mature egg roughly once a month. The maturing egg develops in a follicle which has two functions:

• to produce a mature egg
• to prepare the uterus wall for pregnancy.

The egg is a large cell with plenty of food storage materials and a protective layer of a sticky carbohydrate called mucilage. The egg cannot move itself, but drifts along the oviduct towards the uterus in a current of mucus produced by other parts of the female reproductive tract. The egg may secrete a chemical which attracts sperm.

3 Give at least three ways in which the egg and sperm cells are adapted to their functions.

The **menopause** is a time when the ovaries stop producing eggs. This typically occurs during late middle age, although the range of possible dates varies from woman to woman much more than the time for the onset of puberty.

How do the gametes meet?

4 Draw a flow chart to show how the male and female gametes are brought together.

In humans, fertilisation can only take place in the oviducts. During sexual intercourse, sperm are placed at the entrance to the uterus so that they can swim the rest of the way to the oviduct (figure 2).

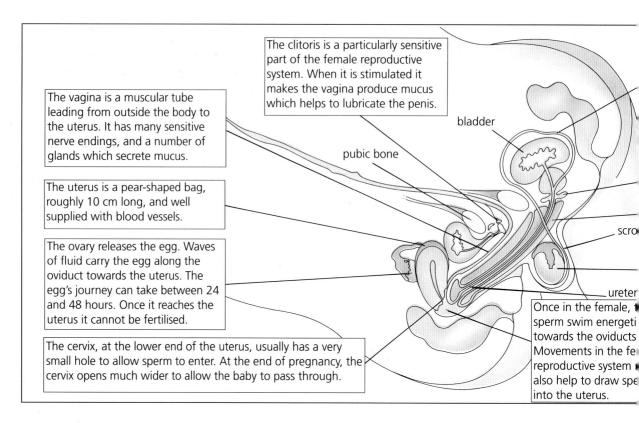

The clitoris is a particularly sensitive part of the female reproductive system. When it is stimulated it makes the vagina produce mucus which helps to lubricate the penis.

The vagina is a muscular tube leading from outside the body to the uterus. It has many sensitive nerve endings, and a number of glands which secrete mucus.

The uterus is a pear-shaped bag, roughly 10 cm long, and well supplied with blood vessels.

The ovary releases the egg. Waves of fluid carry the egg along the oviduct towards the uterus. The egg's journey can take between 24 and 48 hours. Once it reaches the uterus it cannot be fertilised.

The cervix, at the lower end of the uterus, usually has a very small hole to allow sperm to enter. At the end of pregnancy, the cervix opens much wider to allow the baby to pass through.

bladder

pubic bone

scro

ureter

Once in the female, sperm swim energeti towards the oviducts Movements in the fe reproductive system also help to draw spe into the uterus.

Figure 2

What happens between conception and birth?

After fertilisation in the oviduct, the fertilised egg or **zygote** travels on towards the uterus. The journey will take three days, during which time the zygote will grow from a single cell to a ball of 64 cells before it embeds itself in the uterus wall. Over the next 38 weeks it will increase its mass roughly 8 million times. At no other point in the individual's lifetime will it grow at such a high rate. This period of development in the uterus is called gestation, and lasts about 40 weeks in humans, measured from the first day of the woman's last period.

The rapid growth during gestation depends on a constant supply of food and oxygen, provided by the mother. The growing fetus also needs protection from mechanical shocks and a range of chemicals and pathogens which could cause permanent damage or reduced growth. Even with all this care, the newly born human infant is quite helpless and cannot digest adult food. Again the mother has to feed it until the baby can fend for itself. The parents have to:

*   provide a constant supply of food
*   take away all waste products
*   protect against mechanical damage.

It may be because mammals are so good at providing this degree of care for their offspring that they are some of the most successful animals alive today.

Muscle rings squeeze sperm along the sperm ducts rather like toothpaste being squeezed from a tube. Glands along the sperm duct produce secretions which mix with the sperm to form a milky suspension called semem. The semen contains a supply of sugar which provides the sperm with food for the swim to the oviduct.

The bulbo-urethral gland produces a clear mucus which washes away any urine in the urethra. Urine can kill sperm.

Erectile tissue fills with blood and becomes hard when the nerves of the penis are stimulated.

The testes produce sperm continuously and store them in the epididymis (typically about 350 million sperm).

m still in the vagina one hour after ulation stop moving. In the uterus sperm can or up to 24 hours; in the oviducts up to 48 s. This provides plenty of time for fertilisation, healthy sperm can swim from the vagina to oviduct in less than half an hour.

What is the placenta?

The **placenta** (figure 3) is an organ that allows a constant exchange of materials between the mother and fetus. It develops from fetal tissues. The placenta and the uterus wall have a large number of blood vessels which run very close to each other but do not touch. Maternal and fetal blood do not mix. If they did, male children would be damaged by the level of female hormones in the mother's blood, and the higher blood pressure in the mother would damage the fetus. The fetus is a separate individual and has a completely different combination of **antigens** (see chapter 8, *Disease and immunity*). If these antigens leaked into the mother's blood, she would produce **antibodies** that would attack the fetus.

Despite the blood not being allowed to mix, food, oxygen and waste materials are exchanged rapidly across the placenta. The **umbilical cord** is the connection between the growing fetus and the placenta. After birth, the point where the cord joins to the baby constricts and the cord degenerates. All that is left of this important lifeline in later life is the 'belly button' or umbilicus.

The fetus develops inside a bag of fluid which protects it from mechanical damage. This fluid is called amniotic fluid and is produced from the amniotic membrane which forms the outer layer of the bag. One of the signs that birth is imminent is when this bag bursts during **labour**.

What is birth?

Birth is the final part of a process called labour which takes hours, possibly days. Labour starts with contractions of the uterus wall, which goes hard during these contractions. As labour proceeds the contractions become longer, occur more often and become more painful. Another sign of labour starting is a show of blood-tinged mucus which is the plug at the entrance to the uterus. A flow of water from the vagina, often called the 'breaking of the waters', shows labour is near, as does unexpected diarrhoea or sickness.

Placenta

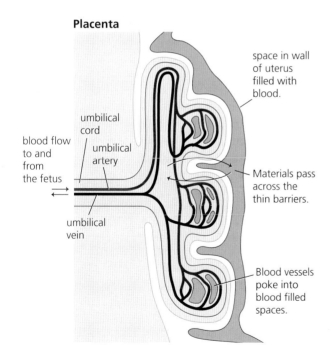

space in wall of uterus filled with blood.

umbilical cord

blood flow to and from the fetus

umbilical artery

Materials pass across the thin barriers.

umbilical vein

Blood vessels poke into blood filled spaces.

Figure 3

At the hospital the mother to be will be checked for any danger signs, and may be linked to monitors which can follow her blood pressure and heart rate as well as her baby's. The next stage of labour can last some hours. During this stage the muscles of the uterus are opening up the cervix so that the baby can pass through. Periodically a doctor or midwife will check to see how far the cervix has opened or dilated. Contractions at this point can become quite painful and doctors can prescribe a number of painkillers.

When the cervix has fully dilated, the mother will feel an urge to push. The final stage of labour is shorter than the earlier part and within minutes the baby is born. In most cases the baby is born head first. A **breech birth** happens when the baby is born feet first. Breech births need to be very carefully managed by the midwife to prevent damage to the mother or baby due to tangling or damage to the umbilical cord.

The baby is followed after 10 minutes or so by the **afterbirth**. This is the placenta. The midwife or doctor will check to see the complete placenta has been delivered to prevent any infection developing in the uterus. Sometimes the baby is too large to pass through the vagina or needs to be helped with forceps, and will tear the outer tissues slightly. Often a few stitches help to keep the torn sides of the wound together after birth to help with healing.

In a few cases the mother or baby is in some danger and the doctor decides to deliver the baby by **Caesarean section**. A Caesarean section is a cut made in the wall of the uterus so that the baby can pass out through the cut rather than through the vagina. Babies born by Caesarean section do not usually have the squashed and wrinkled look of babies that have been squeezed through the vagina. A mother who has had one child by Caesarean section can have another child by normal delivery.

5 Draw a flow chart to summarise the main stages of labour.

How are births induced?

Oxytocin is a hormone produced by the pituitary gland at the base of the brain. The hormone stimulates labour, and is sometimes used to artificially induce labour in mothers who have not gone into labour despite having passed their predicted dates. The placenta begins to work less well after the normal gestation period has finished, and so may cause damage to the baby. Oxytocin is also important after birth because it stimulates muscles in the breasts to squeeze out milk for the baby. Another hormone called **prolactin** stimulates the mammary glands in the breast to produce the milk.

Which is best – breast or bottle?

After birth, the first milk produced by the mother does not look like milk at all. This is the watery colostrum which contains a collection of immunity proteins to protect the baby in the first few days and months of life. It is impossible to produce an artificial colostrum. By about the third day after birth the normal milk begins to come through.

Human breast milk contains a mixture of chemicals that are different from the milk of any other animal. However, doctors can measure the levels of these chemicals and produce an artificial milk by modifying milk from other animals. These are called **formula milks** and can be made from a variety of food sources including plants. It is probably impossible to produce a formula milk exactly like human milk but modern formula milks are very close. Doctors currently believe breast milk is the best milk for growing babies but a good quality formula milk can be almost as good if it is:

- made with sterile water
- delivered in a sterile bottle
- made up to the correct recipe.

How can we prevent pregnancy?

Sometimes people want to have sexual intercourse but not produce children. This is particularly important for couples who want to plan when, and how many, children they have.

Contraceptive methods depend on stopping gametes from joining together to produce a zygote. **Barrier methods** like condoms or diaphragms stop the sperm passing into the uterus and so to the oviduct. Both condoms and diaphragms are used with spermicides which help to kill sperm in case of any leakage. The contraceptive pill is a package of hormones which stops the ovaries producing eggs. The intra-uterine device or IUD is a plastic device which fits in the uterus and interferes with the implantation of eggs into the uterine wall. All of these methods are temporary. When the couple decide they want children they can stop using them and pregnancy should follow as normal.

Surgeons can cut the tubes leading from the ovaries to the uterus to sterilise a woman permanently. A similar operation for men cuts the tube connecting the testes to the prostate gland. These operations are difficult to reverse, and so are only used if people are completely sure they do not want any more children.

Summary of human reproduction

- Sexual reproduction involves two separate sexes, although they can be present in the same individual in certain species.
- The differences between male and female members of a species are controlled by their genes, a selection of hormones and, in humans, a range of cultural and social expectations.
- Males produce the male gametes, sperm, in large numbers from puberty with a general fall-off in production as they get older.
- Females produce a female gamete, the egg, roughly once a month from puberty to the menopause.

- Sexual intercourse brings the gametes together in the oviduct where fertilisation takes place.
- The period between conception and birth is called gestation and lasts about 40 weeks from the start of the last period in humans.
- The amniotic fluid protects the growing fetus from mechanical damage. The placenta exchanges food, oxygen and waste products with the mother's blood.
- Doctors use a range of techniques to monitor babies and mothers during pregnancy and birth.
- Contraception is a way to prevent pregnancy without preventing sexual intercourse.

17.2 Reproduction in other animals

Why do frogs lay so many eggs?

Table 1

Organism	Number of offspring produced per year
Cod	1.85 million eggs released
Herring	20 000 eggs released
Humans	1 or 2 babies
Rats	up to 50 babies
Elephants	over one year from fertilisation to birth
Pigeons	two eggs

Humans are mammals. Mammals tend to produce few offspring, and they invest a lot of energy in the development before birth and care of the young afterwards. This massively increases the chances of survival for each individual offspring. Other organisms adopt a different approach to get as many offspring as possible into the next generation.

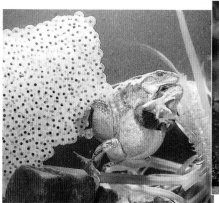

The female frog releases many eggs. The male frog couples with the female as eggs are released and passes sperm directly onto the eggs. The frogs offer no parental care, and most of the tadpoles die before adulthood.

The male giant tortoise transfers sperm directly to the eggs inside the female. Unlike frogs, tortoises do not need water for breeding. After mating the female lays eggs in the sand or earth. The eggs contain a supply of water for the developing tortoise. The hard shell protects against damage, but allows gas exchange with the environment. The eggs and young tortoises are left to fend for themselves.

Pigeons carry out complex courtship behaviour before they mate. During mating, sperm are passed into the female and fertilisation takes place in the oviduct. The male and female share the job of keeping the eggs warm and feeding the young birds, when they hatch.

6 Explain how each of the animals shown have reproductive behaviour that increases the chances of having succesful offspring in the next generation.

Summary of reproduction in other animals

- Animals reproductive strategies vary in terms of number of eggs produced, number of young produced and the degree of parental support. Generally, the more parental support that is provided the fewer young that are produced.

- Larger animals tend to produce fewer offspring than smaller ones and, in mammals, the gestation period lasts longer.

Investigations

1 The cabbage white butterfly lays a number of egg batches throughout the spring and summer. Eggs laid early in spring hatch and grow to adult butterflies in less than two months. Eggs laid late in the summer take much longer. Pupae produced in the autumn will not develop into adults until the following spring.

  a What advantage does the difference in egg growth give to the cabbage white butterfly?

  b What environmental factors control the change in growth patterns for the eggs? Think of as many as possible.

Genetics

Learning objectives

By the end of this chapter you should be able to:

- **explain** what we mean by variation between individuals
- **list** the causes of variation
- **explain** how features are inherited
- **explain** how genes are carried on chromosomes
- **explain** how new genes arise
- **describe** how genes are transferred
- **describe** the social problems that genetic knowledge and technology can cause

18.1 Variation

Why are individuals different?

There are two main sources of difference between individuals:

- Differences may be inherited. These features are passed from parents to their children, for example red-haired parents usually have red-haired children.
- Some differences in features result from our way of life. For example, people might choose to have their ears pierced or their hair dyed. Some people are thin because they exercise and diet, others are thin because they cannot get enough to eat. These are environmental differences.

It is often difficult to tell whether a feature is inherited, environmental, or a mixture of both. One way that has been used to clarify this problem is to study identical twins. Any differences that develop between identical twins brought up together are mainly environmental because the two children have identical genes. Any similarities between identical twins brought up separately are probably genetic.

1 List ten ways in which humans can vary from each other. For each of these differences, decide whether it is inherited, environmental, or whether the environment is influencing an inherited feature.

Continuous and discontinuous variation

Many inherited features are either one thing or another, with no levels in between, for example a person is either male or female, has free ear lobes or has attached earlobes. These are examples of **discontinuous variation**. Many inherited features vary discontinuously because an individual inherits a gene for one feature or its alternative.

The interplay between genes and the environment often causes **continuous variation**. For example, a child may inherit the potential to be tall, but malnourishment will restrict that child's growth. There is a continuous variation in heights across the population (see figure 1). Needles on a Christmas tree branch vary between 1 cm and 2.5 cm in length. The tree needles vary because they are different ages, and those formed during good growing conditions are larger than those formed in colder or drier weather.

Figure 1

Normal curve for height

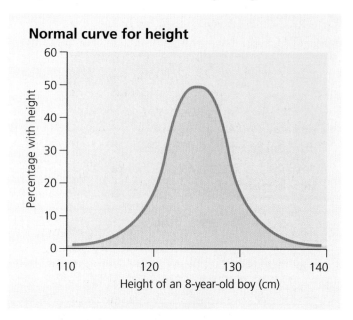

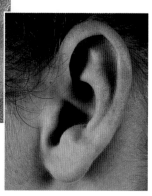

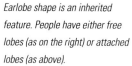

Earlobe shape is an inherited feature. People have either free lobes (as on the right) or attached lobes (as above).

The leaves of plants growing in a shady place are larger than the leaves of plants of the same species growing in a sunny place. This is because the plant in the shade needs big leaves to harvest the same amount of sunlight as a smaller leaf would in a brighter area. At first sight it could look as though there are two different species of plants, a large-leafed woodland plant, and a small leaved plant of open fields. However, if a cutting of a plant from one area is grown in the other conditions it will develop leaves suitable for the new conditions. This is **phenotypic variation**. It can be difficult to decide whether two groups of similar animals or plants, living in different places, belong to the same species with phenotypic variation, or to two related species which share many features.

When ivy grows in full sunlight, its leaves are small (as below). In shaded spots, ivy develops much larger leaves (as on the left) to capture as much light as it can.

Summary of variation

- Individuals of the same species are different.
- Some differences are inherited.
- Some differences are due to the environment in which an individual develops.

- An individual's environment affects how their genetic features are expressed.

18.2 Chromosomes and genes

How are inherited features passed on?

Table 1 *Numbers of chromosomes in different diploid cells.*

Species	Number of chromosomes
Human	23 pairs
Domestic horse	32 pairs
Przewalski's horse	33 pairs
Fruit fly	4 pairs
Onion	8 pairs
Rice	6 pairs

Inherited features are carried as **genes** on chromosomes located in the nucleus. Life starts with a sperm nucleus fusing with an egg cell nucleus. Features are passed from the mother on chromosomes in the egg's nucleus, and anything inherited from the father is carried in the sperm's nucleus.

Every ordinary cell nucleus carries a complete set of chromosomes. Each species has a unique pattern of chromosomes. The number and type of chromosomes a cell carries is called its **karyotype**. If a picture of the chromosomes from a cell is cut up the chromosomes can be arranged into pairs of similar chromosomes, each pair being slightly different from the other pairs. These pairs are called **homologous chromosomes**, or pairs. The numbers of chromosomes in several different species are shown in table 1. Cells with all their chromosomes in homologous pairs are described as diploid cells.

Human cells carry 46 chromosomes, so you might think that fertilised eggs would have 92 chromosomes when the egg and sperm nuclei fuse. In fact, a fertilised egg also has only 46 chromosomes because sperm and eggs don't carry a full set of chromosomes – they are not diploid cells. They have only one from each pair chromosome. Cells that contain only half the usual number of chromosomes are called haploid cells. When the nucleus from an egg combines with the nucleus from a sperm each chromosome gains a partner and homologous pairs are formed. Each homologous pair has one maternal and one paternal chromosome.

Sperm and eggs are the result of specialised cell division called **meiosis** (figure 2). In meiosis the new cells made carry only one member of each pair of chromosomes and develop into sperm or egg cells.

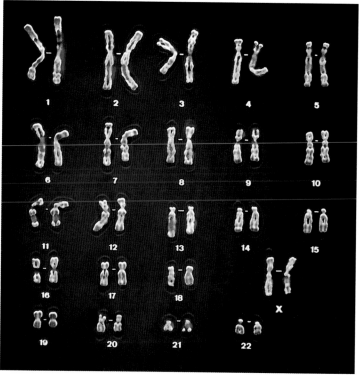

This karyogram shows the full set of chromosomes in a person's cells. This person has two X chromosomes, so she is female.

Meiosis

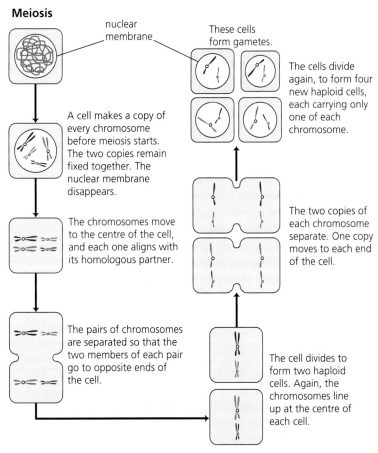

nuclear membrane

These cells form gametes.

The cells divide again, to form four new haploid cells, each carrying only one of each chromosome.

A cell makes a copy of every chromosome before meiosis starts. The two copies remain fixed together. The nuclear membrane disappears.

The chromosomes move to the centre of the cell, and each one aligns with its homologous partner.

The two copies of each chromosome separate. One copy moves to each end of the cell.

The pairs of chromosomes are separated so that the two members of each pair go to opposite ends of the cell.

The cell divides to form two haploid cells. Again, the chromosomes line up at the centre of each cell.

Figure 2 Meiosis produces cells with only half the number of chromosomes of the parent cells.

Very occasionally a pair of chromosomes does not separate during meiosis and both chromosomes go into the same egg or sperm. This can lead to an embryo developing with three chromosomes, called a trisomy, instead of a homologous pair. This usually causes problems, and the embryo often dies because the problems are too severe for it to survive. One of the less damaging conditions is a trisomy of chromosome 21 — children born with this trisomy have Down's syndrome. The extra chromosome causes problems throughout the body, for example the child's nerve synapses are slightly larger than normal and so their nerve impulses are slower, their tongues are larger, which makes it difficult to articulate words, and they may find it harder to keep warm in cold weather.

How is sex determined?

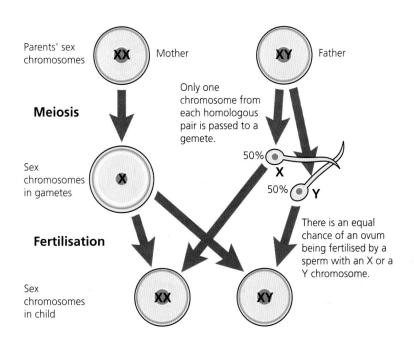

Parents' sex chromosomes — XX Mother — XY Father

Only one chromosome from each homologous pair is passed to a gemete.

Meiosis

Sex chromosomes in gametes — X

50% X
50% Y

Fertilisation

There is an equal chance of an ovum being fertilised by a sperm with an X or a Y chromosome.

Sex chromosomes in child — XX — XY

Figure 3 Boy or girl?

One pair of chromosomes determines sex. Female mammals have a pair of large X chromosomes but males have one X chromosome partnered by a smaller Y chromosome. The Y chromosome triggers the development of male features.

Women can only pass on copies of the X chromosome into eggs but men can pass on copies of either the X or the Y chromosome into their sperm (figure 3). A child's sex is decided when a sperm carrying the X or Y chromosome fertilises the egg. There are no great differences between the two types of sperm and each is equally likely to fertilise an egg.

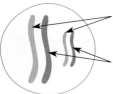

A cell from an organism with two pairs of homologous chromosomes

The pink chromosomes are originally from the female parent

The purple chromosomes are originally from the male parent

There are four possible ways the chromosomes could be reshuffled in the gametes

If the organism had three pairs of homologous chromosomes, there are eight ways the chromosomes could be reshuffled in the gametes

Figure 4 Sex cells carry different combinations of chromosomes.

Boys are boys because their Y chromosome carries genes that switch on male features. Chromosomes carry thousands of genes which control development and metabolism. If you inherit a particular chromosome you get all the genes it carries. Two brothers are not likely to inherit exactly the same combination of chromosomes from their parents. Chance determines which one of each pair of chromosomes passes into a sperm or egg. Some of the possible combinations are shown in figure 4.

2 What type of cell division is found only in gamete production?

3 What kind of cell division takes place when plants are grown from cuttings? Why are all the cuttings taken from a single parent plant identical, but different from the cuttings taken from a different parent plant, even when they are all kept in the same conditions?

4 Look at figure 4. Four different combinations of three chromosomes are shown. Draw the other four combinations possible.

5 What is the probability that two brothers will inherit copies of exactly the same chromosomes from their father?

Summary of chromosomes and genes

- Chromosomes may be grouped into homologous pairs.
- Meiosis is a form of cell division producing gamete cells, which form sperm and eggs.
- A sperm or egg carries only one member of each homologous pair of chromosomes in its nucleus.

18.3 Genes and inheritance

We know that genes are carried on chromosomes. As chromosomes are arranged in matching pairs it follows that we have two copies of each gene, one on the paternal chromosome, one on the maternal chromosome. Gregor Mendel investigated the ways that these pairs of genes interact in an individual. His work is described in figure 5.

The offspring of a cross between two pure breeding varieties is called the F_1 generation, and it is a hybrid. The kind of breeding investigation Mendel performed is a monohybrid cross because it investigates the inheritance of a single characteristic such as the colour of the flowers. Mendel called the inherited characters he was investigating **alleles**.

Mendel's work

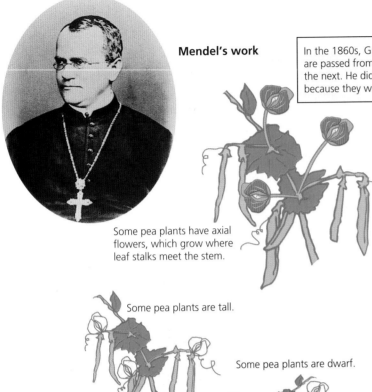

In the 1860s, Gregor Mendel investigated how features are passed from one generation of garden pea plants to the next. He did not know about chromosomes or genes because they were not yet discovered.

Some pea plants have axial flowers, which grow where leaf stalks meet the stem.

Some pea plants have terminal flowers, which grow on the ends of the stems.

Some pea plants are tall.

Some pea plants are dwarf.

Mendel chose varieties of peas (*Pisum sativum*) with distinctive inherited features such as flower colour, flower position, height of the mature plant or pea shape. In **pure breeding** varieties, like those Mendel used, every generation displays the same characteristic – for example, red flowers. Mendel would select peas from two different varieties with clear alternatives – such as red or white flowers, or tall or short stems – to be the parents of the cross.

Some peas are smooth.   Some peas are wrinkled.

Mendel used artificial pollination to carry out control matings, or **crosses**. From analysis of his results, he made predictions about the way features were passed through generations. Then he carried out further investigations to test his hypotheses. Because he used large numbers of plants in his investigations, he obtained reliable results.

Mendel pollinated each flower by hand, using pollen from the other chosen parent plant. He could see which characteristics had been inherited when he grew the seeds produced by the cross in the following year.

Figure 5 Gregor Mendel's work was the starting point for all our understanding of genetics.

Mendel found that only one of the two alternative characteristics could be seen in the F_1 generation. He called this a dominant allele. For example, when Mendel crossed round-seeded peas with wrinkle-seeded peas he discovered that none of the F_1 plants made wrinkled seeds — the allele producing round seeds was the dominant allele.

Mendel let the F_1 plants self-pollinate to produce the next generation, the F_2 generation. No new genes were introduced but the existing combinations were shuffled when pollen and ovules were formed. Mendel noticed that the characteristic that was not seen in the F_1 generation sometimes reappeared in the F_2 generation. For example, his F_1 round seeds produced some plants that carried round seeds, and some plants that carried wrinkled seeds. The gene for wrinkled seeds had not disappeared but had been carried through the F_1 generation. You can see how this works in figure 6. The characteristic which is carried but not seen is called a recessive allele. Mendel also noticed that the dominant allele in the F_1 generation appeared three times as often in the F_2 generation as the recessive allele.

Mendel's experiment

253 seeds were grown to mature plants, and their flowers allowed to fertilise themselves.

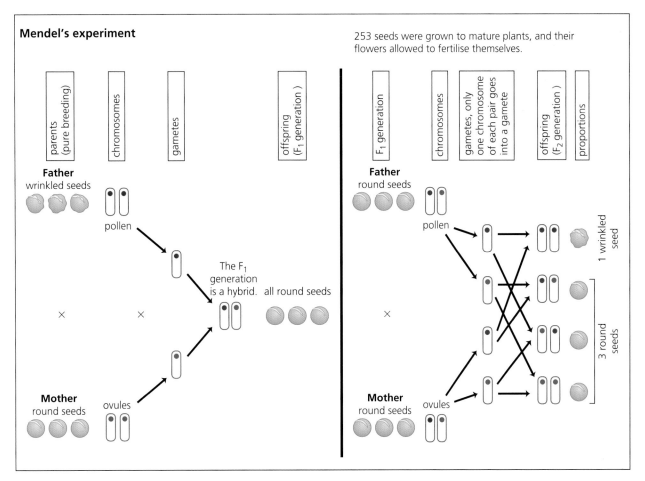

Figure 6 A mendelian cross.

Mendel used his results to work out the pattern of movement of characteristics, or alleles, through generations. He deduced that organisms must have two alleles for a particular feature but that only one goes into the pollen or eggs, and that which one of the pair goes into a particular pollen grain or ovule seems to be random.

We know that alleles are carried on a homologous pair of chromosomes and that parents pass one chromosome, with the allele it carries, to a sperm or an egg. The chromosomes and the alleles they carry pair up at fertilisation. An individual that inherits two of the same alleles, perhaps both for red flowers, is called **homozygous**. A **heterozygous** individual inherits one of each version of an allele, perhaps one for red flowers and one for white flowers.

We now know that what Mendel called alleles are different versions of the gene or genes for a particular feature. For example, the colour of some flowers is caused by a pair of genes controlling the production of a coloured compound in petal cells (figure 7). Many inherited characteristics are due to single genes, but some are the result of two or more genes working together, so the words gene and allele are *not* interchangeable.

6 What is meant by the term 'recessive allele'?

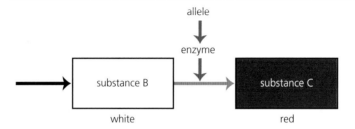

Figure 7 The dominant allele results in the production of the enzyme which converts the white substance B into the red substance C. So the flower petals are coloured red. The recessive allele cannot make the enzyme so the petal stays white.

How do we write down genetic crosses?

When we write down genetic problems we use abbreviations to represent the alleles. For dominant alleles we use a capital letter, usually the first letter of a word describing the character. The lower case letter is used for the recessive allele. We use a checkerboard to show the various combinations of alleles when an egg or ovule is fertilised by sperm or pollen. You can see an example in figure 8.

The test cross

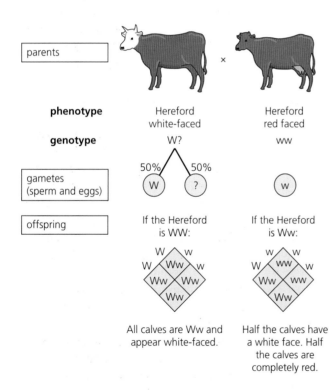

Figure 8 In this genetic diagram, the allele that causes white face is W. The red allele, w, is recessive.

In Hereford cattle a white face is dominant to a red face. We use the capital letter, W, to represent the dominant allele and the lower case letter, w, for the recessive allele.

When two heterozygotes are mated their offspring show a ratio of approximately three individuals with the dominant characteristic to one individual with the recessive characteristic. The ratio will not be exactly 3:1 because we are dealing with the *probability* of a particular chromosome carrying an allele being handed on. The 3:1 ratio will only become apparent when we carry out enough crosses to give reliable results.

A white-faced Hereford calf could be heterozygous or homozygous for the dominant allele because the dominant allele masks any recessive alleles. A black cat could also be a homozygote or a heterozygote for the same reason. If we want to find out, we must carry out a test cross, as shown in figure 8.

Although the dominant alleles can often be detected an organism also carries recessive alleles which are not expressed. The total of the genes that an animal or plant carries is its **genotype**. However, as we saw earlier, an organism's environment also affects the development of its final form and features, its **phenotype.**

What is a genetic disease?

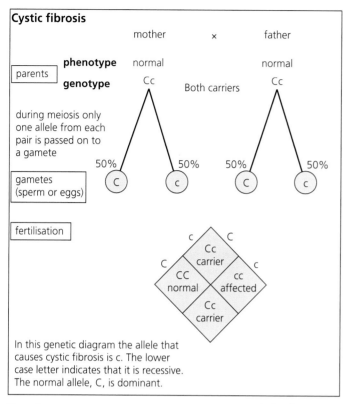

Cystic fibrosis

mother   ×   father

| | parents | | |

phenotype normal   normal

genotype Cc   Cc

Both carriers

during meiosis only one allele from each pair is passed on to a gamete

| | gametes (sperm or eggs) | | |

50%   50%   50%   50%

C   c   C   c

| | fertilisation | | |

c / C

Cc carrier

C   CC normal   cc affected   c

Cc carrier

In this genetic diagram the allele that causes cystic fibrosis is c. The lower case letter indicates that it is recessive. The normal allele, C, is dominant.

Figure 9

Some defective genes cause medical problems, such as cystic fibrosis, muscular dystrophy or phenylketonuria. Many of these alleles are recessive and may not make much difference to the people carrying them as long as there is a functioning allele on the other chromosome. However, some diseases are caused by dominant alleles and anyone inheriting one copy will suffer. An example of this is Huntington's disease (this used to be called Huntington's chorea), which is a condition in which the nervous system deteriorates as people reach middle age.

Problems with recessive alleles arise when a person inherits two of them. The most common disease-causing gene is the cystic fibrosis gene, which affects about 1 in 2000 people in the UK. It is caused by abnormal genes on chromosome 7. The gene is expressed in secretory cells of the lungs and pancreas which produce mucus. Someone with two copies of the malfunctioning gene makes very thick sticky mucus, which blocks the passageways in the lungs and pancreas. Sufferers are vulnerable to lung infections and digestive problems because the enzymes made in the pancreas cannot pass down the pancreatic duct. The inheritance of cystic fibrosis is shown in figure 9.

Sickle-cell anaemia is also a genetic disease. There is an allele that causes abnormal haemoglobin to be produced. This haemoglobin cannot carry oxygen very well and distorts the red cells carrying it into sickle shapes – so it is called sickle haemoglobin. Affected red cells move through the tiny capillaries less easily than normal cells and can block them. Heterozygotes for sickle-cell anaemia have some normal and some sickle haemoglobin, but they are usually able to lead normal lives. Children who inherit the sickle allele from both parents (homozygotes for the disease) are often affected by lack of oxygen for growth, activity and keeping warm, and suffer damage caused by blocked capillaries. Sickle-cell anaemia used to be fatal, but treatment is now possible and blood transfusions have made a dramatic difference in the survival of sufferers.

Some genes present on the X chromosome are not matched by genes on the smaller Y chromosome. These genes are expressed in males, regardless of whether they are dominant or recessive alleles because there is only one copy. If the gene does not function effectively it causes a sex-linked condition. The most well known sex-linked condition is haemophilia. In this disease a recessive allele on the X chromosome results in failure to make a vital blood clotting protein (figure 10). The defective allele is uncommon, but men who carry it suffer excessive bleeding from what should be minor injuries. Women with one copy of the defective allele do not suffer from haemophilia, as they have a normal allele to counter its effects, but are carriers of the disease because they could pass it on to their sons. Female embryos who are homozygous for the disease do not survive.

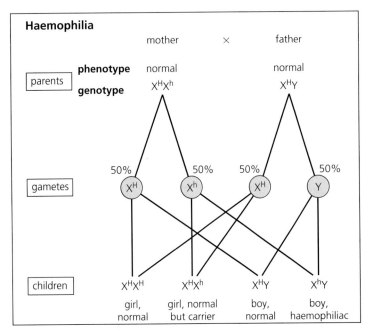

Haemophilia

mother   ×   father

phenotype	normal	normal
parents **genotype**	X^H X^h	X^H Y

gametes

50% X^H   50% X^h   50% X^H   50% Y

children

X^H X^H   X^H X^h   X^H Y   X^h Y

girl, normal | girl, normal but carrier | boy, normal | boy, haemophiliac

Figure 10

Red–green colour blindness is carried in the same way as haemophilia, although its effects are nothing like as serious. About one man in 20 suffers from red–green colour blindness, but a woman must have inherited a copy from each of her parents to suffer from the condition. This is much more rare.

7 The alleles for ginger and black fur colour in cats are neither dominant nor recessive, but equally expressed and are carried on the X chromosome. A female kitten with a ginger allele and a black allele will be tortoiseshell, with a mixture of black and ginger hair. Male kittens have whichever colour is handed on with the mother's X chromosome. Black is a common allele in cats but ginger is much less common.

   a Draw a genetic diagram to show how ginger females arise.
   b Why is it impossible for a male cat to be a tortoiseshell?
   c Why are ginger toms much more common than ginger females?

How can genetic conditions be detected?

All newborn babies are given a blood test to detect phenylketonuria (PKU), which is caused by a recessive allele. In unaffected individuals, an enzyme converts phenylalanine from digested food into tyrosine, but people with PKU cannot carry out this reaction. As a result, phenylalanine accumulates in the body and causes brain damage and restricted growth. If PKU is detected early enough it can be managed and the damage minimised.

Most genetic diseases are very rare and are detected only when children develop problems. Relatives of people suffering from cystic fibrosis, sickle cell anaemia and a similar blood condition called thalassaemia can have genetic counselling to assess the risks of passing on a potentially life-threatening disease to their children. If a high-risk couple is expecting a baby the developing embryo can be screened for some genetic disorders. Genetic testing is also offered to pregnant women over 35 years old because babies of older mothers have a greater risk of a chromosome problem. Down's syndrome is the best known of these, but there are other and more severe conditions. A fetus's chromosomes can be seen by several methods at different stages of pregnancy:

- sampling placental cells at about 11 weeks
- sampling the fluid around a fetus, which contains fetal cells, at 16 weeks
- sampling the mother's blood for circulating fetal cells at 16 weeks.

Summary of genes and inheritance

- Inherited features occur as pairs of alleles carried on homologous chromosomes.
- Alleles are passed to offspring, which inherit a copy of the chromosome that carries them.
- Some alleles are dominant and are expressed if they are present.
- A recessive allele is only expressed if it is paired with another recessive allele.

- A monohybrid cross is a controlled mating between two different pure breeding types.
- The offspring of two heterozygotes show a 3:1 ratio of dominant to recessive features.
- A sex-linked condition is caused by an allele carried on the X chromosome which is not matched by one on the Y chromosome.
- Some genes have harmful consequences when they are inherited.

18.4 How genes work

A gene is a section of DNA carried on a chromosome. It carries the information needed to make a protein. There are also control sections on chromosomes, which switch genes 'on' and 'off'. Although every cell carries a full complement of genes, only the ones it needs to do its job are expressed and most genes in a cell are never switched on. Genetic information is carried as a chemical code along one strand of the DNA molecule, called the sense strand. The other strand is the complementary, or anti-sense, strand. You can read more about DNA structure in chapter 2, *Chemicals of life*. The DNA code is interpreted to make the proteins that cells need for their structure and function. Proteins encoded by genes may be:

- enzymes, which catalyse reactions within the cell
- components of the cell or its cytoplasm
- needed for a particular job – for example insulin, which regulates blood sugar concentration.

How are proteins made?

Protein synthesis starts at the gene which codes for that particular protein. The order of the bases A, C, T and G along the sense strand of the DNA controls the order of **amino acids** in a particular protein molecule. The code uses groups of three bases in a row, called codons, for each amino acid. Each codon in turn codes for the next amino acid to be added to the growing protein molecule. The four bases can be grouped in 64 different ways, to make 64 codons. We use only 20 amino acids in our proteins, so there are several spare codons and several code for the same amino acid. Some codons are used as signals to start protein synthesis and some are full stops to end the protein chain.

When a protein is required cells use their DNA as a template to make complementary copies of the gene in mRNA. This mRNA travels from the nucleus into the cytoplasm where ribosomes attach to it. In the ribosomes the amino acids are joined in the correct order to make the protein needed (figure 11).

Figure 11

How a gene makes a protein

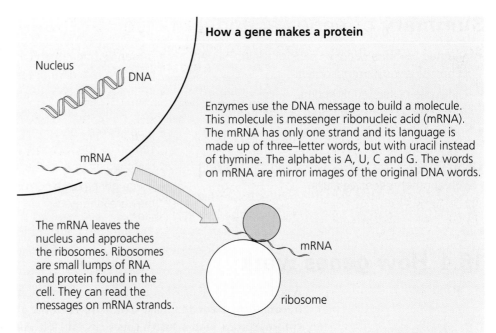

Nucleus

DNA

mRNA

Enzymes use the DNA message to build a molecule. This molecule is messenger ribonucleic acid (mRNA). The mRNA has only one strand and its language is made up of three–letter words, but with uracil instead of thymine. The alphabet is A, U, C and G. The words on mRNA are mirror images of the original DNA words.

The mRNA leaves the nucleus and approaches the ribosomes. Ribosomes are small lumps of RNA and protein found in the cell. They can read the messages on mRNA strands.

mRNA

ribosome

Another type of RNA molecule, called transfer RNA (or tRNA), exists in cells. Each tRNA molecule is a short length of RNA with an aminoacid at one end. The tRNA molecule is twisted, so that a group of three bases sticks out at the other end. These bases are called anti–codons. Anti–codons are the complementary bases to the codons on mRNA molecules. There are enough types of tRNA molecules so that each amino acid can have its own tRNA type and anti–codon.

The sequence of bases on the DNA controls the sequence of codons on the mRNA. This means that only certain tRNA molecules line up, and only certain amino acids join together to make a particular protein.

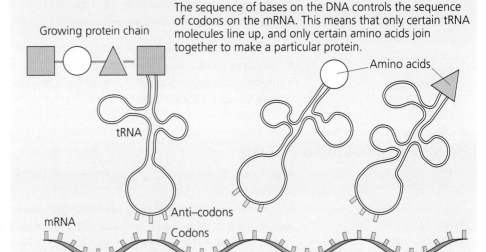

Growing protein chain

tRNA

Amino acids

mRNA

Anti–codons

Codons

When an mRNA molecule approaches a ribosome, enzymes line up the codons on the mRNA with the three bases on the tRNA molecules. Enzymes join amino acids at the other ends of the tRNA molecules. This growing chain of amino acid molecules will form a protein.

Many of the proteins made by ribosomes are enzymes which control important chemical pathways in cells. In this way DNA controls how a cell develops.

Where do new alleles and genes come from?

X-rays can cause mutations in eggs, sperm and developing embryos, so this patient is wearing a protective lead apron.

DNA can be changed or damaged by mutagens, and the changed gene is a **mutation**. Mutagens include ultraviolet light, gamma rays and X-rays, chemicals such as benzene, tetrachloromethane, mustard gas, and many of the chemicals in wood smoke and cigarette smoke. Even very low doses of mutagens can damage genes. We know of many mutagens, and new ones are constantly being added to the list, but a large number of mutations arise for reasons we don't know. These are called spontaneous mutations.

Mutagens cause mutations by:

- breaking chromosomes
- changing a base in a codon
- deleting stretches of DNA
- adding extra bases and changing the grouping of codons.

Most mutations lead to new forms of the gene which do not function very well and can slow down cell activity. However, there is a chance that the change may have no overall effect, or that the new version is better in some way than before. The 'improved' gene will only be passed on if it is passed to the cells which make gametes and used in fertilization (figure 12).

Effects of mutation

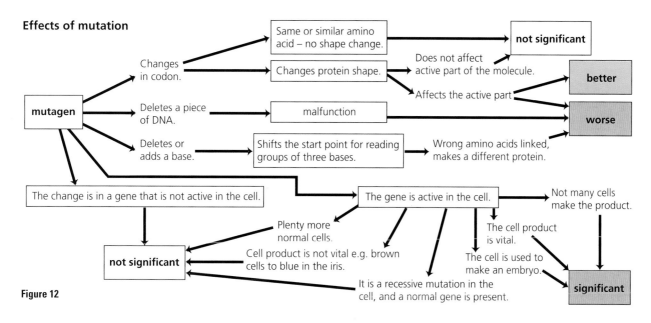

Figure 12

Summary of how genes work

- Genes carry the information needed to make proteins.
- The information on a gene is encoded in groups of three bases. These groups are called codons.

- mRNA is made on the gene's DNA template. It is used by ribosomes to link amino acids in the correct order to make proteins.
- New alleles arise as a result of mutation. Things which cause mutations are called mutagens.

18.5 Moving genes and genetic modification

People have manipulated plant and animal genes since farming began and people had to choose which seeds to eat and which to keep for planting. **Selective breeding** uses natural animal or plant reproduction to produce new, or better, plant and animal varieties. Farmers choose breeding partners with desirable characteristics and hope to produce better offspring. You will find more about selective breeding in chapter 22, *Food and farming*.

Nectarines are a mutation from ordinary peaches that have been selected for a smooth skin. Shetland sheepdogs have been bred from collies over the last century, for features such as height and head shape. (They are only 35 cm tall!)

Scientists manipulate genes in a different and less chancy way than farmers. Directly inserting useful genes into cells is quicker and more accurate than selective breeding. Individual genes are identified and snipped out of the DNA. Millions of copies of the gene are made in a test tube, using a technique called the polymerase chain reaction, and transferred into other cells to function. We can even make artificial genes using mRNA extracted from cells as a template. Direct transfer also lets us do things that are otherwise impossible — like getting yeast cells to make plant chemicals. New genes can be inserted into bacteria, viruses, fungi, plants and animals. DNA carrying the new genes is called recombinant DNA. Even very old DNA from mummified bodies, extinct animals and long dead seeds can be copied and studied.

How do scientists transfer genes from one cell to another?

The enzymes that are used by cells to repair their own damaged DNA can cut and rejoin DNA. Restriction enzymes cut DNA into smaller pieces and ligases join DNA fragments together. Molecular biologists use the restriction enzymes to snip genes out of DNA and the ligases to insert them into other DNA molecules.

Transferring genes into microbes

Scientists know how to grow yeast and some bacteria easily, cheaply and safely. These organisms can be given new genes to make them into 'living factories' and make materials like rennet for cheesemaking, hepatitis B antigens for vaccines or human insulin for treating diabetes, all of which are difficult to obtain from other sources. Genetic engineers transfer these genes into bacteria using a 'carrier' called a plasmid (figure 13).

Figure 13

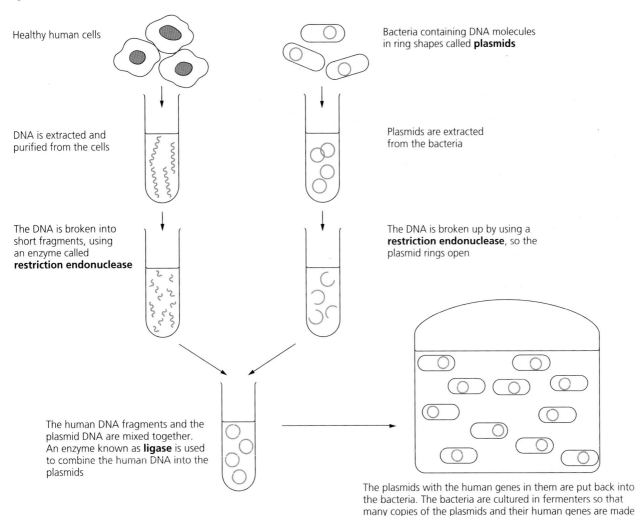

Healthy human cells

Bacteria containing DNA molecules in ring shapes called **plasmids**

DNA is extracted and purified from the cells

Plasmids are extracted from the bacteria

The DNA is broken into short fragments, using an enzyme called **restriction endonuclease**

The DNA is broken up by using a **restriction endonuclease**, so the plasmid rings open

The human DNA fragments and the plasmid DNA are mixed together. An enzyme known as **ligase** is used to combine the human DNA into the plasmids

The plasmids with the human genes in them are put back into the bacteria. The bacteria are cultured in fermenters so that many copies of the plasmids and their human genes are made

Transferring genes into animal cells

Genes can be transferred into animal or human cells by inserting them into retroviruses. The retroviruses have to be disabled first so that they cannot cause an infection. The virus has enzymes that incorporate its genes into a host cell's chromosomes so it can reproduce. The new genes are also incorporated into the host cell's DNA. Several genes may be needed to get a working product but the viruses are very small and can only carry a small amount of DNA.

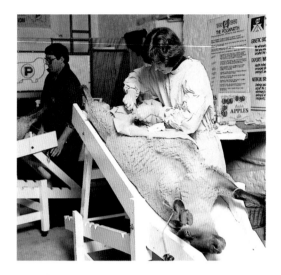

New genes can also be transferred directly into animal eggs. Newly fertilised eggs are injected with hundreds of copies of the gene, and the eggs that survive are implanted into a suitable female. Some of the offspring will have the new gene and, as the transfer took place at the earliest stage of development, all the cells of the new animal will carry the new gene. It will be in the sperm or eggs and can be inherited by the next generation. Injection of genes in this way into human eggs is not allowed.

After eggs have been genetically modified, they are implanted into a suitable host mother to develop in the normal way.

Transferring genes into plants

New genes are inserted into plant cells using a bacterium called *Agrobacterium*, which infects plants. *Agrobacterium* also has a plasmid which can be used to insert genes into plant chromosomes in the same way as new genes are inserted into animal cells by retroviruses. The new genes are transferred into a small piece of plant tissue, not into a whole plant. Each cell with a new gene can be propagated to quickly produce lots of plants with the new characteristic.

Can faulty genes be repaired?

Scientists are investigating gene therapy, which is repairing or replacing faulty genes. So far, genes in animals, plants and bacteria have been changed but there are very strict criteria which have to be met before any work on human cells is allowed. Gene therapy may be used to treat faulty genes in several ways.

- Genes which make unsuitable proteins could be repressed (stopped) by blocking their mRNA synthesis.
- The faulty gene's base sequence could be altered to make a different, less damaging, protein. Bacterial genes in a test tube have been altered but it would be very difficult to change a faulty human gene in a fertilised egg to ensure that the whole body has the new gene.
- Non-functioning genes could be replaced with artificial copies of the normal gene, carried on disabled viruses or in small capsules made from cell membrane which will fuse with cells. The replacement genes should be expressed rather than the defective gene. Doctors are attempting to correct cystic fibrosis by spraying new genes into the lungs of sufferers.

Children whose cells don't make the enzyme ADA cannot resist infections. They have to be protected in special suits or tents. Gene therapy techniques could, in the future, cure such children by inserting ADA-producing genes into their cells.

Genetic modification and gene therapy have tremendous potential but there are many problems involved. Here are a few to think about:

- The transferred gene's activity in the recipient can not be finely controlled and large quantities of its product could be harmful.
- The new gene might need to be in every cell before it can work. Transferring genes into fertilised human eggs is not legal because the new genes would pass into the embryo's developing ovaries or testes and possibly into the next generation.
- Gene therapy might be misused to remove features that our current culture finds unfavourable.
- It could become a 'black market' therapy to produce children with particular features, for example taller or more attractive, and people who are not 'perfect' could become disadvantaged.
- It could reduce the number of different variations of genes in the human population.
- Gene therapy could free families from some unpleasant and fatal diseases and doctors who were not performing this therapy would have to justify why they were not doing it.
- Gene therapy might be the only treatment available for some conditions. Some parents are willing to try any therapy that could help their child and doctors might be pressured to attempt it, even if it is unlikely to work.
- The replaced gene could have other important roles which are not yet understood. By replacing it we could be wiping out important genes through ignorance. The full effects of removing the gene may not be apparent for years.

Summary of moving genes and genetic modification

- Genes can be snipped out of DNA and copied in large quantities using a technique called the polymerase chain reaction. This technique uses bacterial enzymes to make huge numbers of copies of the DNA in a test tube.
- Genes can be made in a test tube from information encoded in mRNA extracted from cells.

- Scientists can transfer genes from one cell to another and from one species to another. A plasmid or a virus is used to carry the gene to its new host cell.
- Genetic modification could be used to treat genetic diseases.
- Genetic modification could cause many social and ethical problems.

Investigations

1 Many genes exist in two or more forms called alleles. They give rise to slightly different proteins which may function differently enough to detect. Potatoes contain an enzyme called catalase. If a small piece of potato is dropped into some hydrogen peroxide the enzyme in cells at the surface breaks down the peroxide into water and oxygen. Oxygen bubbles gather around the potato and buoy it up to the surface. How could you use this technique to investigate whether different varieties of potatoes have different catalase activity.

Ecosystems

Learning objectives

By the end of this chapter you should be able to:

- **investigate** the species present in an area
- **list** the significant abiotic factors affecting an organism
- **recognise** which factors may be limiting
- **explain** distribution of organisms in an area
- **classify** organisms into trophic levels
- **construct** pyramids of number and biomass
- **describe** mineral cycling systems

19.1 Ecology – what lives where

Ecologists try to answer the question: 'Which plants and animals live here, and why?'. The question seems simple, but the answer can be very complex, involving many different branches of science. Chemists identify the chemicals in soil, physicists measure the light levels or temperature in a forest, mathematicians design computer programs to analyse and display the results and biologists try to explain what they mean. Recently, scientists have also had to try to explain how much money a landscape is worth and how a major construction project might change that.

How do ecologists identify the organisms in a habitat?

A typical English woodland contains hundreds of different types of organism. An ecologist could take a lifetime identifying and cataloguing a single area! To make the task easier, ecologists take **samples** in the area and use these to build up a picture of the whole woodland. A sample is a small part of the whole that the ecologist can study in detail.

However, if the sample is too small it could be distorted by unusual features – for example, a single sample of a grassy field might happen to take in the only ant hill in the field. Using only this sample would suggest the whole field was overrun with ants. Normally, ecologists take a number of samples and combine the results.

Before starting to collect a sample, you need to decide:

- *How big* does each sample have to be?
- *Where* can I collect the samples?
- *How many* samples do I need to collect?
- How can I *interpret* the results of my samples?

Why does this plant live here?

A plant needs a supply of water, mineral salts, carbon dioxide, oxygen and light to grow. It also needs space to grow and some protection from grazing animals. If it can get all these things in a particular area it will probably grow there. Normally some of these things will be in short supply and they will reduce the plant's growth. The factors that reduce the growth of the plant are called **limiting factors** (see chapter 4, *Energy transfers*). Ecologists try to find out which factors control the places where plants grow. In effect, they look for the limiting factors.

The mountains of Snowdonia are often wet and cold. The good water supply encourages a rich growth of plants, but the cold stops some plants growing. Water is not a limiting factor, but the low temperature is limiting.

The sandy soils in Dorset do not hold water very well, but the climate there is warmer than Snowdonia. This means the lack of water, rather than the temperature, acts as a limiting factor.

Which plants used to live here?

Scientists use pollen grains preserved in bogs and marshes to work out which plants were most common in the past (see figure 1). In peat bogs, the surface layers are the most recent, covering older layers beneath. It is possible to work out how old a sample of peat is by the distance from the sample site to the surface. Samples from particular depths are examined and the pollen grains they contain identified. The relative amounts of each type of pollen grain give a measure of the relative abundance of the plants that produced them. Luckily, pollen grains have very tough walls and last a long time in the deep, damp parts of the bog away from warmth and oxygen.

Figure 1 The pollen record can show us how abundant different trees were at different times in our history.

1 a Look at figure 1. What effects has the change in temperature had on the forests of Britain over the last 9000 years?

b What other factor do you think has had a major effect over the last 2000 years?

Forest history of Britain, from the pollen record

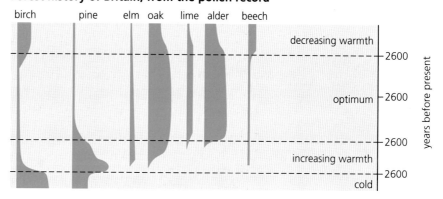

The pollen grain record in figure 1 shows the effects of two factors on the forests of Britain – temperature and human beings. Temperature is an **abiotic** factor which does not depend on the other living things in the environment. Human beings are a **biotic** factor, because they are part of the living environment. Sometimes abiotic factors will change the effect that biotic factors have.

Why does this animal live here?

Animals need food, oxygen, water and shelter. The shelter protects the animal from cold or heat and allows it to hide from predators, to mate and raise its young.

Animals can live anywhere where there is food, oxygen, water and shelter. Different species have adapted different features to help them obtain these resources in their habitat.

Figure 2 Some animals change in response to the changing seasons.

2 List the ways each of the animals in the photographs is adapted to survive in its environment.

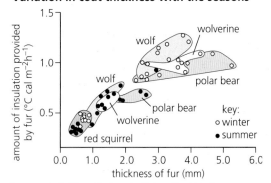

Variation in coat thickness with the seasons

Source: adapted from *Ecology*, by Begon, Harper and Townsend, Blackwell Scientific, 1990.

The environment has a strong effect on the organisms that live there. Sometimes the same species can look very different in different environments. The individuals change slightly to fit in better with their particular environment.

3 Explain what the graph in figure 2 shows about how the species and the environment are linked.

Summary of ecology – what lives where

- Ecologists study relationships between plants and animals living in a habitat, and between living organisms and their environment.
- Plants need water, oxygen, mineral salts, carbon dioxide, oxygen, light, space and shelter to grow. Animals need food, oxygen, water and shelter to grow.
- Environmental factors can strongly affect the way individual organisms develop.
- Limiting factors control the growth and numbers of living organisms in a habitat.
- Limiting factors can be biotic (to do with other living things) or abiotic (to do with the physical environment alone).

19.2 Communities and ecosystems

How do organisms live together?

Organisms do not live alone. They are surrounded by other organisms of the same species called the local **population**. Other organisms of different species also live in the area. Similar habitats often have similar groups of species living together. These common groupings are called **communities**. For example, grassland habitats anywhere in the UK tend to have similar communities of species living there.

The type of community in an area – that is, the plants and animals living there – depends on:

- the abiotic factors (the non-living parts of the environment)
- the biotic factors (the way the living things interact with each other).

Ecologists use the word **ecosystem** to describe the way these living things interact with each other and with the non-living environment. If the term 'community' describes what is present, the term 'ecosystem' describes what is going on.

All ecosystems have:

- energy transfer systems
- systems to recycle materials.

Energy flows through an ecosystem, but materials are cycled round endlessly. The different parts of the ecosystem all work together to make this happen and to keep the ecosystem stable.

How do energy transfer systems in an ecosystem work?

Sunlight is the source of energy that all living things eventually use. Green plants use photosynthesis to transfer energy from sunlight into energy in complex chemicals. These chemicals can be used to build more plant tissues (see chapter 4, *Energy transfers*). The plants that produce these energy-rich compounds are called **primary producers**, and are the first step in the energy transfer system.

Animals cannot photosynthesise and so take in their energy as food. Since animals cannot produce energy they are called **consumers**. Animals that eat plants are called **primary consumers** because they are the first consumer in the consumer chain. A snail is a good example of a primary consumer.

A thrush is also a consumer, but it eats animals not plants. The thrush is a **secondary consumer** because it is the second consumer in the chain. A cat that eats the thrush is also a consumer – it is the third consumer in the chain and so is called the third or **tertiary consumer**.

What are food chains and webs?

One way to follow the flow of energy through an ecosystem is to use **food chains**. A food chain shows what an animal eats and what eats it. **Food webs** show the way that all the food chains in an area link together (figure 3).

Figure 3 This shows a food web for a heathland ecosystem.

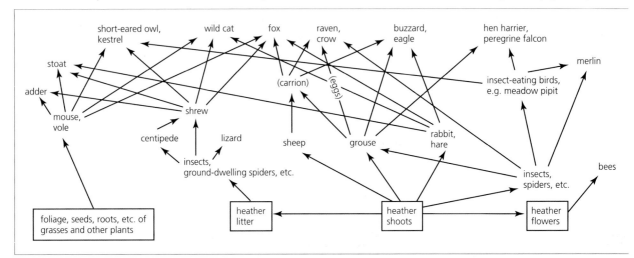

4 Where does the energy in the food web in figure 3 come from?

5 Which animals eat:

   a grouse eggs   **b** insects?

6 **a** Which animal has the widest variety of food?

   b Which animals have the narrowest variety of food?

   c Give one advantage of eating a wide variety of foods.

7 The wild cat is much rarer now than it was in the past. How will this affect the food supply for owls, kestrels and foxes in the heathland ecosystem?

What are trophic levels?

8 **a** Look at the food web in figure 3, and sort the organisms into their correct trophic level.

   b What is the highest trophic level in the heathland ecosystem?

Biologists often sort living organisms into groups. The groups depend on what the person who is doing the sorting is trying to do.

For example, animals that feed at different times of the day can be sorted into groups. The same animals could be sorted into different groups depending on whether they are mammals or birds. Other groups could depend on what sort of food they eat. Ecologists often sort organisms into groups depending on where in the food chain they are. They put the primary producers in one group and the primary consumers in another. These groups are called **trophic levels**. Ecologists number the trophic levels, using level one for the primary producers, level two for the primary consumers, and so on.

How is energy passed from one trophic level to another?

9 Use ideas about energy transfer to explain the shape of the pyramid in figure 4.

10 A single oak tree can support thousands of insects, all chewing away at its leaves. These insects might be food for carnivorous insects, which could be eaten by birds.

a Explain how this situation would produce a pyramid of numbers like the one shown in figure 5.

b What would a pyramid of biomass look like for the oak tree food chain?

When a cow eats grass, it collects energy from level one and builds it into level two. However, there are several reasons why all the energy in the grass does not end up as energy in cow tissue. The cow does not eat the roots of the grass. Some of the energy in the grass passes out in the cow's faeces. Some energy is used to repair damaged cells in the cow, and some is needed for respiration. Respiration drives many other chemical reactions in the body and helps to keep the cow warmer than the environment. In fact, very little of the energy available in trophic level one is used to build new cow tissue. Only the energy used for this extra growth will be available for a secondary consumer at level three to collect. So there is a loss of energy at every transfer, the transfer systems are not 100% efficient. Since the amount of energy available falls as we go up the levels, we would expect the number of animals at each level to get smaller.

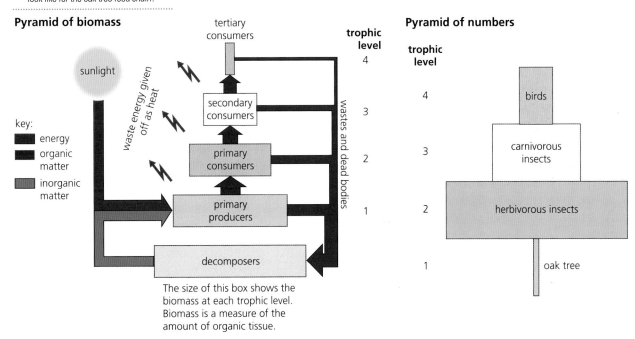

Figure 4 This diagram shows how energy passes up through the trophic levels of a food chain, and how materials are recycled.

Figure 5 This pyramid of numbers shows how many individuals there are at each trophic level in a food chain.

Energy cannot be created or destroyed. The energy that is lost during energy transfers often appears as heat. This energy leaves the Earth as heat. In a way, the Earth is a giant biological machine that converts energy as sunlight into energy as heat. If the balance of energy gained and energy lost is upset, the temperature on the Earth's surface might change.

How are materials recycled in ecosystems?

The living world receives a constant supply of energy in sunlight. However, there are limited amounts of essential chemicals available, and these are used again and again (figures 6 and 7).

Figure 6 Ecosystems recycle important chemicals.

Figure 7 One of the most important minerals cycled through ecosystems is nitrogen.

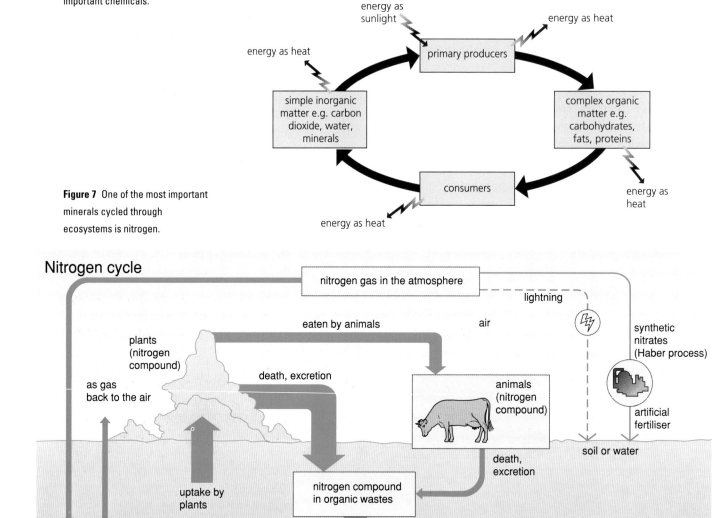

11 Look at figure 7. List the reactions that:
   a increase   **b** decrease
   the amount of nitrogen compounds in the soil.

12 Nitrogen-rich fertilisers are used all over the world, to increase the yield of crop plants. However, there are concerns that the nitrates can damage the environment. Organic farmers have chosen not to use nitrate fertilisers. Explain how an understanding of the nitrogen cycle could help them to maintain high yields without fertilisers.

Summary of **communities and ecosystems**

- A population is a group of organisms of the same species living in an area.
- A community is a group of different species living together in a habitat.
- An ecosystem describes how different species in a community interact with each other and with their habitat.
- All ecosystems transfer energy, and recycle materials.

- A food chain shows what animals eat and what eats them. A food web shows how food chains in an ecosystem are linked.
- Energy is lost each time it is transferred to a higher trophic level. This means there is less biomass, and less energy available, at each successive level in a food chain.
- Important materials such as nitrogen are not lost, but instead are recycled in ecosystems.

19.3 **Competition and adaptation**

Why is competition so important?

Avoiding direct competition

In stable balanced communities, species do not usually compete directly. Many animals feed on tree bark during the winter. Rabbits strip the bark near the ground, Fallow Deer feed about 1.2 m above the ground, and taller Red Deer strip the tree slightly higher up. Squirrels feed on bark at higher levels still. Each is feeding on the same resource but exploiting it in a different, non-overlapping way. Each species occupies a slightly different **niche**.

Figure 8

Plants often arrive in a habitat as seeds carried by the wind, or by birds and animals. Animals come as visitors. These chance arrivals can join the existing community if they can compete effectively with the inhabitants.

Animals and plants compete for resources. Grass might compete with a large tree for sunlight and water in the soil. Animals compete for the best grazing and suitable breeding sites. When members of a species compete they all suffer. Some do not get enough crucial resources and die. Others have less than they need and so cannot reproduce or grow well. Some individuals succeed in getting most of what they need and reproduce most successfully. If the features which helped them compete are inherited, their offspring might cope well with competition too. You can find out more about the effect of this in chapter 20, *Evolution*.

Adults could be competing with their offspring for the same resources so most species have evolved strategies to minimise the effects. Plants disperse their seeds so that seedlings germinate away from the shade of the maternal plant. Young animals sometimes feed on different and smaller food sources to their parents.

13 Look at figure 8. Explain how the animals' behaviour reduces competition.

How are organisms adapted to compete and survive?

Ground-level plants that live in wooded areas are adapted to compete for light. Many ground-level plants complete most of their growth before deciduous trees overhead come into leaf, and cut out the light. They grow very slowly during the coldest months early in the year, but speed up when the ground warms in spring. Bluebells, primroses and anemones flower in spring and die back in early summer when the light levels fall.

Many animals and plants are adapted to avoid being eaten. Plants can often survive a small amount of damage from grazing but, without a deterrent, grazers such as slugs, grasshoppers and snails can completely destroy a plant. Some plants have unpleasant tasting or toxic chemicals in their cells. Clover plants can make a cyanide compound when their leaves are damaged which deters grazers. Other plants have thorns, spines, hairs or stinging cells to stop grazing.

At the next trophic level, primary consumers are adapted to avoid predators. Some are camouflaged to blend in with their background. Most predators have black and white vision, detecting changes of contrast rather than differences in colour, so mottled grey squirrels and rabbits blend well into the background, particularly when they stay perfectly still. Hard-shelled tortoises, spiny hedgehogs and smelly skunks all make it unpleasant for predators to eat them. Table 1 shows some more examples of defence adaptations in plants and animals.

Table 1 *Adaptations to avoid being eaten.*

Organisms	Defence adaptations
Holly bush	prickles on leaves, thick cuticle
Rabbit	eyes at the side of the head can see behind, large ears pick up faint sounds
Housefly	eyes can see all round body, sensitive to air movements
Ladybird	unpleasant taste, warning colours
Geranium	furry coat of hairs and unpleasant taste
Toad	unpleasant tasting chemicals in skin

External parasites such as fleas, ticks and lice have 'claws' to hang on to their victims, and mouthparts which can pierce tough skin. They need to be able to detect a potential meal coming and jump on as it passes by. Internal parasites like the malaria protozoan have very sophisticated mechanisms to avoid a host's immune system.

Predators, unlike parasites, catch and kill their prey. They have to be able to detect their prey using acute sight and stereoscopic vision, by listening, by scent, or by detecting infra-red radiation from its body. Predators have evolved a range of strategies to capture their prey, and then hold and immobilise it for long enough to eat it (see table 2).

Table 2 *Adaptions for capturing prey.*

Predators	Strategies for capturing prey
Shark	Detects prey using acute sense of smell, and vibrations in the water. Many rows of teeth pointing backwards hold prey while biting.
Cobra	Stalks prey, then venom paralyses prey so that it can be swallowed whole.
Crocodile	Waits in ambush below water surface. Large mouth with strong teeth grips prey and pulls it under to drown it. After a period of rotting in the water, prey is ripped up by twisting movements of body.
Spider	Vibrations inform about the prey, sticky web traps insects, venom and web packaging paralyses prey. Prey's body fluids sucked out.
Sparrowhawk	Acute vision spots prey from a distance. Dives rapidly onto prey, which is gripped in sharp talons. Hooked beak tears into prey's flesh.

Summary of competition and adaptation

- If a population is too large for the available resources the members suffer in competition.
- Animal and plant species can co-exist with competitors when they have slightly different needs.
- Animals and plants have strategies to avoid competition with their own offspring.
- Plants have mechanisms to reduce grazer damage. Grazers have protective mechanisms to deter predators.
- Predators have to be able to detect, catch and subdue prey.

19.4 Population changes

How do populations change?

Ecologists re-visiting sites find that the numbers of animals and plants living there fluctuate over time. The birth of young, germinating seeds, and immigrants arriving from other areas swell the populations. At the same time other individuals die from accidents, starvation or disease, get eaten, or leave the area. Populations are stable if the numbers arriving equal the numbers leaving. A harsh winter or a summer drought can reduce populations drastically. A warm moist year boosts vegetation growth so everything benefits and populations boom.

Birth rate

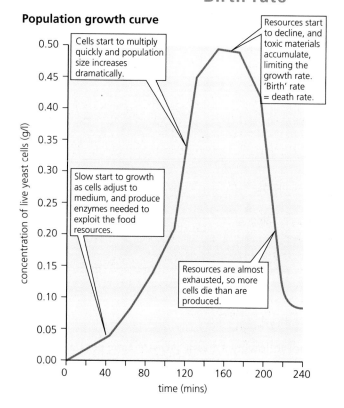

Population growth curve

Cells start to multiply quickly and population size increases dramatically.

Resources start to decline, and toxic materials accumulate, limiting the growth rate. 'Birth' rate = death rate.

Slow start to growth as cells adjust to medium, and produce enzymes needed to exploit the food resources.

Resources are almost exhausted, so more cells die than are produced.

If a population is not affected by external factors, as the members reproduce, it follows a growth curve like that shown in figure 9. Asexual reproducers such as yeast, bacteria, fungi and greenfly can generate enormous populations in a very short time in favourable conditions. For sexually reproducing organisms, the population growth is slower, but as long as each individual produces two replacement offspring over its reproductive lifetime, the growth curve follows the same basic shape.

When there is plenty of food, water, warmth, light and shelter in a habitat, populations grow quickly. Well-fed parents produce more offspring, which are usually larger and more successful. Plants produce more seeds, and birds lay larger clutches of eggs in a year with favourable conditions. However, in poor conditions there are fewer offspring, and fewer survive to maturity, so the population growth rate drops. Birth rates, and therefore population growth rates, depend heavily on environmental conditions.

Figure 9

14 Bluetits lay a clutch of eggs in spring, and often have a second brood later in the year. They raise about nine nestlings in each brood. The youngsters can breed the following year. If four pairs breed one spring, calculate the size of the population at the end of the second year, if all the birds survive and reproduce successfully.

Death rate

A population of garden birds is stable because there is only enough food, roosts and nesting sites for a certain number of individuals. In the competition, very few will get everything they need, but most will get enough to reproduce. Some will die or go to forage elsewhere. Parasites and diseases spread easily through large crowded populations. Parasites do not usually kill, but they are a drain on the host so that it is more likely to die from other diseases.

When conditions become unfavourable – for example, when there are not enough resources, or when the population has become overcrowded – more individuals die and the population declines. Charles Darwin was interested in the minute differences between individuals, that made some better able to compete than others. In crowded populations, these tiny differences can mean that some individuals pass on their successful features to their offspring, while other individuals breed less successfully. This led to Darwin's ideas on **natural selection** (see chapter 20, *Evolution*).

How do predators affect prey populations?

The populations of two species are linked when one species eats another as a main food source. Predators eat a range of prey, but most have a preferred prey and affect the size of the prey population. Scientists have constructed models of the relationship between predator and prey populations using observations of animals in natural situations and in some laboratory studies (see figure 10). In real life, the situation is more complex – for example, predators can usually eat something else if the prey population declines, or migrates. In addition, prey numbers are affected by how much food they have, the climate, and disease, as well as the size of a particular predator population.

Figure 10

Predator–prey relationship

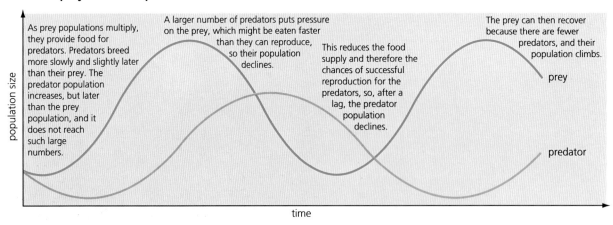

As prey populations multiply, they provide food for predators. Predators breed more slowly and slightly later than their prey. The predator population increases, but later than the prey population, and it does not reach such large numbers.

A larger number of predators puts pressure on the prey, which might be eaten faster than they can reproduce, so their population declines.

This reduces the food supply and therefore the chances of successful reproduction for the predators, so, after a lag, the predator population declines.

The prey can then recover because there are fewer predators, and their population climbs.

prey

predator

population size

time

How does the human population change?

The human population is not following a classic growth curve because we are no longer subject to the same natural controls as other animals and plants (see figure 11). Until a few thousand years ago the human population is thought to have grown very slowly, but the development of agriculture and animal husbandry massively increased our food supply, which meant the same amount of land could support many more people. Other developments over recent centuries have also meant that humans can resist many factors which normally control population size.

Figure 11

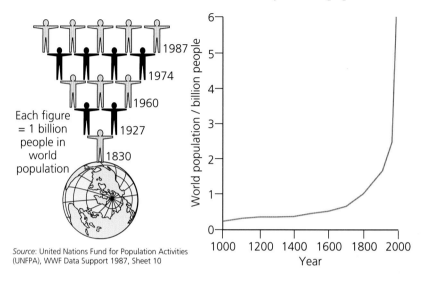

Each figure = 1 billion people in world population

1830
1927
1960
1974
1987

Source: United Nations Fund for Population Activities (UNFPA), WWF Data Support 1987, Sheet 10

The most important factor which has changed for humans is a huge drop in the death rate. More of us live longer and swell the population. More children survive the early years and fewer mature individuals die at an early age. Fresh food is more widely available so people's diets are of higher quality, and people are able to resist illnesses better. More sanitary housing, better hygiene and vaccines have reduced the spread of diseases, while drugs and antibiotics have improved people's chances of surviving any infections they do contract. Modern medical technology also allows people to survive for longer with other conditions such as heart disease, diabetes or major injuries. Social systems support more vulnerable individuals in many societies.

Reliable contraception affects population size, and the age structure of populations. Where contraception is freely available and family incomes are reasonable, family size has gradually declined.

Summary of population changes

- Population size results from a balance between the numbers of individuals recruited to a population and the numbers emigrating or dying from accidents, diseases and food shortage.

- The populations of predators and their main prey are closely linked. They fluctuate together, the numbers of prey determining how well predators survive and reproduce.

Investigations

1 Duckweed is a small green plant often found floating in ponds and waterways. It has two small leaves which float on the surface with a thin root dipping into the water. Duckweed can multiply very quickly and can clog a waterway with thousands of plants. It seems to be a particular problem in ponds which have been polluted with farmyard manure. Explain why the duckweed is such a problem in these ponds. Plan an investigation to check your explanation.

2 Weeds are plants which grow well in areas where they are not wanted. What makes them so successful? List factors that makes a weed like dandelion so good at colonising areas of waste ground. Arrange your reasons in a list with the most important one first.
Plan a series of investigations to check whether your predictions are correct.

Evolution

20

Learning objectives

By the end of this chapter you should be able to:

- **recall** that living things have changed during the Earth's history
- **explain** what fossils are
- **list** evidence for the past existence of life forms
- **explain** how the environment can encourage changes in organisms
- **explain** why different populations can become different species

- **understand** Darwin's main ideas
- **explain** what is meant by 'survival of the fittest'
- **describe** the evolution of one species
- **understand** why organisms which cannot adapt to change may become extinct
- **list** the reasons for conserving wild plants and animals

20.1 The changing Earth

The Earth has changed a great deal since its formation about 4500 million years ago. Living things have had to cope with these drastic changes. Simple life forms have evolved into complex multicellular organisms, and a huge variety of living things has appeared, flourished and disappeared. The study of evolution describes how living organisms change with time.

The Earth's crust is still changing very slowly. The continents are carried on overlapping, slow-moving plates of rock (called tectonic plates) which make up the crust. When the first living things colonised the land from the oceans, the plates formed just one huge landmass, across which the animals and plants spread. Then, about 150 million years ago, the supercontinent split into blocks, separated by seas. Each block carried living things, which became less and less able to interbreed with populations on the other blocks. In each area species changed in different ways.

What can we learn from fossils?

Preserved remains of ancient plants and animals, called **fossils**, give us clues about what has lived on Earth in the past. Preserved burrows, nests, footprints, tracks and feather marks provide indirect evidence, and direct evidence comes from preserved body parts. A fossil's age can be estimated roughly by:

- finding the age of the rocks in which it is found
- comparing it with other fossils in the same sorts of rock.

Amber is fossilised sticky resin which oozed from the bark of trees about 300 million years ago. Animals preserved in amber look as they must have done when they were alive. They are so well preserved that, using an electron microscope, scientists can even examine their cellular structure.

Fossils of marine molluscs, like these ammonites, are fairly easy to find because these animals were hard shelled, abundant and died in sediments. But scientists might find only single fragments of less common species.

When an animal or plant dies its soft parts decompose, but its hard parts (bones, teeth, lignin and shell) resist decay and are more likely to be preserved. These parts can become encased in rock as the sandy or clay sediments around them are gradually compressed. Animal and plant material can also become petrified – minerals gradually replace the dead material as it disintegrates. Some fossils show very fine details such as scale patterns and tree rings.

Remains are best preserved by conditions which slow down or stop decomposition – even soft tissues can be preserved if decay is slowed down. Very well preserved fossils have been found in waterlogged bogs where there is little oxygen, in glaciers, and in tar pits where chemicals inhibit decay.

Piecing together a skeleton, or a sequence of fossils, is very difficult because skeletons are often scattered, distorted, and even lost through being compressed into rock by earth movements, and through erosion.

We know how animals and plants work from studying living things. We can apply this sort of knowledge to fossils, to work out what ancient species were like, and how they lived. For example, we know that a flat-topped fossil tooth with ridges is likely to have come from a herbivore, because we know that this shape is an adaptation for crushing vegetation. If the fossil tooth is 10 cm wide it is likely to have come from a large jawbone, in a very large head. Pollen fossils trapped in peat bogs and sediments tell us about the type of vegetation nearby, and so what the local environment was like. The climate at the time can be deduced from the vegetation. However, fossils can't tell us everything about extinct species. For example, dinosaurs are often pictured in green, sandy and brownish colours, like modern crocodiles and turtles, but they could just as easily have had red, yellow and black stripes like some snakes.

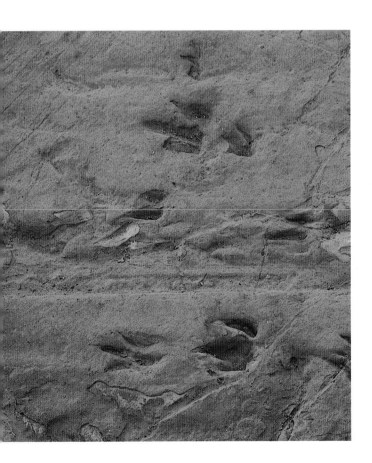

Dinosaur footprints in fossilised dried mud give us evidence of how heavy the dinosaur was, how fast it was running and how long its legs and stride were.

We know that the blood pressure needed to push blood to the top of a giraffe's neck is very high. So we think that dinosaurs like this diplodocus, which had very long necks, probably carried them horizontally, or had very large hearts.

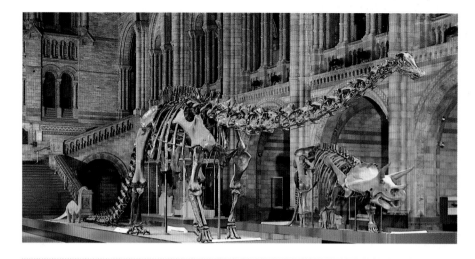

LORETO COLLEGE LIBRARY MANCHESTER

1 Look at the photograph of the diplodocus skeleton, above, and work out as much as you can about the creature.
   a How big was it?
   b Do you think it walked on two legs or four?
   c What do you think it might have eaten?
2 Look at the photograph of dinosaur footprints on page 189.
   a How many toes did the dinosaur have?
   b Do you think the dinosaur was walking or running?
   c What modern animal makes similar footprints? What clues does this give you about the way the dinosaur might have held its body and tail while running?

Summary of the changing Earth

• The Earth's shape and climate have changed much since it was formed.

• Fossils are the preserved remains of plants and animals. Tracks, nests and burrows may be preserved as well as bones and teeth.

• Fossils are formed when minerals replace the organic materials of dead animals and plants.

• We interpret fossils to reconstruct the structure and way of life of animals and plants which died millions of years ago.

20.2 **Development of species**

Why do species change?

In order to grow and reproduce successfully, living things have to be able to cope with the world around them. Many different species compete for the same habitat. Organisms with features which allow them to survive in a particular habitat are adapted to that habitat. Unfortunately the environment does not stay stable for long – it is changed by physical forces and by the effects organisms have on it. Species must also be able to adapt to environmental changes. Species which cannot adapt could become extinct.

Polar bears have many features that make them well adapted to their freezing habitat.

Adaptation to the environment involves many features of an organism's body. Some individuals have better combinations of features than others and are more likely to survive and reproduce. For example, adaptation to a cold environment involves many different inherited features, which all contribute to effective heat generation and conservation:

- thick insulation, such as fat layers
- different types and lengths of hair or feathers, which trap air
- an ability to retain heat within the body instead of losing it through exposed skin, feet or beak
- a surface colour that absorbs the Sun's warmth
- an ability to use a wide range of food sources to obtain energy
- a body shape that reduces heat loss
- oily surfaces that prevent water reaching the skin.

Improving any one of these features increases the chances of survival and reproductive success in a cold climate. If the features are heritable, they could be passed to the next generation. Individuals with favourable features have a selective advantage. Less well adapted individuals are less successful in the struggle for resources. They may breed less well, producing fewer or smaller offspring in riskier sites, or they may not get the chance to breed at all.

What is natural selection?

Darwin found a species of marine iguana on the Galapagos islands that lives on the shoreline and eats seaweed, instead of living in trees, eating fruit and vegetation as mainland iguanas do. This species is not found anywhere else in the world.

Our current ideas about the way species develop and adapt were put forward by Charles Darwin and Russell Wallace during the 19th century. Since then further scientific discoveries have supported their main points and given us an understanding of how changes in species come about.

Charles Darwin sailed round the world aboard *HMS Beagle* on a mapping voyage. The ship visited little-known places, including South America and the Galapagos Islands. Darwin's job was to record the plants and animals they encountered. The voyage provided much new and thought-provoking information and raised many questions.

- Fossilised remains of sea creatures were found near the tops of South American mountains. Darwin realised that the Earth must be much older than was generally believed at the time for the dead animals and surrounding sediments to have turned to stone, then be thrust upwards to become part of the Andes mountains. Life had been on Earth for longer than people originally thought. What had happened during that time?
- The diversity of animals and plants, many very different from those in Europe and Africa, was great, even though the climates were quite similar in many places. Why were there so many kinds of animals and plants?
- There were fossils of giant animals which resembled living animals. Why had they died out? Why were the 'modern' animals smaller than the extinct ones?

Darwin was particularly interested by the animals living on a very isolated group of islands, the Galapagos Islands, in the Pacific ocean. The animals were similar to some South American species but in some ways they were very different. Some Galapagos species, like the marine iguanas and the giant tortoises, are not found anywhere else in the world. Each island in the Galapagos had its own population of animals which were slightly different from similar species on other islands in the group. Some species were found on only one remote island, some colonised several neighbouring islands.

Darwin wondered how and why differences between species arose, and what determined whether a particular plant or animal survived. Wild animals and plants have to struggle to survive against the climate, compete for food and space, resist disease and evade predators. Darwin reasoned that individuals with favourable features are better able to exploit their surroundings, survive and successfully raise offspring. He knew that differences between domestic breeds of animals and plants are caused by people selecting particular individuals as parents. Could some sort of selection be happening in the wild?

Another scientist at the time, Russell Wallace, had similar thoughts as he observed the diverse wildlife and intense competition in South East Asia where he worked as a forester. Darwin and Wallace jointly put forward their ideas on **natural selection** as the force which brought about changes in species. Natural selection is a mechanism of evolutionary change, as described in figure 1.

Natural selection

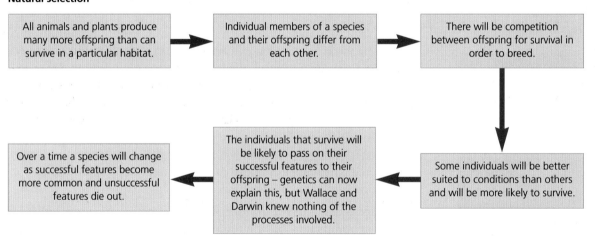

Figure 1

Darwin called this idea the **survival of the fittest** – organisms with favourable combinations of features are more 'fit' to survive than others. In this context 'fitness' means being able to survive and bring up young in a particular environment. Some of the critical features and differences which make an organism better adapted to its environment are inherited and successful organisms are likely to pass these features on to their offspring. Gradually these features become more common in a population, and less favourable features disappear. The environment effectively forces a genetic change in the population.

Darwin and Wallace thought that species changed gradually in response to their environment. After a very long time a population of plants or animals

3 Explain what is meant by the terms 'natural selection' and 'survival of the fittest'.

might be so different from its ancestors that it would be a new species, more 'fit' to survive in its habitat. Two populations of the same species living in different environments may change in very different ways, in response to their own local conditions and ultimately the two populations may become different enough to be considered as two different species. So, the populations of animals on the Galapagos islands adapted to their particular environment. They could not breed with animals on other islands because of the deep, cold water and the distances between the islands, so new features were not shared between islands. Darwin saw life on Earth as a gradual progression, with living things constantly developing to exploit the wide range of available habitats.

The case of the peppered moth

The peppered moth, *Biston betularia*, rests on tree trunks with its wings spread out. Its markings camouflage it well against the bark of silver birch trees encrusted with lichen. Until 1848 naturalists found only light-patterned moths but then a black, or melanistic, moth was found in Manchester. More and more black moths turned up in the industrial cities, and fewer light moths. By the end of the 19th century nearly all the moths found in Manchester were black. However, in the country most moths were light and very few dark forms were found. What could have caused this rapid change in the cities?

In the 1840s Manchester bacame an industrial region and tree trunks became coated with black soot. The few mutant black moths in the population were better camouflaged against the tree trunks than the light moths, which stood out and were easily visible to predators. The black moths had a selective advantage and survived longer to breed – and to pass on their black gene. The dark form is due to a dominant mutation (see chapter 18, *Genetics*) so it spread quickly through the population.

These light and dark peppered moths are two different forms of the same species, which are suited to different habitats.

4 Why were light forms of the peppered moth still common in the country regions? Light forms still turned up in Manchester – how or where did these come from?

5 Explain why the black coloured moth spread more rapidly as a dominant mutation than it would have if it were recessive.

Do disadvantageous features always die out?

At first sight a genetic disease would not seem to be an advantageous variation. The gene causing sickle-cell anaemia (see chapter 18, *Genetics*) is found in people in West Africa and the eastern Mediterranean, and in people whose ancestors came from these areas. The sickling gene makes a haemoglobin that does not carry oxygen well. People with a normal gene from one parent and the faulty gene from the other are not badly affected because they have some normal haemoglobin. But people with two copies of the faulty gene are severely affected and may die without medical intervention.

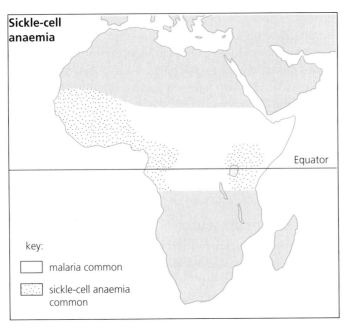

Sickle-cell anaemia

Equator

key:

☐ malaria common

⬚ sickle-cell anaemia common

Figure 2

If this gene is so disadvantageous, why is it still so common in some parts of the world? People with two sickle genes obviously have no advantage because they die before they have children but perhaps having one copy of the gene is advantageous. If you look at the map in figure 2 you will see that the distribution of the sickling gene covers areas where malaria is common. Malaria is caused by a protozoan that lives in red blood cells and digests haemoglobin. Children become infected with it soon after birth, and many die. Children with a single copy of the sickling gene were found to have a significantly better chance of surviving this malaria. The parasite seems to be less able to infect red cells with some sickle haemoglobin than normal red cells.

How can two populations become two species?

It takes more than one difference to make a new species. The development of a new species takes tens of thousands of generations. Even with short-lived organisms such as bacteria, the evolution of penicillin resistance took many years and millions of generations of bacteria. Fossils can show the changes which produce new species, where we have a complete enough record (figure 3).

Biologists think that new species can develop from isolated groups of animals or plants. The isolated group has only a small selection of the gene variations found in the whole species, and some inherited features might not be carried by any of the group. The isolated group interbreeds and passes its genes onto future generations. Features that improve adaptation to the local environment are more likely to be passed on and become more common, while less favourable features become more rare. Rare genes could disappear altogether, while new features could come from chance mutations to existing genes. After a long time the balance of genes in the isolated population becomes very different from that of the original species elsewhere, and they may possess unique new features. Darwin discovered that this had happened to the finches living in the Galapagos islands (figure 4)

Since Australia and Europe separated from the main supercontinent 150 million years ago, their mammal species have followed different evolutionary paths. Both kangaroos and deer are large, grazing mammals, but a young kangaroo develops in its mother's pouch while young deer develop for much longer inside the mother's uterus.

Figure 3

6 Look at figure 3. Describe how the horse's foot has evolved over the generations, as indicated by the fossils found.

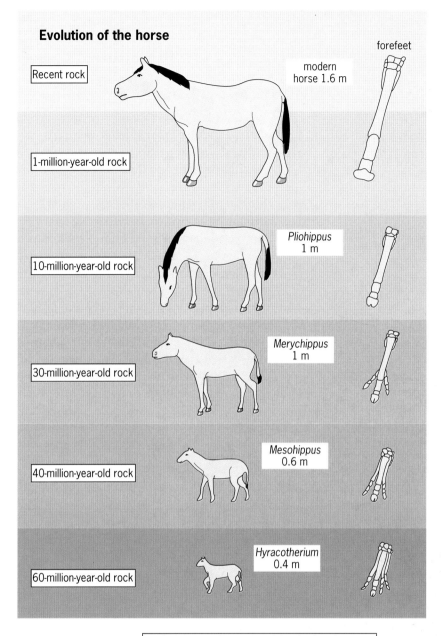

Evolution of the horse

Recent rock

1-million-year-old rock — modern horse 1.6 m — forefeet

10-million-year-old rock — *Pliohippus* 1 m

30-million-year-old rock — *Merychippus* 1 m

40-million-year-old rock — *Mesohippus* 0.6 m

60-million-year-old rock — *Hyracotherium* 0.4 m

7 Why do you think the Galapagos finches show such a wide variety of adaptations compared with finches on the South American mainland, which is only 600 miles away?

Figure 4

Galapagos finches

Darwin suggested that, following their volcanic origin, the Galapagos islands were colonised by plants and animals from the mainland – including a small group of finches.

The finches gradually spread to all the islands in the group, but the finches had to adapt to the different feeding conditions on their particular island. Some ate only seeds (like their mainland ancestors), while others developed into wood borers, fruit eaters and insect eaters.

The finches spread over widely separated islands did not interbreed and developed into separate species.

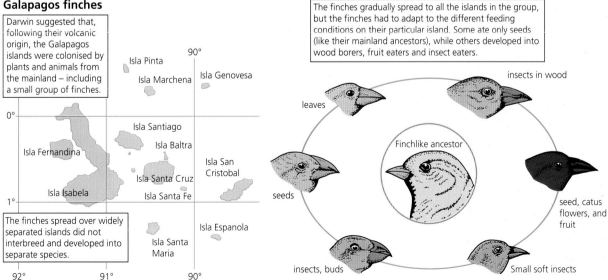

leaves

insects in wood

seeds

Finchlike ancestor

seed, catus flowers, and fruit

insects, buds

Small soft insects

How do we know that species have shared ancestors?

Each of us has genes that we have inherited from our grandparents through our parents. Our grandparents' genes have also been passed to our aunts and uncles, so we have genes in common with our relations. Trace your family tree, and you will find that you have genes in common with the descendants of your great-great-aunts, whom you might not even know — you are related through your common ancestry. Animal and plant species inherit genes from their ancestors, which are passed on to the ever-widening range of offspring. Species that have evolved from the same ancestors are related and have genes in common. The more closely they are related the more genes they have in common (figure 5). These genes can be detected by examining the DNA, and the structure of vital proteins.

Related species also share successful features and body structures. However, the structures may have adapted differently for different ways of life. The pentadactyl (or 'five-fingered') limb pattern is shared by all the vertebrates that evolved after the fishes. Although they all have the ability to make the basic limb pattern, it is heavily modified for different ways of life.

Figure 5

Looking at relatedness

Biologists examining fossil bones had to use similarities in bone shape to group together the ancestors of apes and humans, and to work out when ape ancestors diverged from human ancestors. This 'traditional' family tree shows very early branching.

gibbon
pygmy chimp
chimpanzee
human
gorilla
orang-utan

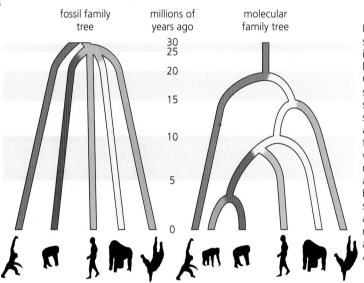

fossil family tree

millions of years ago

molecular family tree

30
25
20
15
10
5
0

Now we can look at similarities between important biochemicals, like haemoglobin, or RNA. Chemicals with the same structure are made by the same genes, inherited from shared ancestors. This allows a wider range of features to be evaluated when deciding the relationships between ancestral species. The tree based on these techniques shows that humans and apes diverged more recently, and that humans are close relatives of the African apes.

How quickly can species change?

Some species, like sharks, which live in a stable environment, may not change in millions of years – there isn't much pressure to change a species if it is optimally adapted to its environment. However, the fossil record shows that changes *can* be quite rapid. Extinctions are often followed by evolution of huge numbers of new species. These bursts often coincide with major climatic changes, such as the retreat of ice after the ice ages. Perhaps the environmental changes forced animals and plants to adapt rapidly. The fossil record is not very precise – a fossil that is slightly earlier than another in a sequence could be 75,000 years older. This is a long time compared with the 50 years it takes for colour changes in peppered moths, or the 25 years required to evolve insecticide resistance in insects.

Summary of development of species

- Charles Darwin explained how new species develop from pre-existing species.
- Darwin recognised that the environment was a key factor in the survival of species. Individuals which are well adapted to their environment are able to survive and reproduce better than less favoured individuals.
- Favourable features can be passed on to offspring to give them an advantage over other members of a species.

- In a sooty industrial city, dark peppered moths are better camouflaged against predators than light forms and will eventually replace the light form.
- Even harmful genes such as sickle haemoglobin can have an advantage in a particular environment.
- New species can arise from populations which are separated from the rest of their species. They adapt to their particular habitat.
- Different species which have developed from the same ancestral species share genes and structures in common.

20.3 **Extinctions**

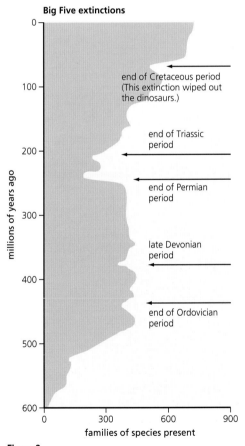

Big Five extinctions

end of Cretaceous period
(This extinction wiped out the dinosaurs.)

end of Triassic period

end of Permian period

late Devonian period

end of Ordovician period

millions of years ago

0   300   600   900
families of species present

Figure 6

We think that about 50 billion species have evolved on the Earth, but fewer than one in a thousand of these are around today. Fossil records show that species survive for an average of about 4 million years and then disappear.

- Some evolve into something else, different enough to be a new species.
- Some live in just a few places and disappear when hit by a series of natural disasters such as disease and floods.
- Some species are out-competed by others with better adaptations to a changing environment.

There is evidence for five periods of mass extinctions in the past, when a very large proportion of fossil species disappeared at the same time (figure 6). There was one mass extinction about 65 million years ago when the big reptile groups were declining. Up to 50% of the aquatic and 20% of the land-dwelling animal species died out, including dinosaurs, many mammals, marine animals and plankton. A large proportion of plants disappeared at the same time. A mass extinction which affects a wide range of habitats and ways of life has to be caused by something that normal adaptability cannot cope with. A popular hypothesis is that the Earth was hit by giant meteorites which threw dust into the atmosphere, blocking light and warmth from the Sun. The rocks formed at the time of the extinctions contain plenty of an unusual element called iridium, found in meteorites, which supports this hypothesis.

Should we try to prevent extinctions?

The giant mammals of prehistoric times, such as mammoths and giant elk, disappeared as the human population started to expand. We might have hunted them to extinction.

Many species have died out because of human activity.

- Some have been hunted to extinction for food or because they threatened humans or their farms.
- Some did not have enough suitable habitat left to maintain reasonable populations.

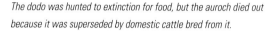

The dodo was hunted to extinction for food, but the auroch died out because it was superseded by domestic cattle bred from it.

If the number of individuals in a species becomes very low, we say the species is endangered. Many people believe that we should try to conserve such species, and organisations all over the world work hard to prevent them becoming extinct (see chapter 21, *Human effects*). Conservation sites can be set aside as habitats for endangered species but they must be able to support breeding populations.

There are very few black rhinos left in the wild, despite efforts to save the species' habitat and protect the animals from poachers.

The European lynx is endangered. To help preserve the species, animals from a captive breeding programme are being released into the wild.

- The population must be big enough to carry the full range of genes — including rare genes.
- Breeding members of the population must be able to choose unrelated mates, to avoid having only a small selection of gene varieties passing to the next generation.
- There must be enough different groups in the population so that animals can move from one to another. Many social animals leave their own group to find a mate in another.
- There should be enough refuges and breeding places for animal species. This can be difficult for migratory species that need overwintering sites or resting places on a migratory route.

Some animals are nearly extinct in the wild. A zoo can help a species to survive by breeding it and reintroducing animals into the wild. The breeding population is likely to be small and closely related, even if animals from several zoos are collected together, because zoos send their surplus animals to other zoos. A well planned breeding programme tries to keep the range of genetic features as wide as possible.

What are gene banks?

Crops have been **selectively bred** from wild plants for increased yield and easier harvesting. Unfortunately useful genes can be lost during the process. Crop breeders need the wild relatives of crop plants for useful genes like resistance to disease.

Small plant colonies in the wild are vulnerable to all kinds of dangers, including trampling, flooding, careless collecting or hungry slugs. Endangered plants are grown and propagated in botanical gardens but large populations take up space so seeds of some rare plants are conserved in gene banks. A gene bank is a collection of seeds kept in cool dry conditions. It allows plant scientists to keep a large number of potential plants in a small space. Some of the seeds are used to raise new plants from time to time to replenish the stocks. Although many seeds keep for a few years some plants will only grow from very fresh seed so these have to be grown continuously. A wide range of specimens has to be grown to keep as much genetic diversity as possible.

Frozen sperm and embryos can be stored in animal 'gene banks', and used in breeding programmes for endangered animals. A small sample of frozen rhino sperm can be sent to a zoo half way round the world more easily and safely than an adult male! At the destination zoos the sperm is used to artificially inseminate females.

Summary of extinctions

- Genetic resources are lost when species become extinct or endangered.
- Genes of some species can be maintained in a gene bank.

Investigations

1 As dark forms of the peppered moth became more common scientists attempted to find an explanation for the increase. Three explanations were offered:

a Dark moths absorbed warmth from the Sun better than light forms and were able to complete their life cycles more quickly. In smoky cities where little sunlight penetrated dark moths had an advantage.

b The change in colour was due to caterpillars eating dark-coloured pollutants on leaves in cities.

c Dark moths would be better camouflaged in cities than light forms and would be better able to survive predation by blue tits.

Plan an investigation to test each of these hypotheses.

21

Human effects

Learning objectives

By the end of this chapter you should be able to:

- **explain** the term 'ecological footprint'
- **explain** how human impact on the environment relates to population size and consumption per person
- **define** and use the term 'biodiversity'

- **list** the factors that tend to reduce biodiversity
- **describe** measures that attempt to preserve and extend biodiversity
- **describe** the factors that affect the size of an ecological footprint for people, buildings and transport systems

21.1 People and the environment

How do people affect the environment?

Just like other animals, human beings need food and water, clean air supplies and shelter to stay alive. We also produce a range of waste products. It is because we use things and produce wastes that we have an effect on the world around us.

When the human population was small, the impact on the global environment was small. As the population increases, its effects become more widespread and more serious.

Population size is not the only factor affecting the environment. Different people consume different amounts of raw materials and produce different amounts of wastes. The more sophisticated our technology becomes, the greater the effect of human populations on the world. For example, a few people with electric chain saws can cut down more trees than a much larger number of people with axes. Environmentalists use the term **ecological footprint** to describe the effect we have on the world (figure 1). The size of the footprint depends on how much we *take out* and how much we *put back*.

----

1 a What do the figures in this table say about the ecological footprint of a typical person living in the USA, and in Ghana in Africa?

b How important are **i** population size, and **ii** consumption per person, in terms of human impact on the global environment?

	USA	Ghana
population (millions)	246.3	15.5
energy consumption (GJ per person, per year)	278	3
steel consumption (thousand metric tonnes per person, per year)	103	779

Figure 1

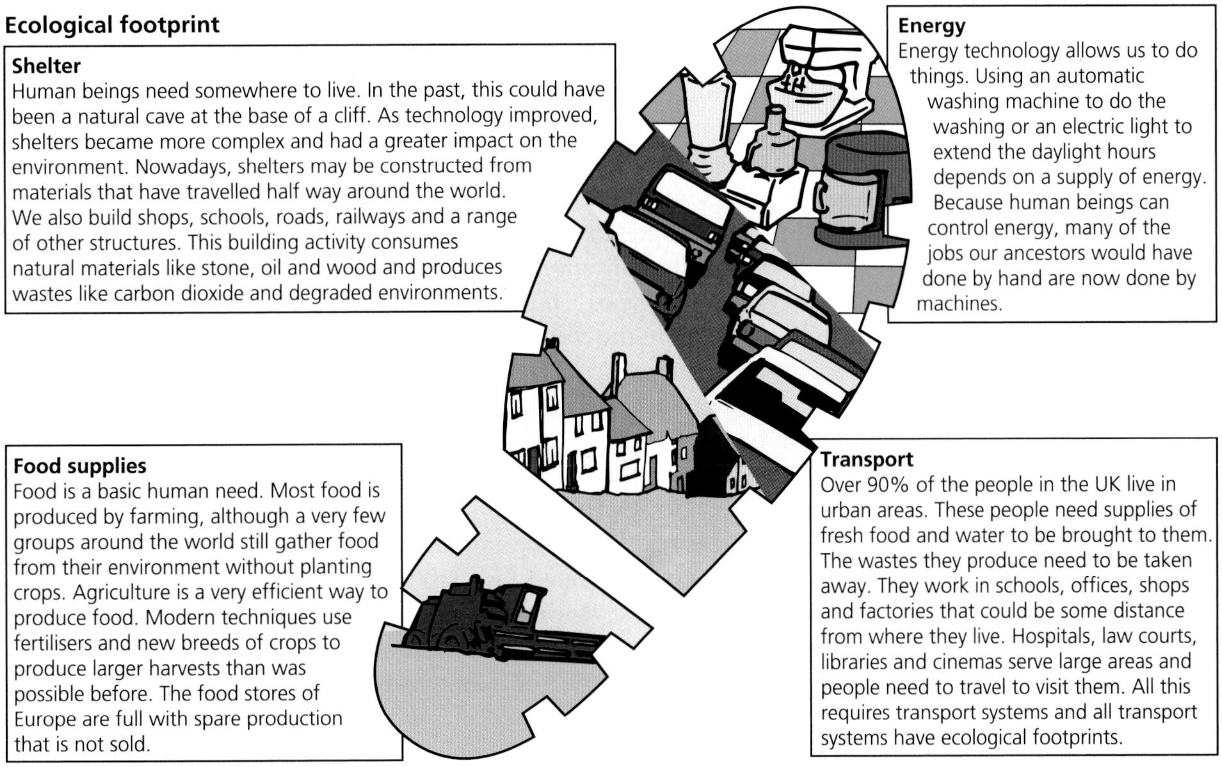

Ecological footprint

Shelter
Human beings need somewhere to live. In the past, this could have been a natural cave at the base of a cliff. As technology improved, shelters became more complex and had a greater impact on the environment. Nowadays, shelters may be constructed from materials that have travelled half way around the world. We also build shops, schools, roads, railways and a range of other structures. This building activity consumes natural materials like stone, oil and wood and produces wastes like carbon dioxide and degraded environments.

Energy
Energy technology allows us to do things. Using an automatic washing machine to do the washing or an electric light to extend the daylight hours depends on a supply of energy. Because human beings can control energy, many of the jobs our ancestors would have done by hand are now done by machines.

Food supplies
Food is a basic human need. Most food is produced by farming, although a very few groups around the world still gather food from their environment without planting crops. Agriculture is a very efficient way to produce food. Modern techniques use fertilisers and new breeds of crops to produce larger harvests than was possible before. The food stores of Europe are full with spare production that is not sold.

Transport
Over 90% of the people in the UK live in urban areas. These people need supplies of fresh food and water to be brought to them. The wastes they produce need to be taken away. They work in schools, offices, shops and factories that could be some distance from where they live. Hospitals, law courts, libraries and cinemas serve large areas and people need to travel to visit them. All this requires transport systems and all transport systems have ecological footprints.

Quarrying and mining

Modern buildings contain rocks. These rocks have been dug from the Earth's crust in a quarry, shaped, processed and finally transported to building sites. Some types of rocks change dramatically between quarrying and use. For example, bricks are made of clay but look nothing like the raw clay extracted from the ground. The ecological footprint for a building depends on the materials used to build it, the way they were extracted, modified and transported, and any waste produced during the process.

Quarries can be very large and can change the shape of the landscape dramatically. After the quarry is worked out and no useful rock remains, the area is usually landscaped so that it looks as natural as possible. The mineral industry prides itself on the care it takes to restore land.

Unfortunately, some of the most valuable quarries are in areas of outstanding natural beauty. Quarries in the Peak District National Park extract limestone for buildings and for the chemical industry. It is very difficult to decide whether it is better to have new buildings and roads or an intact National Park. Many complex issues must be faced when deciding whether to develop a new quarry, or to extend an existing one.

Energy consumption

Everyone in the world uses energy to get things done. All this energy use has an ecological footprint.

Most of the world uses wood for heating and cooking. In the past the low consumption meant that trees could grow so that a new supply of wood was created as quickly as existing stocks were used up. Wood is a good example of a renewable resource. A renewable resource constantly replaces itself, so it should never run out. However, consumption has increased recently. In many areas of the world local supplies of wood are being used up more quickly than they can be replaced. The loss of trees has important ecological effects, including changes in the climate which can convert low-productivity drylands into non-productive desert. A renewable resource is becoming a non-renewable one. Non-renewable resources can only be used once and are then gone forever.

Oil and gas are non-renewable resources. They were produced millions of years ago by the decay of plants and animals, and are now available for use. Energy is used in manufacturing and maintaining the machinery that extracts the oil. Energy is used to move the oil to the consumers, and to process crude oil into useful products. However, the largest part of the ecological footprint is probably the wastes that oil and gas produce when they burn. Changes in the atmosphere created by increased energy use may be the biggest single threat to the Earth's biosphere.

The ecological footprint of a technology depends on how efficiently it does its job. An efficient technology will have a smaller footprint than an inefficient one because it uses less raw materials and produces less waste. Intermediate Technology is a charity that is trying to reduce the ecological footprint of cooking stoves in India. IT has worked with university departments and local people to produce a more efficient cooking stove, which uses much less fuel than traditional stoves. Table 1 shows the effects of some different technological industries.

In Burkina Faso people use fuel wood for cooking. The consumption is four times faster than the forests can sustain – local damage to the environment is inevitable.

The damage to the atmosphere by excessive use of fuels in the developed world has global implications.

Table 1 Products and effects of some modern technological industries.

Industry	Useful products	Negative effects
Mining	metal ores which can be refined to produce metals, materials for construction	spoil heaps of contaminated rock, contamination of water supply, loss of landscape
Farming	food and drink, clothing (e.g. cotton, flax), timber	animal wastes, loss of diversity, loss of habitats
Chemical industry	useful products (e.g. plastics, drugs, foods)	industrial pollution (e.g. acidic solutions, toxic solutions)
Energy industry	heating, transport, entertainment	waste gases such as carbon dioxide and other acidic gases

Year	Consumption (kW)
1500	0.9 – 1.9
1800	0.9
1900	0.4
1950	0.9
1975	2.3

2 The table (left) shows the average daily fuel use per person in Denmark, for heating and cooking.

a Explain how changes in technology might be responsible for changes in energy consumption in Denmark between 1500 and 1975. How are these changes likely to have affected the ecological footprint of energy use in Denmark?

b Predict likely changes in the ecological footprint of energy use in Denmark *since* 1975 and give reasons for your predictions.

Summary of people and the environment

- An ecological footprint is an estimate of the impact a person, a country or a technology has on the Earth.
- Ecological footprints include measures of resources used, wastes produced and the efficiency of any technology involved.

- Ecological footprints tend to get larger as population size and consumption per person rise.
- Efficient technology can reduce the size of an ecological footprint.

21.2 Managing wastes

How can we manage our biological wastes?

We consume food and produce faeces and urine just to stay alive. When the human population was small, this waste could be allowed to decompose naturally in the environment. Now that our population is so large, and that so many of us live in crowded urban areas, our wastes must be carefully managed. The organic waste produced by humans is called **sewage**. However, most of what flows through sewers is water rather than sewage, so it is now known as **waste water**.

Waste water from homes contains a very dilute mixture of human faeces and urine (table 2). Industrial waste water is a more complex mixture containing a range of other chemicals. Sometimes these extra chemicals can cause major problems for waste water treatment engineers.

Table 2 *Average water use per person in the UK, per day, in litres. Source: Severn-Trent Water.*

Activity	Use
Washing and bathing	42
Toilet flushing	37
Washing clothes	24
Dish-washing and cleaning	13
Drinking and cooking	6

3 Use table 2 to answer these questions.

a An average toilet flush uses 9 l of water, and an average person uses the toilet five times a day. If during that time they produce 1 l of urine, what is the concentration of urine in the waste water from the toilet?

b Use other relevant figures from table 2 to calculate the eventual concentration of the urine in waste water.

Human sewage is very rich in nitrogen-containing compounds. A range of micro-organisms called decomposers can digest these chemicals and convert them to nitrites, nitrates and harmless nitrogen gas which is released into the atmosphere. At the same time the micro-organisms break down other organic chemicals to carbon dioxide and water. In a carefully managed sewage treatment works, the outflow should be clean water. When the works is overloaded or damaged in some way, problems can occur.

Decomposers need oxygen to break down sewage. The biochemical oxygen demand, or BOD, is a measure of how much oxygen is needed to convert the sewage to harmless chemicals (see table 3).

Table 3 *Typical BOD levels in different liquids.*

Liquid	BOD (mg/l)
Treated domestic sewage	20 – 60
Raw domestic sewage	300 – 600
Dilute dairy parlour and yard washings	100 – 2000
Liquid sewage sludge	10 000 – 20 000
Cattle slurry	10 000 – 20 000
Milk	140 000

When water with a high BOD is discharged into a river, decomposers in the river try to finish the job begun at the works. As they do so, they use up a great deal of oxygen in the river water. This changes the ecology of the river dramatically (figure 3).

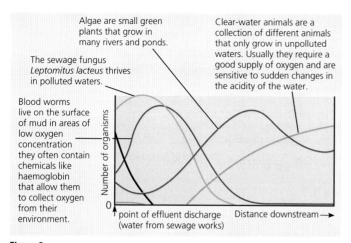

Algae are small green plants that grow in many rivers and ponds.

The sewage fungus *Leptomitus lacteus* thrives in polluted waters.

Blood worms live on the surface of mud in areas of low oxygen concentration they often contain chemicals like haemoglobin that allow them to collect oxygen from their environment.

Clear-water animals are a collection of different animals that only grow in unpolluted waters. Usually they require a good supply of oxygen and are sensitive to sudden changes in the acidity of the water.

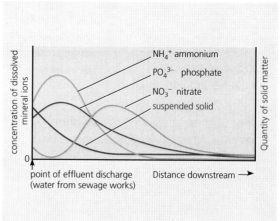

Figure 2

4 **a** Sketch a rough graph to show the amount of oxygen dissolved in river water at increasing distances downstream from a sewage outlet discharging water with a high BOD.

   b Use information from the graphs in figure 2 to explain the shape of the oxygen graph you have drawn.

5 Explain the distribution of each of these organisms in the river described in figure 2.

   a algae   **b** sewage fungi   **c** blood worms   **d** clear-water animals

What is acidic gas pollution?

Problems with sewage and waste water tend to be local. Other waste problems occur on a larger scale. For example, acidic gases produced by our energy technology can do damage many hundreds of miles away from the area where they were produced.

Most of the energy human beings use comes from burning fuels in oxygen. These fuels can be derived from living plants (wood, straw) or from the remains of long dead plants and animals (coal, oil and natural gas). One thing that all fuels have in common is that they produce acidic gases when they burn. These acidic gases are a source of dangerous pollution.

When fuels burn, they react with oxygen to produce a range of compounds. These compounds depend on:

• the type of fuel
• the combustion temperature
• the supply of oxygen.

All fuels contain carbon, which burns to form carbon dioxide. Unfortunately, some of them also contain sulphur which reacts with oxygen during combustion to give sulphur dioxide.

In the past, people got rid of the sulphur dioxide by building tall chimneys which took the gas high into the air. By the time it drifted to ground level again, it had been diluted so that it was less dangerous. It had also been blown a distance of some miles so that the original producer of the pollution did not have to suffer its effects!

Fuels need oxygen to burn, and this is usually supplied as a blast of air. But air also contains the gas nitrogen, and at certain temperatures nitrogen and oxygen react together to produce a range of compounds called nitrogen oxides, often abbreviated to NOx. The major source of nitrogen oxides in the UK now is motor vehicles.

carbon + oxygen → carbon dioxide

sulphur + oxygen → sulphur dioxide

nitrogen + oxygen → nitrogen dioxide

What are the effects of acidic gas pollution?

The effects of acidic gas pollution depend on the concentration of the gases in the mixture and how readily the victim reacts to the pollution. Lichens are simple, slow-growing plants that have a large surface area and absorb a lot of chemicals from the air, so they are very sensitive to air pollution. Some grow on trees, others on rocks, gravestones and buildings. Lichens have been used to monitor the amounts of air pollution in an area, and have disappeared completely from some badly polluted cities (figure 3).

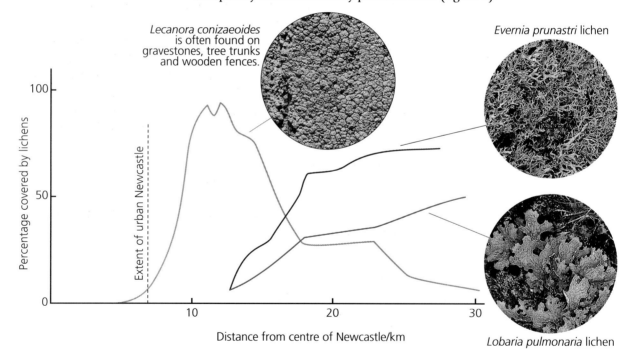

Figure 3 Cover of ash trees by lichens in relation to distance from Newcastle city centre.

6   The levels of sulphur dioxide in the air have been found to be high in the centre of Newcastle, and to decrease with distance from the city centre. Look at the graph in figure 3.

a Describe any pattern you can see in the growth of lichens and the distance from the centre of Newcastle.

b Why do you think different species of lichens show different patterns?

c Explain how the growth of lichen could be used to assess air quality in a city.

Among human beings, it is the young, the old and people with breathing difficulties that are most easily hurt by acidic gas pollution. In 1952 a particularly bad smog killed 4000 people in five days in London. Smog is a mixture of smoke and fog. The smoke contains the acidic gases from burning fossil fuels. Fog is a suspension of tiny water droplets in the air. When the acidic gases dissolve in these, they produce tiny droplets of sulphuric acid. The smog in London was particularly dangerous because the lack of wind at the time kept it at ground level and did not disperse the pollution over a wider area. The smog increased the death rate for Londoners by more than the cholera epidemics of the 19th century. It was as if London was in the middle of an acidic rain cloud.

What is acid rain?

In most cases the acidic gases from burning fossil fuels rise and are diluted by winds. But if the gases react with water droplets in rain clouds, the rain falls as a dilute solution of acid. This is called acid rain.

Rain is naturally slightly acidic because it reacts with carbon dioxide from the air as it falls. However, the extra acidity produced by burning fossil fuels can have major, long-term effects. These effects depend on the concentration of the acid in the rain and the area where it falls. Some areas of a country are much more easily damaged than others.

Acid rain can fall straight into lakes, or drain through the soil into them. At first an affected lake becomes very clear, because the acid kills the microscopic plants and animals that live in the water. Then some of the larger plants and animals die. Some organisms benefit from this dose of acidity, because their competitors die out. For example, dragonfly nymphs and whirligig beetles grow in larger numbers than normal. However, this change in the ecology of the lake can lead to the death of fish, as their food supplies are reduced overall. The acidity can also help toxic aluminium salts to dissolve in the water. Aluminium ions are particularly dangerous and kill fish and fish-eating birds like osprey. Even birds nesting around acid-damaged lakes are affected, and tend to produce eggs with weaker shells which break before the young bird is ready to hatch.

How can the effects of acid rain be reduced?

There are two ways to deal with acid rain:

- repair the damaged lakes
- prevent the formation of acid rain.

Lime is used to neutralise excess acidity in many lakes. This treatment is expensive and needs to be done regularly. Few environmentalists see this as a permanent solution. One Norwegian activist said it was 'like taking an aspirin to cure cancer'.

Since acid rain forms when there are excess acidic gases in the air, the way to prevent it forming is to prevent the gases from being released. This means reducing the sulphur content of fuels and carefully controlling the combustion conditions in boilers and furnaces. If low-sulphur fuels cannot be used the waste gases can be cleaned before they are released. The gases are passed through a basic mixture which absorbs the sulphur and nitrogen oxides to give a cleaner exhaust gas. This is called **scrubbing**. Many scrubbers also include systems to clear fine dust and ash particles from the gases.

The European Union has passed laws which insist that all industrial boilers over a certain size, including power stations, must be fitted with acid gas scrubbers. This should reduce the emissions of acidic gases at source and so reduce acid rain. A similar initiative now means that all new cars are fitted with **catalytic converters** which convert nitrogen oxides into nitrogen.

The other way of reducing acidic gas production is to reduce our dependence on energy from fossil fuels by developing more energy systems with smaller ecological footprints.

7 **a** List the ways the problem of acid rain can be tackled.

b Which method is most likely to have the greatest effect? Give reasons for your choice.

c Why do you think acidic gas pollution became a major problem before people began to think seriously about solving it?

Summary of managing waste

- Renewable resources can last forever because they regenerate themselves at least as quickly as they are used up.
- Non-renewable resources can only be used once, because they do not regenerate.
- All human beings and other animals produce organic wastes that are rich in nitrogen compounds.
- Increases in populations of humans or other animals can overload the environment with nitrogen-rich wastes, and so lead to local pollution.
- Waste water treatment works use natural processes to treat large amounts of organic waste.
- All fuels produce acidic gases when they burn in the air.

- The amount of acidic gas pollution depends on the type of fuel, the combustion temperature and the amount of oxygen supplied.
- Sulphur dioxide (SO_2) and nitrogen oxides (NOx) are the most dangerous acidic gases.
- Acid rain forms when acidic gases dissolve in falling rain.
- Acid rain can be prevented by reducing emissions of acidic gases. Acid-damaged lakes are treated by liming.

21.3 Global warming

What is global warming?

Acid rain is a problem that affects complete countries and travels across national borders. **Global warming** is a pollution problem that has a global effect. The average temperature of the Earth changes according to rules we do not completely understand. It seems that human beings might be causing a rise in temperature that they cannot control, and which could lead to catastrophic changes in the living conditions on our planet. This rise in temperature is called global warming.

Most incoming sunlight passes straight through the atmosphere to the Earth's surface. The Earth's surface absorbs roughly half of this energy and converts it to heat. The heated Earth radiates this energy back into space as infra-red radiation, which has a longer wavelength than sunlight. As long as the overall rate at which heat energy is absorbed from the Sun is matched by the overall rate at which energy is radiated into space, the global temperature will not change.

The atmosphere and oceans redistribute energy across the Earth as they move. This reduces temperature differences between the various regions of the globe, and helps to create the weather conditions in all parts of the Earth. The energy transfer system is stable, but chaotic – it shows continual, unpredictable changes that always fall within particular limits.

Some scientists think that changes in the atmosphere caused by industrial pollution are damaging the Earth's energy transfer systems. They believe that increased levels of some gases in the atmosphere reduce the amount of energy radiation from the Earth's surface back out into space. They predict that this **greenhouse effect** could lead to a rise in the global temperature and melt the polar ice-caps. Sea levels would then rise and many low-lying land areas would be flooded.

Gases that tend to reduce energy radiation from the Earth are called **greenhouse gases**. Greenhouse gases include carbon dioxide, methane and water vapour.

8 a Study the charts in figure 4 on pages 210 and 211, and list the factors that will tend to:

   i increase global temperature

   ii decrease global temperature.

b Which factors are easiest for human beings to control?

How does the Earth respond to changes in the atmosphere?

9 a What feedback loops can you find in figure 4?

b Sort these loops into positive and negative loops.

c Choose one of the positive loops to explain why they are so dangerous.

10 What evidence can you find to link global temperature and carbon dioxide levels in the atmosphere?

An increase in the level of carbon dioxide in the atmosphere will raise the Earth's temperature. However, an increase in the carbon dioxide level will also increase the rate of photosynthesis in plants. This will reduce the levels of the gas in the atmosphere, which in turn lowers the global temperature. This link is called a **negative feedback** loop because an increase in one factor (the carbon dioxide level) makes the system work to reduce the levels of that factor.

A **positive feedback** loop happens when an output tends to increase the production of itself. Positive loops are very dangerous because, once they start to act, they can be very difficult to stop.

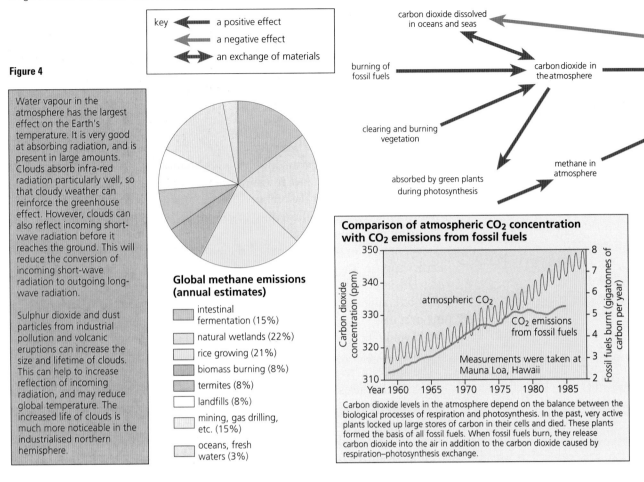

Figure 4

key ⬅ a positive effect

← a negative effect

⬌ an exchange of materials

Water vapour in the atmosphere has the largest effect on the Earth's temperature. It is very good at absorbing radiation, and is present in large amounts. Clouds absorb infra-red radiation particularly well, so that cloudy weather can reinforce the greenhouse effect. However, clouds can also reflect incoming short-wave radiation before it reaches the ground. This will reduce the conversion of incoming short-wave radiation to outgoing long-wave radiation.

Sulphur dioxide and dust particles from industrial pollution and volcanic eruptions can increase the size and lifetime of clouds. This can help to increase reflection of incoming radiation, and may reduce global temperature. The increased life of clouds is much more noticeable in the industrialised northern hemisphere.

Global methane emissions (annual estimates)

intestinal fermentation (15%)

natural wetlands (22%)

rice growing (21%)

biomass burning (8%)

termites (8%)

landfills (8%)

mining, gas drilling, etc. (15%)

oceans, fresh waters (3%)

carbon dioxide dissolved in oceans and seas

burning of fossil fuels

carbon dioxide in the atmosphere

clearing and burning vegetation

methane in atmosphere

absorbed by green plants during photosynthesis

Comparison of atmospheric CO$_2$ concentration with CO$_2$ emissions from fossil fuels

atmospheric CO$_2$

CO$_2$ emissions from fossil fuels

Measurements were taken at Mauna Loa, Hawaii

Carbon dioxide (ppm) concentration — 350, 340, 330, 320, 310

Fossil fuels burnt (gigatonnes of carbon per year) — 8, 7, 6, 5, 4, 3

Year 1960 1965 1970 1975 1980 1985

Carbon dioxide levels in the atmosphere depend on the balance between the biological processes of respiration and photosynthesis. In the past, very active plants locked up large stores of carbon in their cells and died. These plants formed the basis of all fossil fuels. When fossil fuels burn, they release carbon dioxide into the air in addition to the carbon dioxide caused by respiration–photosynthesis exchange.

Summary of global warming

- The levels of certain gases, called greenhouse gases, affect the way radiation passes through the atmosphere.
- Radiation trapped by the atmosphere probably tends to raise the temperature of the Earth, although conclusive proof of this is not yet available.
- Plants and animals maintain a balance of carbon dioxide concentration in the atmosphere.
- Burning fossil fuels has upset the balance of carbon dioxide in the atmosphere over the last few hundred years.

21.4 Biodiversity

What is biodiversity?

Damage to the Earth by humans reduces the chances of survival for many species – and increases the survival chances for others. Humans seem to have reduced the variety of organisms alive, and this is now causing concern. Biologists use the word **biodiversity** to describe the range of living things.

It is easy to encourage people to protect individual species, particularly cute, furry ones like harp seals or attractive ones like tigers. It is much more difficult to encourage protection for a complete collection of animals and plants, some of which appear to have no use.

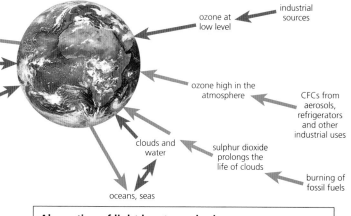

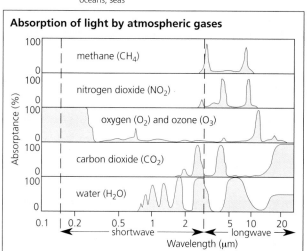

Ozone absorbs mainly in the ultraviolet (UV) range of the spectrum. CFCs are chemicals that react with ozone in the higher levels of the atmosphere and break it down. This means that more UV light can penetrate to lower levels. This UV light may be involved in the increase in skin cancers across the globe. Another effect of ozone layer destruction is that the lower levels of the atmosphere tend to cool more quickly. This reduces global warming. However, ozone in the lower atmosphere can act as a greenhouse gas and absorb some infra-red radiation. At the moment, scientists think that the cooling effect of ozone loss at the top of the atmosphere is slightly greater than the greenhouse effect of ozone at the bottom.

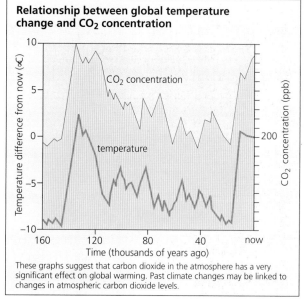

Relationship between global temperature change and CO_2 concentration

These graphs suggest that carbon dioxide in the atmosphere has a very significant effect on global warming. Past climate changes may be linked to changes in atmospheric carbon dioxide levels.

Maintaining biodiversity is really about maintaining ecosystems. Tropical rainforests contain between 50% and 90% of all species, although they only cover about 7% of the land on Earth. The only way to preserve this enormous biodiversity is to preserve the rainforest intact, rather than selecting certain organisms that are worthy of protection. This all-or-nothing approach can be expensive, as even careful development of rainforests can damage biodiversity.

When all the members of a species have died, the species is said to be **extinct**. Extinction is a natural part of the living world. Species have been becoming extinct for millions of years and will continue to become extinct in the future. At the same time, new species develop. However, the rate of extinction, particularly of large mammals, seems to have accelerated over the last few thousand years. This is probably linked to the way human beings use the world.

Elephants and rhinos are two species of large mammal that are threatened with extinction. Human beings have helped to make extinction more likely by:

- hunting the animals for valuable products
- destroying their natural habitat.

Both of these factors also affect the number of primates in South East Asia and the fate of whales across the oceans.

This brazil nut tree has died because the forest around it has been cleared to create pasture. Essential parts of the tree's biotic environment have been destroyed, so it could not survive. Protecting individual species is impossible if their habitat is destroyed.

African elephants

The African elephant is one of the largest land mammals. The number of living elephants is now so low that the species is classified as in danger of extinction by the United Nations Environment Programme. The total number of elephants in the whole of Africa fell from 1.2 million in 1981 to 764 000 in 1987.

People are now much more aware of the need to protect species and their habitats, and the African elephant story looks as though it will turn out to be a success. One of the reasons is that much of the elephant's natural habitat is now in protected areas, as shown by table 4.

Table 4 *Data on the African elephant's habitat. Source: World Resource, 1989.*

Habitat	Original range (x 1000 km^2)	Percentage of original range remaining	Percentage of original range now in protected areas
Forest	26 512	72	<5
Bushland/grassland	4126	29	31 – 40
Mountain	6086	14	11 – 20
Woodland	62 672	38	21 – 30
Forest/grassland	27 726	35	5 – 10
Bushland	29 447	21	21 – 30

11 Calculate the date when African elephants would become extinct, if their numbers continued to fall at the steady rate described in the text.

Elephant tusk and rhino horn are extremely valuable in the markets of South East Asia. Elephant tusk provides the ivory for a range of decorative uses while rhino horn is an essential ingredient in some traditional oriental medicines.

The elephant has been protected for years by the Convention on Trade in Endangered Species (CITES) but the amount of money that can be made has encouraged organised crime to take up elephant hunting. Ivory from Zaire, Angola, Zimbabwe, Botswana and Malawi is shipped through South African cities like Johannesburg, Durban and Cape Town to world markets. In 1992 the South African police confiscated 1300 ivory cubes. In 1993 the number rose to over 22 000 cubes — the equivalent of 2700 tusks. The poachers cut the tusks into cubes because they are easier to hide. Sometimes they dye them brown to make them even more difficult to detect. The best hope for elephants and rhinos is an agreement signed in Lusaka in September 1994. It sets up a special police force to tackle poaching of ivory and rhino horn and hopes to reduce elephant hunting throughout Africa as effectively as it has done in Tanzania and Kenya. The success of this body depends to some extent on funding. It needs to attract one million dollars a year, at 1995 prices, to operate. This sum of money may be all that stands between the elephant and extinction.

Summary of biodiversity

- Biodiversity is the name given to the range of different species alive at any one time.
- Human beings have tended to reduce biodiversity by destroying habitats and hunting individual species to extinction.
- Protection of individual species and biodiversity depends on international agreements.
- CITES is the international organisation that tries to control the trade of products from endangered species, such as ivory from elephants.

Learning objectives

By the end of this chapter you should be able to:

- **explain** how farming has changed the landscape
- **describe** how a farmer can improve the soil
- **list** ways in which a farmer can increase the yield of crops and animals
- **explain** how breeders improve crops and animals

22.1 Development of farming

When did farming begin?

Agriculture started in the Middle East about 10 000 years ago. Before this, people gathered plants growing wild and hunted animals for their food. During the Stone Age people learnt to cultivate the wild ancestors of beans, peas, chickpeas and lentils. The practice of growing crops such as these spread to the Mediterranean and reached Britain by the Iron Age. There are very few hunter-gatherer societies left in the world today.

Farm animals were developed from wild species that live in social groups and have a way of life that can be manipulated to suit humans. Domestic dogs came from wolves, which live and hunt co-operatively. A pup's instincts allow it to fit in with human family structure. Sheep, goats and cattle became domesticated by the Stone Age. Cattle were used for pulling carts as well as for their milk, meat and leather. Farmers learned to neuter male animals to make them easier to handle. Other species, such as camels and llamas, were domesticated in other parts of the world. Some animals, like deer and bees, are exploited without being fully domesticated.

How did farming affect our landscape?

After the last Ice Age, Britain was covered by forest and small communities farmed in natural clearings. Gradually, the woods were cleared for crops, grazing, fuel and building material. People tended their animals while they grazed and moved them from place to place to take advantage of the best grazing.

By medieval times land was being cultivated in strips using **crop rotation**. In a rotation, crops are planted in a particular order to allow for their differing needs and to reduce pests and diseases. You can see an example of a crop rotation system in figure 1.

Figure 1

Crop rotation

Year 1 onions, peas and beans. Peas and beans enrich the soil's nitrate content.

Year 2 root crops, such as carrots and beetroot.

Year 3 brassicas, such as cabbages and kale.

Year 4 The land is rested by allowing it to lie fallow. Animals are grazed on the fallow field to add manure before the cycle begins again.

Between 1346 and 1665, plagues reduced Europe's population by about a third. There were fewer people to look after the livestock so farmers created fields with hedges or walls to keep the animals in one place. This made the landscape of woods, fields and hedgerows that we are familiar with in Britain today.

How can different terrains be used?

Soils and land vary, and some areas are more useful and productive than others. Loamy soils are excellent for grass (as long as there is enough rain), which supports dairy and beef cattle. Light soils are more suitable for growing cereals and root crops. Steep hillsides are difficult to cultivate unless they are terraced, but grapevines grow well on them and sheep are agile enough to graze them. Sheep and deer do well on moorlands, which are unsuitable for crops. Moorlands are also used for forestry.

Land with only limited agricultural potential is described as marginal. In some cases areas that are not suitable for agriculture can be improved – for example, wet land can be drained to improve grazing or crop yield. Some land is set aside for forestry and leisure uses instead of agriculture so surplus crops are not produced.

Fields are enlarged by removing hedgerows to accommodate machinery for ploughing, sowing, tending and harvesting crops.

Do animals and plants have to be cultivated to be useful?

1 List the qualities that would make a species useful for cultivation. Give reasons for your choices.

Some species of plants and animals are very common in their natural habitat and no special effort is needed to fulfil the demand for them so they are collected from the wild. Examples of these include herbs, scented and medicinal plants, frogs, cockles and winkles. Collecting provides a useful income for families in many parts of the world. However, the demand for some products has increased so much that they are over-collected. Eels and sturgeons are disappearing from European rivers because they are caught before they can reproduce. To prevent species from dying out because of over-collection, they must be cultivated. Many products, for example medicinal plants, are being brought into cultivation, particularly if they are collected from a remote part of the world, grow in adverse climates or in parts of the world that are politically unstable.

Plants

Hundreds of different plant species have been cultivated by humans over the centuries, to produce a whole range of different products (see table 1).

By cultivating plants and animals, we can obtain large amounts of the materials we need without depleting the wild stocks. The amount of crops and farm animals that can be produced by farming depends on:

- their genetic capacity for growth
- how well the conditions the animals or plants are kept in match their needs
- how many are lost due to the effects of other organisms – animals feeding on the crops, parasites or disease
- how well competitors, such as weeds and grazing wildlife are controlled.

Table 1 *Products that can be obtained from cultivated plants.*

Product	Part of plant		
	Tubers and roots	Stem and leaves	Flowers and seeds
Staple foods	potatoes	rice, wheat,	barley, maize
Flavours	ginger, garlic	chives, dill	fennel, cumin
Food garnishes/luxuries	radish	maple syrup	chocolate, dates, strawberries
Medicines	yam	foxgloves	poppies
Perfumes	orris	sandalwood	lavender, roses
Textiles and fibres		sisal, sea grass	cotton, hemp, jute, flax
Materials		latex, paper	kapok
Construction materials		wood for planks, poles, posts, fences, chipboard, MDF, thatch	
Pasture, animal fodder	mangold	grass, clover, alfalfa	
Pleasurable items		tobacco	tulips, lilacs, chrysanthemums

Fisheries

The demand for fish has increased as the human population has increased but recently the total mass of fish being caught has dropped. Wild fish must reproduce as least as quickly as they are caught if the population is to survive. Fish breed when they are big enough, but they take longer to mature in unfavourable conditions. Fish lay their eggs in spawning grounds, usually in the warmer shallower waters relatively close to the shore which are the main fishing grounds. The sea is full of hazards for eggs and young fish, and very few survive long enough to reach breeding age. For example, only about one in every 85 000 North Sea cod survives past its first birthday.

Fewer young fish are surviving long enough to breed and replace those caught and the numbers of fish such as the herring have plummeted because of over-fishing. Fishermen have been set limits, or quotas, on the amount of fish they are allowed to catch in an effort to halt the decline. Quotas limit the size and total mass of a fish species that can be landed, but they do not control what the fishermen actually catch and throw back into the sea.

It is difficult to manage stocks of wild fish well because we don't know:

- how many fish there are
- the age structure of the populations
- how many young fish survive to spawn
- whether there is enough food for the fish at their different life stages.

About 12% of fish supplies come from farmed fish. Several species are farmed, although trout and salmon have replaced the very bony perch, which were kept in fish ponds for many centuries. Shellfish, such as oysters, scallops and mussels, are also being cultivated. Farmed fish live in large mesh cages in the open sea or in lakes and are fed a balanced pelleted diet. When the female fish are ready to spawn their eggs are carefully squeezed out and mixed with sperm taken from male fish. The fertilised eggs are kept in controlled tanks so that a large proportion will survive.

2 How does artificial fertilisation improve the productivity of a fishery?

3 Some fish farms take advantage of waste warm water from power stations to improve yields. Why do they get a better yield?

4 Explain what is meant by the terms 'quota' and 'over-fished'.

5 Haddock and cod are very different in size when mature but they swim together in mixed shoals of various ages. What would the effects on the larger species be if the fishing net size that was used was the right size for catching the smaller species? What do you think would happen to fish of the 'wrong species' that were caught?

6 Cod are important predators of shrimps, scampi, dabs and other commercially valuable fish. What effect could measures to conserve cod stocks have on these other species?

7 In the North Sea the most important fish predators of other fish are whiting and cod. Devise a fisheries policy which makes use of this information.

8 Construct a list of ten products that are collected from the wild, rather than farmed.

Bees

Bees that are kept for honey production still live in a semi-wild state in hives, where thousands of sterile female workers tend the queen, eggs and young bees. They also forage for food, defend the nest and build the honeycomb. The queen stays in the nest, tended by the workers. She is specialised for egg-laying. A grid keeps the queen in the lower part of the hive – the smaller workers can pass through the grid to fill the cells with honey stores.

Each day worker bees fly out to collect nectar and pollen from flowers and carry it to the nest where it is used as food for the young bees. The bees convert nectar into honey at night. Nectar tastes of the flowers it comes from and flavours the honey, so beekeepers will often move the hives to different areas to obtain different flavours of honey. Towards the end of the season the combs are taken out of the hive and the honey extracted by centrifuge. The bees are allowed to keep some honey to last them over the winter.

Visiting hives are an advantage to orchard growers because bees are important pollinators. As bees forage, thay take pollen caught on body hair to the next flower they visit. Bees tend to visit one type of flower at a time, which improves fertilisation and, therefore, fruit and seed production.

Honey bees comb the pollen they have collected from flowers into a **basket** made of long hairs on each hind leg.

9 Why is the queen bee barred from most of the honeycomb?

10 The flowers of runner beans have a long tubular structure and only heavy bees with long tongues get at the nectar. Some bees have learned to stick their tongues through the back of the flower to get the nectar. Explain why this will lead to poor yields.

Summary of development of farming

- Farming practices change the landscape.
- Wild plants and animals can be exploited as well as cultivated or domesticated species.
- The proper management of fish stocks has become critical with increased demands.
- Managed bees are important pollinators of commercial orchards.

22.2 Improving crop yield

What conditions do crop plants need to grow well?

Crop productivity is measured by the mass, or yield, of saleable plant material harvested from a given area of land. The harvested material, whether it is wheat seeds, lettuce leaves or fence posts, is the result of successful photosynthesis by the crop plants.

Factors that affect the rate of photosynthesis are important in crop growth. Some of these, such as the carbon dioxide concentration and the temperature around crops can only be controlled in greenhouses, but other factors such as water and mineral supply can be improved outdoors. However, anything that increases yields costs money, so farmers have to make a trade-off between the money they spend on improving yield and the extra money these improvements will earn.

Plants grown too close together compete for light and soil water and will not grow as well as plants grown further apart. However, if the spaces between plants are too large the farmer won't get the maximum yield from that field. There is usually an optimum spacing for each crop variety that the farmer needs to use to get the best yield.

How can a farmer improve the nitrate content of the soil?

Plants need minerals to grow (see chapter 9, *Water balance*) and the concentration of nitrate and ammonium ions in the soil often limits crop growth. Most of the nitrate in the soil comes from decaying plant and animal material. Plants are able to take up this released nitrate, but it is very soluble and is quickly washed through the soil by rainwater. To overcome the lack of nitrate in the soil, farmers add extra nitrate in the form of inorganic fertilisers and manure. Adding nitrate to the soil is an important way of increasing yield.

11 What do plants use nitrate ions for?

Inorganic fertiliser

Adding inorganic fertilisers to the soil is the quickest way of improving crop yield. Specially formulated fertilisers are sprayed onto crops at the appropriate times in the crop's growth cycle. Modern high-yielding crops need a high fertiliser input to obtain the best yield. The exact amount needed depends on the crop being grown – about 190 kg is applied to each hectare growing winter wheat. Farmers in developing countries may not be able to afford to grow the more modern crop varieties because of the high cost of fertilisers.

Manure

Manure is a mixture of animal faeces and bedding materials and contains partly digested plant material. When farm animal housing is cleaned out the dung is piled up and allowed to rot and mature. As it matures micro-organisms in the manure begin to break down the large nitrogen-containing compounds into smaller, more soluble compounds. Once the manure has matured, it is spread onto fields and microbes in the soil complete the breakdown into nutrients that plants can use. These microbes act most quickly when the soil is warm and moist, but this may not coincide with the time that crops need fertilising.

Adding manure to crops has other advantages as well as feeding the plants:

- The decomposing bulky material in manure holds water and improves the water supply to a crop.
- It sticks the soil particles together into granules. Air spaces between the granules allow roots to respire. Soil that is held together like this is also less likely to be eroded away by wind and rain.
- The soil surface stays soft so seedlings can emerge more easily.
- Manure provides food for earthworms and other soil-dwelling organisms. Earthworm tunnels act as drainage channels for water and allow air into the soil.

Many farms only grow crops and do not have a ready supply of animal dung. 'Green manure' is plant material which is ploughed into the ground while it is still growing. Soil microbes break down this material and release nutrients into the soil. Farmers can grow a green manure crop such as clover or alfalfa and grass as part of a crop rotation.

Can nitrogen-fixers improve crop yield?

Plants can't use nitrogen gas from the atmosphere for growth but a few bacteria and fungi living in the soil can. These are called 'nitrogen-fixers'. When these organisms die and decay nitrogen-containing compounds are released into the soil. Some of the organisms, such as *Rhizobium* and a few others are able to live independently in the soil, but grow better *inside* the roots of certain host plants. *Rhizobium* is found in nodules on the roots of legumes — peas, beans, clover and their relatives. Both partners benefit from this arrangement — the *Rhizobium* gains sugars and other materials made by the plant, and the plant uses the nitrogen compounds made by the bacteria. This is called a **mutualistic relationship**.

When they replant a field of grass, farmers sow a mixture of grass and clover seeds. The clover stimulates the nitrogen-fixing bacteria in the soil and they provide up to 175 kg of fixed nitrogen per hectare, improving the soil for the next crop. Scientists are attempting to transfer nitrogen-fixing genes into crop plants so that they don't need extra fertiliser.

12 What advantage does clover have as a green manure over other plants?

13 Draw up a table of the advantages and disadvantages of the various ways of increasing the nitrate content of soils.

How can the water-holding capacity of soil be improved?

Different soil types have different capacities for holding water, as figure 2 shows.

The amount of water in the soil depends on rainfall in the area and the structure of the particular soil. The soil's water-holding capacity can be improved by adding **humus** in the form of manure or plant wastes such as straw stubble. Humus improves clay soils by sticking the particles together into larger granules. Adding lime (calcium hydroxide) to clay soils has a similar effect and also reduces the soil's acidity.

Figure 2 Different soil types have different characteristics and hold water in different ways.

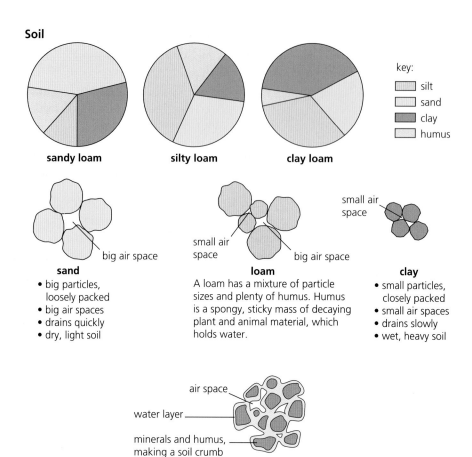

Soil

key:
- silt
- sand
- clay
- humus

sandy loam

silty loam

clay loam

sand
- big particles, loosely packed
- big air spaces
- drains quickly
- dry, light soil

big air space

loam
A loam has a mixture of particle sizes and plenty of humus. Humus is a spongy, sticky mass of decaying plant and animal material, which holds water.

small air space

big air space

clay
- small particles, closely packed
- small air spaces
- drains slowly
- wet, heavy soil

small air space

air space

water layer

minerals and humus, making a soil crumb

soil crumbs (enlarged)

Wet fields can be drained by land drains, which take advantage of any slope to drain water away to a lower area or stream. In dry areas irrigation ditches carry water to the fields in a network of channels from a stream or well.

Why are some crops grown in greenhouses?

Crops can be watered using overhead sprinklers while they are seedlings or when the crop is maturing. Black membrane placed between rows of crops reduces competition by weeds and evaporation from the soil.

A greenhouse traps the Sun's warmth so plants grow faster than they do outside. Greenhouses are used for crops that need extra warmth, are being grown out-of-season, fetch high prices or, like cut-flowers, have to be free of blemishes. The environment within a greenhouse can be completely controlled. It can be heated by electrical soil warming cables or hot water pipes if the weather is cold. Crops are regularly watered and fed by automated sprays and mists. Artificial lighting can supplement natural light or be used to change a plant's growth patterns. A greenhouse can be kept free of disease and pests by good hygiene and screens. Pests are easy to spot and are easily controlled by sprays or biological controls.

14 What expenses will the owner of a large automated greenhouse incur? To start you off:
  • cost of soil heating cable
  • electricity to warm the cable.

How are crop pests controlled?

Competition from weeds, and damage caused by insects, viruses and fungal diseases reduces the productivity of a crop. Farmers have to take measures to control these pests so they can obtain optimum yields from their crops.

Controlling weeds

Weeds compete with crops for light, soil nutrients and water and after harvest because they harbour pests and disease. They have to be separated before the crop can be sold or processed. Weed seedlings are ploughed under the soil to kill them before sowing crops. Weeds that appear later are removed or are killed with a herbicide. Herbicides which kill broad-leaved plants can be used safely on wheat and other cereals because cereals are not broad-leaved and are not affected by the herbicide. Some herbicide chemicals affect people. Workers must wear protective clothing when using them and they should only be used on food crops well before harvest so there is no risk of chemicals getting into the food.

15 Look at the graph in figure 3. Why is MCPA a useful weedkiller for farmers who want to grow wheat?

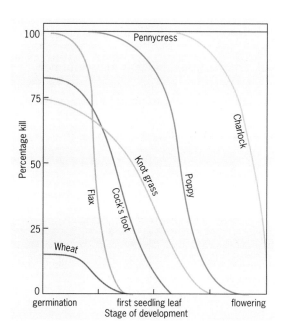

Figure 3 The effect of MCPA weedkiller on plants.

Controlling plant diseases

Most plant diseases are caused by viruses or fungi growing in the leaves and stems (see table 2). Fungi take the nutrients the plants make by photosynthesis so there is less available for the plant to grow or produce seeds, fruits and root stores. Viruses divert plant cells from their normal occupations into making more virus cells, and so reduce the yield. Fungicides are used to treat fungal infections but there are no cures for virus diseases. Old crop varieties often carried viruses but plant breeders have used micropropagation to raise disease-free plants (see Chapter 23, *Microbiology and biotechnology*).

These discoloured ears of wheat are infected with a fungus that produces a toxin, or ergot. A disease like this could seriously reduce a farmer's wheat yield.

16 What problems might a farmer face using a fungicide spray?

Table 2 Microbes and the ways they can damage crops.

Organism	Effect on crops
Potato blight *Phytophthora*	Blighted and virus-infected potatoes are smaller than healthy potatoes. The potatoes are inedible.
Potato leaf roll virus *Aspergillus flavus*	Mould grows on crops stored in warm, damp conditions. It produces a toxin (ergot) which harms animals or people who eat peanuts and grains contaminated by the mould.
Chocolate spot of beans	Fungi divert sugars away from roots, shoots, seeds and tubers, reducing growth and storage.

Plant diseases can be controlled in a number of ways:

- Using disease free seeds, tubers or bulbs to start the crop. Some varieties of plant may not legally be grown because even the seeds are heavily infected with the viruses.
- Dusting seeds with a fungicide before sowing kills germinating fungal spores before they can infect the crops.
- Burning diseased plant material left over from old crops to prevent new outbreaks.
- Controlling aphids, which carry many viruses from plant to plant as they feed.
- Removing wild plants, such as chickweed, because they harbour diseases.
- Using fungicide sprays to limit disease outbreaks.

Controlling pests

In warm parts of the world a locust swarm can ravage a farm in a day. The swarm travels from country to country, devastating crops. If the swarms are spotted they are sprayed from the air with an organophosphorus insecticide.

Wild animals – from greenfly to deer – eat crops and seeds. The larger animals can be discouraged by physical means such as fences, bird scarers and rabbit or squirrel-proof tubes round saplings. Insects and soil pests are very difficult to control and cause enormous amounts of damage. Aphids (greenfly) carry virus diseases and damage young shoots as they feed. They overwinter on wild plants and winter wheat, then infest newly sown crops the following year.

Farmers use chemical insecticides to control insect pests once their numbers pass a threshold level. Insecticides undoubtedly improve farmers' crop yields, but there are disadvantages to their use, especially in the longer term.

- Insecticides are expensive to use, so some farmers, especially those living in poorer areas, can't afford to use them.
- The insecticide might not actually hit the target pest.
- The chemical might degrade too quickly and therefore not be fully effective.
- The chemical might not degrade quickly enough and could leave harmful residues in the crops and soil.
- Many insecticides affect a wide range of insects, so indiscriminate spraying could kill beneficial insect predators such as lecewings and ladybirds as well as the pests.
- Insecticides such as malathion are toxic to humans. If they persist in crop food they could cause harm.
- Sprays can drift onto people, their gardens, their beehives and their pets, causing unforeseen damage.

What is biological control?

Biological pest control uses natural predators or diseases instead of chemicals to control pests. Biological controls are often used in greenhouses where the conditions are controlled and the concentration of predators can be kept high. Crops such as tomatoes, cucumbers and peppers are successfully protected by biological controls. Predatory mites are used to control red spider mite, *Encarsia*; a parasitic wasp controls whitefly by laying eggs in their larvae, and nematode worms are used to keep down populations of vine weevils and slugs.

Some animals can become pests when natural population controls are not in place. This is a particular problem if a new species is introduced into a country. European rabbits became a serious pest in Australia because there were few natural predators or competitors to keep their numbers in check. To control these animals a European rabbit virus, myxomatosis, was introduced, killed most of the rabbit population. Also in Australia, 60 years ago a beetle caused major damage to Australian sugar cane and cane toads were introduced to control the beetle. This they did successfully, but unfortunately the toads thrived too well, eating the native Australian wildlife. Their numbers have now reached pest proportions.

17 What are the advantages of using a biological control instead of an insecticide to control whiteflies in a greenhouse?

How can foods be stored after harvest?

After harvest, food crops may be spoilt before they can be used. They should be stored in cool, dry, rodent-proof stores because damp encourages moulds, warmth encourages grain sprouting, insect activity, and rats and mice may eat or seriously damage the crop. Grains are sprayed with insecticide to kill insect pests. Use of technology and an understanding of the causes of food spoilage have enabled us to develop methods of preserving foods after harvest. Some of these methods are described in table 3.

Table 3 *Methods of food preservation.*

Preserving method	How it works
Freezing (-20°C)	Very low temperature stops microbial growth.
Refrigeration (4°C)	Low temperature slows microbial growth.
Bottling/salting/making jam	High sugar and salt concentrations draw water from microbes. Boiling kills microbes, sealed jar bars entry to other microbes.
Drying	Too little water to support microbial growth in dried food.
Canning	Heating food to a high temperature kills microbes and a sealed tin prevents further entry.
Pickling	Vinegar lowers the pH of the food and inhibits microbial growth.
Smoking	Heat and the chemicals in smoke kill microbes. Smoked food is too dry to support microbial growth.
Pasteurisation	Heating to 72°C for 15 seconds then cooling rapidly reduces the numbers of souring microbes.
Irradiation	Gamma radiation from cobalt-60 kills microbes, spores and insects which infest grain. It also prevents stored grain from sprouting. Irradiation through sealed packaging prevents further contamination. Only limited use of irradiation is allowed on food in the UK.

18 UHT milk is heated very quickly to temperatures greater than 100 °C, then cooled. How does this help keep the milk fresh for longer?

19 Why does food stay fresh for much longer in the freezer than in the fridge?

20 Why does pasteurised milk go sour in the fridge?

Salmon can be preserved by smoking, but most is stored in tins.

Summary of improving crop yield

- Farmers must provide the best growing conditions for crops to achieve maximum yields.
- Farmers can change the water-holding capacity of their soil.
- Soil nitrate content can be increased by adding manure, compost, inorganic fertiliser, or by boosting nitrogen-fixing bacteria.
- Crops can be grown in controlled environments in greenhouses.
- Weeds compete with crops for resources.

- Insects and other pests eat or damage crops, causing losses. They are controlled using insecticides.
- Some pests can be controlled using biological controls.
- Fungi and viruses cause plant diseases, which lead to crop losses.
- Crops need to be protected from pests after harvest, to control losses.

22.3 Farming animals

Can animal husbandry be made more efficient?

Only a small proportion of the energy animals obtain from their food is stored in new biomass. They use much of this energy to keep warm, to graze and to interact with other animals. **Intensive rearing** is a way of making meat and egg production more efficient for a given food input. Intensively reared animals are kept in an environment where the ventilation, food supply, and the temperature are all carefully controlled. They spend less energy keeping warm and moving about so have more for growth. Fewer people are needed to care for them and only a small area of land is used directly so this system of animal production is more efficient. However, it does have extra costs for feed, heating and ventilation that standard farming practices don't have.

Animals have been bred especially for intensive rearing. Laying hens are bred for high production of brown eggs, while chickens reared for the table grow quickly to oven-ready weight and offer maximum breast meat yield because customers apparently do not like leg meat. Pigs have been selected to give birth to large numbers of young and to gain weight rapidly.

How are chickens farmed intensively?

Battery chicken farming is very highly controlled to obtain the maximum possible yield.

Most chickens are kept in battery cages to save land and labour in looking after them. The chickens break fewer eggs, and fewer gut pathogens such as *Salmonella* pass between birds, their faeces and eggs. Hens naturally lay fewer eggs in the winter so artificial 'summer' lighting is used to ensure year round production. Small amounts of food are mechanically distributed to the birds throughout the day, which reduces the energy they need to spend in looking for food. Automated spill-proof dispensers provide enough water for the birds' needs, but not so much that they develop leg problems from urine in their bedding. An egg collection system takes the eggs to a packing station.

21 Animals eat grain and vegetation. Review the section on pyramids of biomass and energy in chapter 19, *Ecosystems*, and then explain why more food is produced by land growing crops than land used for keeping animals.

22 Explain why chickens in battery cages really need more agricultural land than just the area covered by the shed.

23 The cost of feed accounts for about 70% of the cost of producing eggs. What other costs are there?

24 Why can dirty eggs be a health hazard?

How do animals cope with intensive rearing?

Domesticated animals have a complex social behaviour. Chickens have a pecking order in which a dominant chicken pecks less dominant chickens in competition for nest boxes, food and water. Birds at the bottom of the pecking order are pecked by the others and get least access to resources.

Intensive rearing does not suit chickens and they suffer feather pecking, broken bones and even cannibalism. Pigs naturally prefer to live in small groups and fight to establish their position in the hierarchy. In large intensively farmed groups, pigs that lose fights cannot escape and get badly injured. Pigs kept in individual stalls suffer because they need company and get bored. Pigs bred intensively do not make good mothers. The piglets often die because the sow lies on them, so she is kept in a farrowing crate, which stops her turning round and moving too quickly. The sow suffers because she cannot behave naturally by making a nest, and she may be kept in the crate all the time she is suckling the piglets.

Free-range systems of producing eggs, such as percheries and barns, where chickens are able to move around and have access to the outside, cost more to set up than intensive systems. The animals might also have problems with gut microbes and parasites, and eggs might get damaged and dirty, but they allow the hens to behave in a more natural way. Pigs allowed to live outdoors make better mothers and are more successful at raising piglets, although they have smaller litters than the breeds reared intensively.

Pigs that live in the open can root in the ground for forage and shelter in pig arks.

25 Draw up a table of the advantages and disadvantages of intensively rearing animals.

How do hormones improve yield?

Some animals are given growth hormones to improve the yield obtained from them – whether it's meat or milk. Bovine somatotropin (BST) is a natural hormone in cows and affects how the nutrients are used in a cow's body. Cows naturally have differing amounts of this hormone. The best milkers (which also tend to have leaner meat) often have more BST than other cows. This hormone can be made commercially by bacteria that have been genetically modified to carry genes for it (see chapter 18, *Genetics*, for more about genetically modifying bacteria). A cow given extra BST produces up to 25% more milk from the same amount of food.

There is controversy about the use of BST. Some consumers do not wish to drink milk which might contain BST residues because they think that it might harm them. There are reports that cows given BST are less healthy, and suffer more udder inflammation.

26 Construct a table of the advantages and disadvantages of using BST to increase productivity.

How are animal pests controlled?

Animals are plagued by blood-sucking ticks and lice which can carry disease, and warble flies which lay their eggs under the skin. Dipping an animal in insecticide helps to prevent infections. However, resistance to pesticides is appearing among insect pests as more and more of them are exposed to these chemicals. Often two or three pesticides are used in combination to overcome this resistance. Workers need to take precautions when using the chemicals.

Summary of farming animals

- Intensive farming aims to get more meat or egg production for a smaller energy input. There are animal welfare problems with intensive rearing.

- Farmers can manipulate an animal's metabolism to improve yield.

22.4 **Improving the breed**

What can be done to propagate the good features of plants?

Seeds grow into plants that are different from their parent plants because they carry a mixture of genes from each parent. The young plants may be better than, as good as, or worse than their parents in any particular feature – growth, resistance to pests, etc. Many plants with good characteristics are reproduced, using cuttings or tubers, to ensure that the good features are passed on. This is called **vegetative propagation**. Cuttings are genetically identical to the plant they were taken from – they are clones of the original. Geraniums and chrysanthemums are propagated from cuttings while strawberry plants are propagated by runners (this is shown in figure 4). Many horticulturally important plants are now produced by **micropropagation** (see chapter 23, *Microbiology and biotechnology*). Micropropagation needs more skill to perform than taking cuttings, but it is quicker and needs less space per plantlet.

Propagation

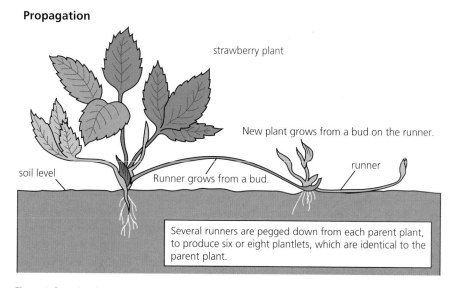

strawberry plant

New plant grows from a bud on the runner.

runner

soil level

Runner grows from a bud.

Several runners are pegged down from each parent plant, to produce six or eight plantlets, which are identical to the parent plant.

Figure 4 Strawberries are propagated vegetatively using runners.

Surprisingly, vegetative propagation can be used to produce plants that are *not* identical to their parents. For instance, fruit growers prefer to use small trees because they take up less space (so more can be grown in a field) and the fruit can be picked mechanically. Scientists have developed strains of fruit trees that are strong but which lead to a small tree. These are called dwarfing rootstocks. Cuttings from the desired full-sized apple or cherry strain are grafted onto the roots of a dwarfing rootstock, which restricts the final size of the tree but produces full-sized fruit (see figure 5).

Fruit trees

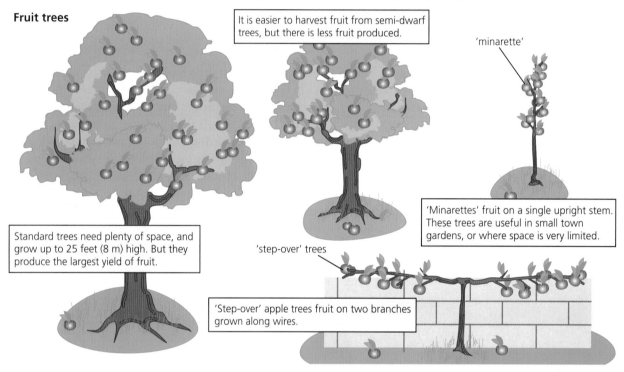

It is easier to harvest fruit from semi-dwarf trees, but there is less fruit produced.

'minarette'

Standard trees need plenty of space, and grow up to 25 feet (8 m) high. But they produce the largest yield of fruit.

'Minarettes' fruit on a single upright stem. These trees are useful in small town gardens, or where space is very limited.

'step-over' trees

'Step-over' apple trees fruit on two branches grown along wires.

Figure 5 Fruit trees are grafted onto specially bred root stocks which affect the final shape and size of the tree.

How does selective breeding improve breeds?

The plant and animal species used in agriculture exist as thousands of different breeds, varieties and strains. They differ from each other in a few key characters, which may be as small as the colour of the pods or a plant's final height. One breed of cow can easily mate with another breed, even though they may look very different, so they are not different species. Some breeds, such as Ronaldsway sheep, are very old and have become specialised for a particular environment. Farmers, and the environment, gradually select and develop a strain which suits them and which has distinctive features. Landraces are breeds that farmers have developed from local animals or plants. As agriculture has become more industrialised fewer breeds are being used and many of the older breeds are dying out.

Landraces may have unique adaptations. The ancient breed of Ronaldsway sheep can cope with cold weather and poor food.

Selective breeding of animals

Hereford cattle were originally developed 200 years ago to mature quickly and have meat that was marbled with fat and that had a high energy content and a fine flavour. However, today's consumers want lean meat and the Hereford is no longer considered an ideal breed. Cattle are now being bred for leaner meat by introducing genes from other breeds like the Charolais. Dairy cows have been developed by selective breeding to give nearly four times as much milk as older breeds, but now a different milk content is desirable and the breeders are at work again.

Breeders choose bulls and cows with desirable features, such as docility or good weight gain, to be parents. Nowadays, most bulls are kept at a stud farm, which provides sperm samples for artificially inseminating cows. The calves from the cross will probably inherit some of the desirable features of each parent and will be bred from in their turn, gradually improving the herd's quality. However, passing a good feature from adult to calf is governed by the same laws of chance as any other genetic feature. Calves may not inherit the desired features – even worse, they might inherit one desirable feature but lose others. Traditional breeding programmes take a long time to change the characteristics of a breed. Some important features are controlled by many genes and simple breeding programmes cannot change them much in the short term.

27 Give one advantage and one disadvantage of a farmer using artificial insemination to improve a herd of cows.

28 Why don't farmers keep their own bulls?

Selective breeding of plants

Cultivated wheat, rice and other cereals are very different from the wild grasses that were their ancestors. Farmers developed them by saving seeds from the tallest plants with the best seed heads, selecting for and encouraging genetic changes. Plant breeders want to improve certain aspects of crop production. For example, blackcurrant plants have been developed that produce their fruit on the edge of squarish bushes, which are therefore much easier to pick by machine.

In a traditional breeding programme, plants with the desirable characteristics are chosen as parents. Their seeds are grown on and assessed. The breeder hopes that the new young plants will have a better combination of features than either parent. A flow chart of a plant breeding programme is shown in figure 6.

29 Why are the male parts of flowers removed in plants chosen to carry seeds?

Commercial pea strains were bred not to waste energy growing tendrils.

Plant breeding programme

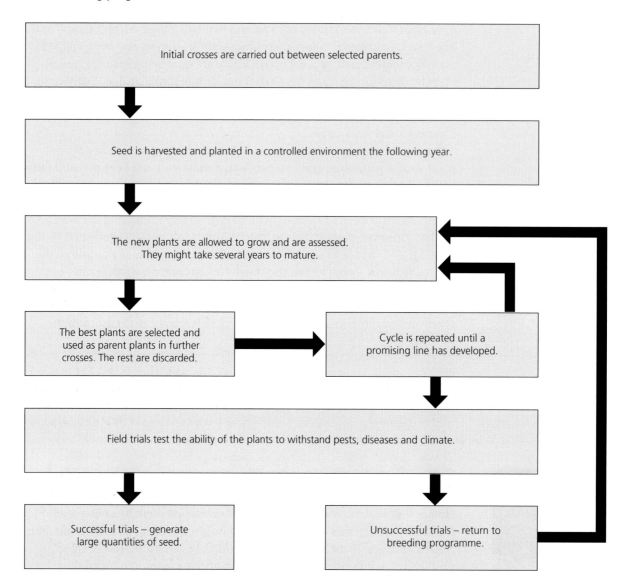

Figure 6 Careful breeding programmes can be developed to improve crops.

Is there a quicker way to improve a species?

It can be very difficult to introduce good features or remove undesirable features from plants that will not cross-breed. For example, the chromosomes of the broad bean are incompatible with those of other bean species so they won't cross-breed. Scientists have learned how to transfer genes from one plant species to another, and from microbes into plants to partially overcome this problem. Plant breeders can transfer a single desirable gene into an plant instead of carrying out a complex breeding programme.

The breeders' targets are to develop plants that:

- grow better in poor conditions
- are larger
- are more pest-resistant: a hybrid maize has been bred that can make a microbial toxin which kills stem-boring beetles
- have a longer shelf-life or are able to survive packing and transport
- have a better nutrient value
- have a higher yield
- are resistant to herbicides so farmers can use herbicide sprays to control weeds
- are more able to grow in soil contaminated with salt and metals
- can fix nitrogen.

Improving tomatoes

Tomatoes are difficult to get to market because they go soft shortly after ripening. They are picked before they are ripe so that they are firm enough to survive packing and distribution but they haven't much flavour at that stage. Just before they are sold the tomatoes are treated with a hormone to ripen them. Plant breeders have lengthened the shelf life of one tomato variety by inserting an extra copy of the gene for a ripening enzyme – but they deliberately put it in backwards. This reversed gene makes mRNA that neutralises the normal gene mRNA and results in less ripening enzyme being made. This is called 'antisense' gene technology. The modified tomatoes stay firmer when ripe and can be picked later with more flavour. The modified tomatoes also make thicker purees, which will make it cheaper for manufacturers to make soup and ketchup.

Many people are concerned about using genetically modified crops. Some say these products are unnecessary – for example, if people want less fat in chips then they should eat fewer chips and not genetically engineer potatoes to absorb less oil. Some plants are being genetically engineered to have a stronger resistance to viruses. This causes concern, since such plants could encourage the evolution of stronger, more harmful plant pathogens.

Can animals be genetically modified?

Plant breeders have succeeded in transferring new genes into plants, but it is much more difficult to transfer genes into whole animals. The aims of genetically modifying animals are:

- to improve the weight gain of animals
- to make animals more fertile
- to increase their ability to live in more marginal areas
- to increase their resistance to parasites
- to make new products.

Most genetic modification in animals has not yet passed the research stage. Some animals have been altered so that they produce human blood products in their milk, and soon there could be sheep that carry an insecticide in their skin cells and shear their own wool with a keratinase produced in follicle cells. You can find out more about animal gene technology in chapter 23, *Microbiology and biotechnology*.

Why should we conserve genes?

30 Look at table 4 below. Why should we be worried about the loss of vegetable varieties?

31 Some older breeds, which have fallen out of use, are conserved in special rare breeds farms. What are the advantages of conserving these species?

Selective breeding has led to each type of farming using a particular breed. For example most dairy farmers keep Friesian–Holstein cows and 60% of a region's rice crop may come from just one variety. Older breeds are disappearing, taking with them their potentially valuable characteristics (see table 4).

Monocultures, – areas where only one crop variety is grown in large expanses – are very vulnerable to disease. A fungus infecting a few plants in one part threatens the whole crop because all the plants are equally vulnerable. In wild populations, members of the same species are genetically different and some are naturally more resistant to infections than others. Efforts are being made by some groups to try to conserve species in gene banks so that genes can be reintroduced to vulnerable species (see chapter 19, *Evolution*).

Table 4 Reduction in commercial vegetable varieties in the 20th century.

Vegetable	Number of varieties available in 1903	Number of varieties available in 1992
Artichoke	34	1
Asparagus	46	1
Runner bean	14	1
Lima bean	96	8
Garden bean	578	32
Beetroot	288	17

Summary of improving the breed

• Large stocks of plants can be propagated vegetatively.

• Breeders use conventional techniques or genetic modification to improve crops and animals.

• Monocultures are very vulnerable to disease and whole crops can be wiped out.

Investigations

1 Farmers frequently put fertilisers containing nitrogen compounds on their fields in an effort to improve crop yield. List three forms of fertiliser. Devise an investigation into the effect of fertiliser on seedling growth.

2 Farmers need to get the spacing of their crops right. Planted too close together they compete for essential resources and their growth is reduced, plants spaced too far apart reduce the yield per acre. Devise an investigation into the effect of spacing on the yield of a crop.

Microbiology and biotechnology

23

Learning objectives

By the end of this chapter you should be able to:

- **explain** why microbes are so useful
- **describe** how bacteria and fungi are grown commercially
- **list** products that can be made by microbes
- **describe** how products are made by microbes

- **explain** the advantages of using tissue-cultured plant cells
- **explain** why genes are transferred into other organisms
- **discuss** some of the social and ethical problems raised by genetic manipulation

23.1 Manufacturing with microbes

Lactic acid bacteria make milk proteins into curds. Yoghurt is eaten straight away, but cheeses are left to mature. Microbes make thickners for low fat foods, and for meat substitutes.

Farmers grow plants or animals but biotechnology uses microbes or individual plant and animal cells. The newest processes use organisms with new genes transplanted into their chromosomes to give them new abilities. We have used microbes to make wine, bread and dairy products for thousands of years but most biotechnological products have only been developed in the last quarter of the 20th century.

The most widely prescribed drug in the world is penicillin, made by the fungus Penicillium. About a hundred different antibiotics are now made by bacteria and fungi. Microbial enzymes are also used in glucose sensors, diagnostic tests and washing detergents.

Yeast ferments the sugars in dough or beer wort to produce alcohol and carbon dioxide. Carbon dioxide produced in breweries and bottled under pressure is used in industry. The left-over yeast is made into vitamin pills or a tasty spread.

Why do we use microbes to make products?

We use microbes for many reasons.

- Microbes reproduce very quickly. Bacteria multiply rapidly by binary fission, so a large population quickly builds up. In favourable conditions, fungi grow a mass of hyphal threads and make spores within days.
- Since microbes can digest ethanol, mashed stalks, waste pea pods and even wet cardboard, biotechnological processes often use cheap waste as raw materials. This solves a waste disposal problem at the same time as producing useful materials.
- Microbes convert raw material to products very quickly. It takes weeks for a chicken to grow from hatching to oven-ready size, but microbes make the same mass of protein food in a few days. They are efficient at turning raw material into a product without wasting energy in moving about, making flowers or other activities.
- Microbes flourish in large warm steel tanks on an industrial estate – they don't need green fields or fresh air.
- Microbial enzymes make fewer by-products that need to be removed before a product can be packaged.
- New genes can be inserted into microbes by genetic engineering to change the products much more quickly than by breeding animals or plants.

1 a If two bacteria each split into two by binary fission once an hour in favourable conditions, how many bacteria will there be in 24 hours?

b Draw a graph to show how the population changes during that time.

How are microbes grown commercially?

In biotechnological industries, fermentation means growing any microbe to make a product. The large vessels used to grow microbes are called **fermenters** (see figure 1).

Useful microbes are collected from the wild, or special strains are developed from those already used. For example, microbes living in hot volcanic springs have enzymes that are suitable for making biological washing powder, because they are able to work at high temperatures while ordinary enzymes are **denatured** above 45 °C. Thousands of wild fungi are screened to find those which make antibiotics. Sometimes a microbe with the right features can't be found, or is too difficult to grow in a fermenter. Genetic engineers can transplant useful genes into another microbe that is easier to grow. There are now strains of yeast that produce enzymes for cheese making, or antigens for hepatitis vaccine.

Bacteria and fungi secrete enzymes into their surroundings to break down food materials into smaller, nutrient molecules that they need. We can harvest these enzymes, or the substances they produce.

Many bacteria and fungi need plenty of oxygen to grow. Fungi grow fine hair-like hyphae over the surface of the substrate (the material on which they grow). Yeast is an unusual fungus because it doesn't grow hyphae or need oxygen. The useful waste products made by bacteria and fungi include: ethanol, lactic acid, acetone, butanol and methane.

Once a useful microbe has been identified, scientists investigate how to make it grow and make product as quickly as possible. The microbe is grown in a small-scale fermenter (a pilot fermenter) under various conditions and with different nutrients. The conditions that produce the best growth rate, economically, are used for large-scale production. The conditions that can influence growth rate in fermenters are shown in table 1.

Table 1 Factors influencing growth rate in fermenters.

Condition	Effect on growth rate
Temperature	The warmer it is, the faster microbes grow – up to a limit. Keeping to temperature can be expensive.
pH	Most microbes grow best in slightly acid conditions, but carbon dioxide and other waste products make the conditions inside the fermenter very acid. Alkalis may have to be added.
Food materials	Starchy materials may need more steps to break down and turn into product than sugars, but they may be cheaper. Microbes may also need protein, mineral or vitamin supplements.
Oxygen	Some microbes need a supply of oxygen while they grow. Others are poisoned by it and may need an atmosphere of nitrogen.

Figure 1

Industrial fermenter

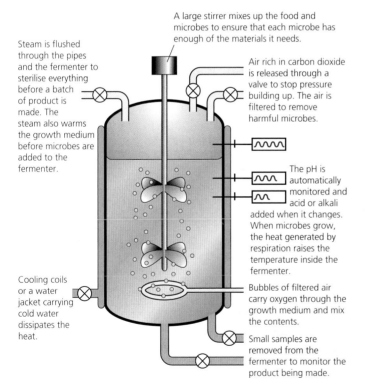

A large stirrer mixes up the food and microbes to ensure that each microbe has enough of the materials it needs.

Steam is flushed through the pipes and the fermenter to sterilise everything before a batch of product is made. The steam also warms the growth medium before microbes are added to the fermenter.

Air rich in carbon dioxide is released through a valve to stop pressure building up. The air is filtered to remove harmful microbes.

The pH is automatically monitored and acid or alkali added when it changes. When microbes grow, the heat generated by respiration raises the temperature inside the fermenter.

Cooling coils or a water jacket carrying cold water dissipates the heat.

Bubbles of filtered air carry oxygen through the growth medium and mix the contents.

Small samples are removed from the fermenter to monitor the product being made.

Fermenters

The microbes are grown in large steel fermenters which hold thousands of litres of liquid nutrients – the growth medium. The fermenter and its pipework is sterilised by flushing with steam. The growth medium may also need sterilising. Small batches of microbes are grown in a laboratory to get them growing at their maximum rate before they are put into the fermenter. Once the fermentation is over the fermenter is washed out and sterilised again. People who come into contact with the microbes and their products often wear protective clothing. Most processes are done in batches because it is hard to keep conditions ideal in the fermenter – toxic wastes build up and nutrients are used up. Brewers and cheese-makers have to keep several batches on the go at the same time to get a continuous supply of product.

2 Name three factors that need to be carefully controlled when growing microbes in an industrial fermenter.

Summary of **manufacturing with microbes**

- Bacteria and fungi are used to make products. Viruses are used to carry new genes into cells.

- Microbes are used because they grow quickly on cheap food materials.

- Microbe genes can be altered to increase the yield of product or to make entirely new products.

- Microbes are grown in sterile fermenters. The environment inside the fermenter is monitored and adjusted to give the best conditions for making the product.

23.2 Products from microbes

How do we use enzymes from microbes?

Enzymes made by microbes are widely used in industry to change raw materials into valuable products – for example, a bacterial carbohydrase is used to break down waste carbohydrate into sugars. Another bacterial enzyme, glucose isomerase, acts on these sugars to make a valuable glucose and fructose syrup. The syrup is much sweeter than cane sugar and so less needs to be used.

Enzymes are expensive and it is wasteful to add them to a batch of material, then throw them away when the product is purified. Instead the enzymes are trapped, or immobilised, inside a rod of spongy porous material. The rod is dipped into the substrate material, or the substrate is slowly trickled down the rod, and the enzyme does the conversion. When the process has finished the rod is washed ready for the next batch. Yeast cells and plant cells have also been immobilised this way. Some of the uses that microbial enzymes can be put to are shown in table 2.

Table 2 Enzymes from microbes and how they can be used.

Enzyme	Uses
Carbohydrases	Converts starch syrup to sugar syrup.
Isomerase	Changes glucose into sweeter fructose.
Protease	Pre-digests proteins in baby food. Tenderises meat, also changes flour to get crisper biscuits.
Pectinase	Used in extracting fruit juice.
Protease, lipase	Used as active enzymes in 'biological' washing powders.

Brewing and baking

Yeast can respire aerobically but if there is plenty of sugar around it doesn't carry out the whole process. Instead it breaks down sugars to ethanol and releases some carbon dioxide. This **anaerobic respiration** is fermentation, and does not need oxygen.

$$\text{glucose} \rightarrow \text{ethanol} + \text{carbon dioxide} + \text{energy}$$

3 Look at figures 2 and 3. Make a list of the useful products which are made from wastes of the yeast industries.

Brewers grow yeast on a sugar source to make ethanol (figure 2). Wine is made using the natural sugars in fruits, but beer uses sugars made from grains such as wheat or barley.

Bakers make bread from some kind of grain flour, yeast and water. Enzymes in the flour release sugars from starch, though a small amount of sugar may be used to start the process. Carbon dioxide bubbles are trapped in the dough and make it rise. Ethanol is driven off during baking.

Figure 2

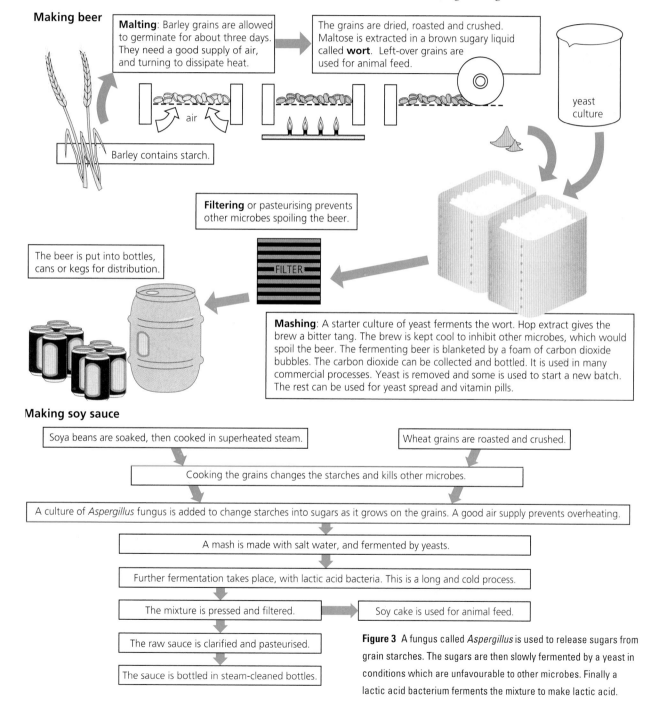

Making beer

Malting: Barley grains are allowed to germinate for about three days. They need a good supply of air, and turning to dissipate heat.

The grains are dried, roasted and crushed. Maltose is extracted in a brown sugary liquid called **wort**. Left-over grains are used for animal feed.

yeast culture

air

Barley contains starch.

Filtering or pasteurising prevents other microbes spoiling the beer.

FILTER

The beer is put into bottles, cans or kegs for distribution.

Mashing: A starter culture of yeast ferments the wort. Hop extract gives the brew a bitter tang. The brew is kept cool to inhibit other microbes, which would spoil the beer. The fermenting beer is blanketed by a foam of carbon dioxide bubbles. The carbon dioxide can be collected and bottled. It is used in many commercial processes. Yeast is removed and some is used to start a new batch. The rest can be used for yeast spread and vitamin pills.

Making soy sauce

Soya beans are soaked, then cooked in superheated steam.

Wheat grains are roasted and crushed.

Cooking the grains changes the starches and kills other microbes.

A culture of *Aspergillus* fungus is added to change starches into sugars as it grows on the grains. A good air supply prevents overheating.

A mash is made with salt water, and fermented by yeasts.

Further fermentation takes place, with lactic acid bacteria. This is a long and cold process.

The mixture is pressed and filtered.

Soy cake is used for animal feed.

The raw sauce is clarified and pasteurised.

The sauce is bottled in steam-cleaned bottles.

Figure 3 A fungus called *Aspergillus* is used to release sugars from grain starches. The sugars are then slowly fermented by a yeast in conditions which are unfavourable to other microbes. Finally a lactic acid bacterium ferments the mixture to make lactic acid.

How are microbes used in the dairy?

4 List two things a cheese manufacturer can do to ensure that only the right kind of bacteria grow in cheese.

Milk acquires lactic acid bacteria from the cow's milk ducts and skin as she is milked. Lactic acid bacteria use lactose in anaerobic respiration and release lactic acid, which makes milk taste sour. When lactic acid accumulates and changes the pH, milk curdles – the proteins are denatured and clot into curds.

The dairy industry uses lactic acid bacteria in a controlled way to make cheese and yoghurt. Other bacteria make the flavours that give cheeses their distinctive tastes. Pasteurised milk is used for yoghurt and cheese because milk naturally contains bacteria that could spoil the product and these are killed during pasteurisation. Laboratory-grown starter cultures of lactic acid bacteria are inoculated into the milk. Yoghurt and cheese-making use the same processes to start with. The yoghurt-making bacteria need warm conditions to grow, but most cheese-making bacteria develop best in cooler, slightly salty surroundings (figures 4 and 5).

Figure 4

Industrial cheese-making

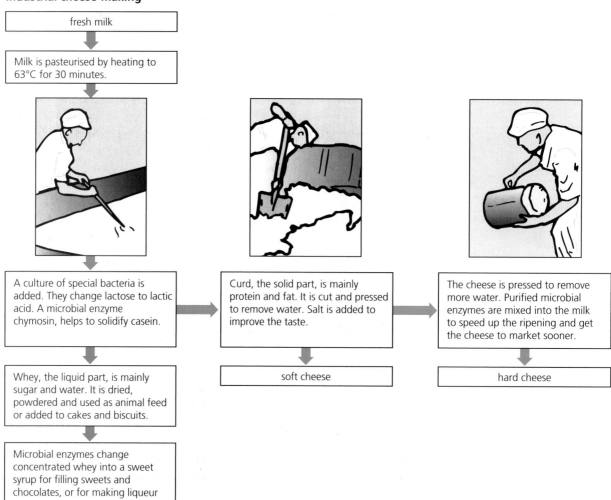

fresh milk

Milk is pasteurised by heating to 63°C for 30 minutes.

A culture of special bacteria is added. They change lactose to lactic acid. A microbial enzyme chymosin, helps to solidify casein.

Whey, the liquid part, is mainly sugar and water. It is dried, powdered and used as animal feed or added to cakes and biscuits.

Microbial enzymes change concentrated whey into a sweet syrup for filling sweets and chocolates, or for making liqueur drinks.

Curd, the solid part, is mainly protein and fat. It is cut and pressed to remove water. Salt is added to improve the taste.

soft cheese

The cheese is pressed to remove more water. Purified microbial enzymes are mixed into the milk to speed up the ripening and get the cheese to market sooner.

hard cheese

Yoghurt making

> Pasteurised milk is thickened with skimmed milk powder or other thickeners. Pasteurised milk makes thicker yoghurt than unpasteurised milk.

> The milk is warmed to 45°C to thicken the milk proteins, reduce the oxygen and provide the best temperature for the bacteria.

> A starter culture of *Lactobacillus bulgaricus* or *Streptococcus thermophilus* bacteria is added.

either

> The yoghurt is dispensed into pots and incubated for four hours until set.

or

> The yoghurt is incubated, stirred and then dispensed into pots.

Figure 5

Can we turn waste into profit?

Wastes are often incinerated. Plenty of energy is released which could be used to heat water, but most just goes up the chimney. Microbes can ferment many sorts of wastes in an oxygen-free atmosphere and convert them to methane. Landfill waste disposal sites can cause problems because methane produced in them accumulates underground and can catch fire.

Many different bacteria are involved in methane production — some start breaking down proteins and carbohydrates, others convert the breakdown products to simpler materials. The final stages of breakdown are done by methane-generating bacteria, which need warm, oxygen-free conditions to work in. The early stages of the breakdown use up any oxygen and generate heat, which warms the mixture.

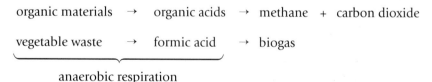

organic materials → organic acids → methane + carbon dioxide

vegetable waste → formic acid → biogas

anaerobic respiration

Biogas is made from animal and vegetable wastes in a simple fermenter called a digester (figure 6). Biogas is used like bottled gas for heating, lighting, cooking and driving cars. To obtain a steady supply of biogas, food factories, sewage works, and households in a community, can pool all their animal manure, human sewage and vegetable waste in a digester. When the digester is emptied the remaining material makes an excellent fertiliser for crops.

5 What kind of organisms make methane? What biological process in their cells results in methane?

Figure 6 A biogas digester.

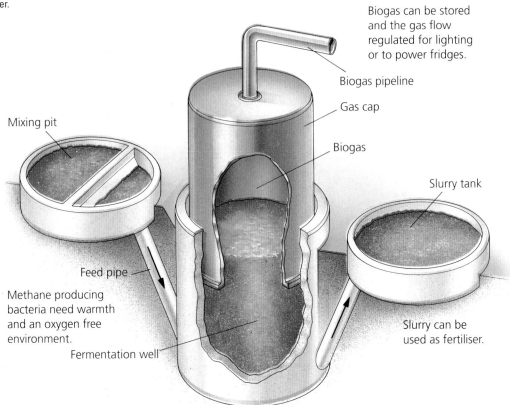

Biogas can be stored
and the gas flow
regulated for lighting
or to power fridges.

Biogas pipeline

Gas cap

Biogas

Slurry tank

Mixing pit

Feed pipe

Methane producing
bacteria need warmth
and an oxygen free
environment.

Fermentation well

Slurry can be
used as fertiliser.

When cars were first developed some used alcohol for fuel, but the cheapness of petrol made them uneconomic. Since then, oil prices have risen, and importing oil and petrol for fuel is very expensive. Countries that do not have their own supply are working out ways of finding alternative fuel sources. Alcohol is a good alternative to petrol because it has a high energy content, can be made from a variety of sources and its chemistry is well known. It can also be used to make other useful products that are usually made from oil.

In Brazil the waste products from sugar processing are too valuable to dump. The sugary liquid left after sugar crystals are made (called molasses) is fermented by yeast into a weak alcohol solution. This is not valuable – in fact the molasses is worth more for baking and animal feed – but when waste sugarcane stem is burned to power a distillery the dilute alcohol is turned into valuable fuel alcohol. Cars and trucks can run on pure alcohol, or on a mixture of petrol and alcohol.

6 In the 1930s Americans used to use corn to make fuel alcohol. Why is this process uneconomic now?

7 In some parts of the world wood and dried animal dung are the main fuel source. Think of ways in which a communal biogas digester could help a small rural village without electricity.

8 Putting human waste into a digester has health benefits. How can a digester help reduce intestinal diseases?

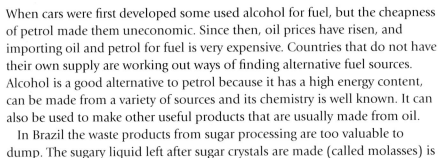

This woman is cooking using biogas from a fermenter in Gujarat. If they had no biogas, she and the other villagers would have to collect scarce and valuable wood for their cooking fires.

Can waste be turned into food?

9 Who is likely to eat mycoprotein?

10 What objections are people likely to have to this new food?

11 Eating mycoprotein is eating food lower down the food chain than meat. What advantages does this have over eating meat?

A search for high-protein animal feed using microbes led the way to entirely new human foods. A bread has been developed that is made from single-celled algae, and there is a protein-rich food (**mycoprotein**) that comes from a fungus called *Fusarium*, which grows on liquid flour waste in a fermenter. Bubbles of oxygen passing through the fermenter supply the fungus and mix the fermenter's contents. Agitation breaks up the fungus mycelium into pellets of hyphal filaments. The fungus is separated from the medium and the fine filaments are pressed together to give it a fibrous texture like meat. The microbial cells are rich in protein but low in cholesterol and are a good meat substitute.

How are antibiotics made?

Figure 7

Penicillin is the most widely used antibiotic. Several forms of penicillin are made by different strains of *Penicillium* fungus. Since it was first found, higher yielding fungus strains have been bred. These are grown in fermenters on waste sugary liquids, as shown in figure 7.

Making penicillin

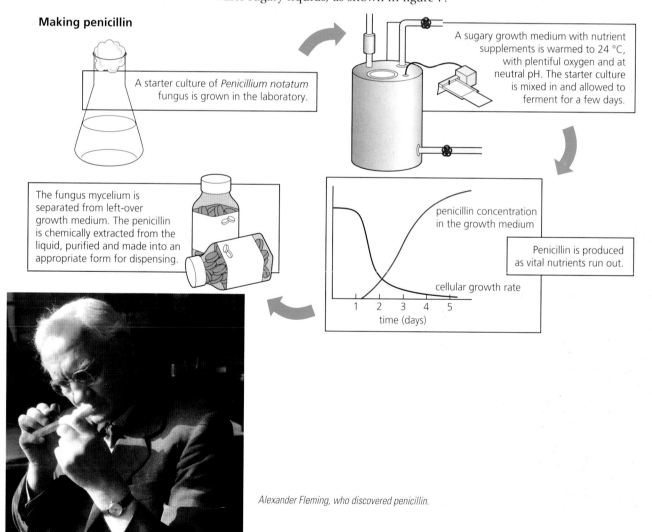

A starter culture of *Penicillium notatum* fungus is grown in the laboratory.

A sugary growth medium with nutrient supplements is warmed to 24 °C, with plentiful oxygen and at neutral pH. The starter culture is mixed in and allowed to ferment for a few days.

The fungus mycelium is separated from left-over growth medium. The penicillin is chemically extracted from the liquid, purified and made into an appropriate form for dispensing.

penicillin concentration in the growth medium

Penicillin is produced as vital nutrients run out.

cellular growth rate

time (days)

Alexander Fleming, who discovered penicillin.

Penicillin was discovered accidentally in 1928 by Alexander Fleming, who was investigating bacteria that cause septic wounds. A fungus had contaminated one of his nutrient agar plates and seemed to have destroyed the bacteria around it. His laboratory notes were followed up ten years later when Howard Florey and Ernst Chain isolated a tiny amount of penicillin, the antibacterial substance made by the fungus *Penicillium notatum*.

12 From the information in figure 7, what is the best time to stop the process and extract penicillin?

Summary of products from microbes

- Enzymes made by microbes are used to make useful products and to speed up manufacturing processes.
- Yeast can be used to make bread or beer by growing it in different conditions.

- Lactic acid bacteria grow on milk sugar. The acids they make convert milk into yoghurt or curds, which are made into cheese.
- Penicillin is an antibiotic made by a fungus.

23.3 Plants and biotechnology

What is micropropagation?

Gardeners generate plants by taking cuttings from good parent plants. They get a clone, of young plants that are genetically identical to the parent plant. Commercial plant breeders also use this **micropropagation** to produce new plants.

One technique used is like taking cuttings. A stem with plenty of side buds is wiped with a mild disinfectant and cut into tiny bud sections. Each section is placed into a tube of sterile agar growth medium containing rooting hormones. The bud develops into a tiny plantlet with roots, which then grows in a moist hazard-free atmosphere. When it is big enough the new plant is potted up in a greenhouse to toughen up.

How is tissue culture performed?

Individual plant cells can be grown in a laboratory – this is known as tissue culture, which is outlined in figure 8. The cells can be persuaded to multiply and regenerate whole plants. Tissue culture allows plant breeders to produce very large numbers of plants from a single parent. If a good parent plant is infected with a virus, bud cells can be used to get new virus-free plants. The cells inside the bud divide rapidly but the viruses can't multiply as quickly, and so some cells will escape infection.

Plants can also be raised from genetically modified cells. Because there is sucrose in the agar, the regenerating plants don't have to photosynthesise and so they can be kept on a shelf in a room instead of in a greenhouse.

Micropropagation

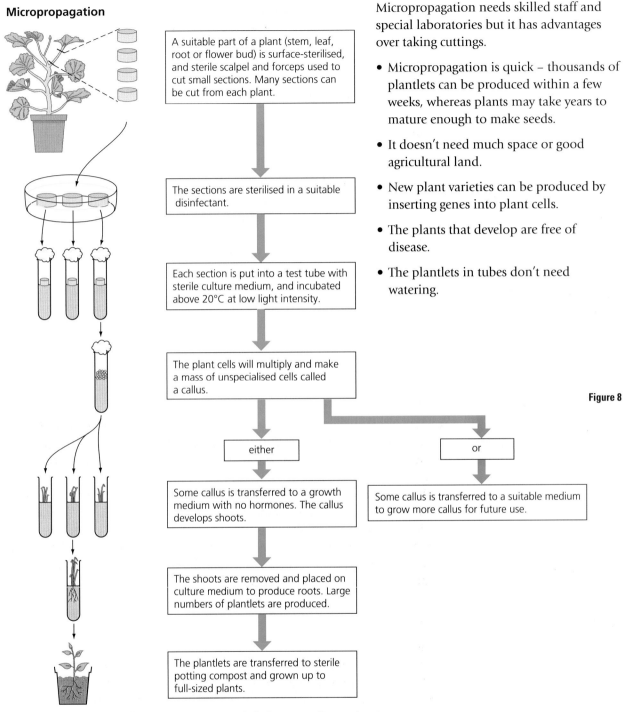

A suitable part of a plant (stem, leaf, root or flower bud) is surface-sterilised, and sterile scalpel and forceps used to cut small sections. Many sections can be cut from each plant.

The sections are sterilised in a suitable disinfectant.

Each section is put into a test tube with sterile culture medium, and incubated above 20°C at low light intensity.

The plant cells will multiply and make a mass of unspecialised cells called a callus.

either

or

Some callus is transferred to a growth medium with no hormones. The callus develops shoots.

Some callus is transferred to a suitable medium to grow more callus for future use.

The shoots are removed and placed on culture medium to produce roots. Large numbers of plantlets are produced.

The plantlets are transferred to sterile potting compost and grown up to full-sized plants.

Micropropagation needs skilled staff and special laboratories but it has advantages over taking cuttings.

- Micropropagation is quick – thousands of plantlets can be produced within a few weeks, whereas plants may take years to mature enough to make seeds.

- It doesn't need much space or good agricultural land.

- New plant varieties can be produced by inserting genes into plant cells.

- The plants that develop are free of disease.

- The plantlets in tubes don't need watering.

Figure 8

Summary of plants and biotechnology

- An individual plant cell is capable of regenerating an entire plant.

- Plant growers use micropropagation to generate thousands of identical plants from a single good parent plant.

23.4 Genetic manipulation

How can genetic manipulation 'improve' microbes?

Certain bacteria and yeasts are easy to grow, but others making useful products are much more difficult to grow. Genetic engineers have isolated genes for useful products from these organisms and transferred them into the more easily grown bacteria or yeast. Microbes with new genes have been genetically modified. The modified microbes grow well in fermenters and make the new product. Using the modified bacteria is better than trying to use the original microbes for several reasons.

- The modified bacteria may use cheaper or more easily available nutrients than the unmodified ones.
- They may grow in an environment which is less difficult to maintain. For example, the original bacteria may need very warm or very acid conditions.
- The modified bacteria may be less dangerous to people working with them. For example, many bacteria that are grown to make vaccines are harmful to humans. Yeasts, which are less dangerous than the original organism, are modified to make the antigens required, and the vaccine made from those antigens may also be less dangerous.
- Bacteria can be modified to make human or mammalian biochemicals which are usually extracted from blood or from slaughtered animals. Examples of these are **insulin** and chymosin.

Insulin

Human biochemicals are difficult and expensive to obtain in large amounts from human blood or tissue. Hormones were the first products to be made from genetically modified microbes. Insulin used to be extracted from pig pancreases, a process that was expensive – and some people couldn't use the insulin. The human insulin gene and its controlling genes were transferred into bacteria, which then released insulin into their culture medium as they grew. Microbial insulin is cheaper than insulin extracted from pigs, and it suits many users better. Microbial hormones are less likely to carry a hidden infection than hormones from animal or human tissues.

Chymosin

Traditionally, an enzyme called rennet which was extracted from calves' stomachs, was used to coagulate milk proteins in cheese-making. The quality of this rennet was very variable, and it became difficult to obtain because of changes in dairy farming. The active enzyme in rennet is chymosin. The gene for chymosin was extracted from calf cells and transferred into a type of yeast called *Kluyveromyces*. This yeast secretes the enzyme in large quantities. The microbial enzyme is packaged to give a product with consistent characteristics, and is now widely used to make cheese.

Rape seed has been genetically modified to produce an oil which is used in the soap and cosmetics industry, and which is usually extracted from coconuts or palm oil. Rape seed can be grown in parts of the world where coconuts do not usually survive.

13 A modified yeast was licensed for bread making. The yeast makes bread rise more quickly. Should the bread be labelled as containing a genetically modified product?

How can animals be used as biochemical 'factories'?

Animals or plants carrying genes that have been transplanted from other species are called **transgenic**. You can read about how crops are improved by genetic engineering in chapter 22, *Food and farming*. Scientists are investigating ways of using transgenic animals as 'living factories' to make human biochemicals on a large scale. Microbial products carry risks associated with taking in 'foreign' chemicals, but because humans have been eating animal meat and drinking milk for thousands of years, products from animals should be safer. Also, a modified bacterium or virus could escape into the environment, and cause infections or even revert to a virulent form, whereas the risks to humans and the environment from sheep or chickens are low and well known. Making products in microbes involves fermenters and high-technology equipment but getting a cow to secrete chemicals into her milk is low technology. The first successful transfers were genes for human biochemicals such as α_1-antitrypsin, which is used to treat lung problems.

It is difficult to transfer genes into whole animals. The new genes have to make the product exactly as they would in their original cells. Some of the problems are listed below.

- The new gene needs to be regulated. The animal may have suitable regulators or they may have to be transferred with the main genes.
- The new gene must be present in every cell making the product, so it must be transferred into the early embryo.
- The gene must be fixed in the chromosomes, ideally as a homozygous gene, and passed on to the next generation.
- The gene must function and make its product in a way that allows it to be collected easily. For example, genes active in breast tissue could make products secreted in milk. The product must be stable in milk and resist milk enzymes. Transgenic chickens could be developed which secrete chemicals into egg yolks.

To transfer new genes into the cells of an early animal embryo eggs are collected from an ovulating female and fertilised with sperm in a dish. The fertilised eggs are microinjected with hundreds of copies of the new genes. The eggs that survive are implanted into the oviduct of a specially prepared host mother. Some of the young animals that are born will have the new gene in their chromosomes. As the transfer happened at a very early stage of development the new genes will be present in the ovaries and testes of these animals, and may be passed to the next generation.

Tracey is a transgenic sheep. Her genes have been modified so that she secretes useful chemicals into her milk. Tracey's milk is worth over £2000 per litre.

Summary of genetic manipulation

- New genes can be inserted into bacteria and fungi so that they make new products.
- New genes are inserted into animal cells by microinjection, at an early embryo stage.
- Genetic manipulation is a recent development which has raised many ethical questions.

Classification

What is a species?

Animals and plants are found in a bewildering array of forms. Some have developed from shared ancestors and have features in common. Scientists group living things into sets based on the number of important inherited features they share, so we talk about 'the big cats' or 'the dinosaurs', which are large groups containing many different animals.

Animals or plants that share many features are members of the same species. Because they are so alike members of the same species can breed together, and will produce offspring that can interbreed. Members of one species cannot breed with members of another species, so foxes can't breed with domestic dogs or with jackals for instance.

Each species is given a two-part Latin name to identify it. This name is the same all over the world, no matter what the local name for the species might be (table 1).

Table 1 *Some Latin species names.*

Latin name	Common English name
Theobroma cocoa	Cocoa tree
Quercus suber	Cork oak
Bufo marinus	Cane toad
Ovis aries	Sheep
Canis lupus	Wolf

Closely related species are grouped together in a genus. All species in the group share the same first, or genus, name. For example, *Lasius niger*, the black ant, and *Lasius umbratus*, the yellow lawn ant, belong to the same genus. All species are assigned to larger groups within one of five kingdoms:

- The Monera – bacteria and their relatives
- The Protoctista – single-celled organisms
- The Fungi
- The Plantae – green plants
- The Animalia – animals.

Plants and animals have very distinct features and there is no doubt about which kingdom they belong to, but some microbes have both plant and animal features and can be very difficult to classify. Viruses do not have a cellular structure and cannot reproduce or be active outside another living cell so they are not included in any kingdom.

The kingdoms

Monera (bacteria)

These are single-celled organisms with a cell wall. They do not have a nucleus, mitochondria or chloroplasts, and they reproduce by binary fission. Examples are *Salmonella* and blue-green bacteria.

Protoctista

These are single-celled organisms with normal cell structures such as a nucleus, mitochondria and so on. This kingdom includes the protozoa and the single-celled algae. Examples are *Amoeba*, a pond-dweller and *Pleurococcus*, an alga that forms a green powder on damp tree trunks.

Fungi

Fungi grow as fine threads called hyphae. They release enzymes into the environment to obtain nutrients. Fungi do not have chlorophyll. They reproduce by spores. Examples include *Penicillium*, which makes penicillin and mushrooms.

Plantae

Typical plants have chlorophyll and cell walls made of cellulose. This kingdom is subdivided into the following:

- **Algae** have no true roots, stems or leaves and live in water.
- The **mosses** and **liverworts** also have no true roots but are anchored to the ground. These have simple stems with no xylem or phloem, no waterproof cuticle and reproduce by spores. Mosses and liverworts are restricted to growing in damp places. Examples include *Pellia*, found by streams and sphagnum moss.
- **Vascular plants** reproduce by spores or seeds, have xylem and phloem, and their leaves have a waterproof cuticle. *Ferns* have waterproofed 'leaves'. The young 'leaves' coil in a bud at ground level. Spores are clustered in structures beneath the 'leaves'. Buckler fern is an example. *Gymnosperms* are seed-bearing trees and shrubs that do not bear flowers or fruits. Their seeds are often carried in cones. Examples are larch, pine and cypress. *Angiosperms*, or flowering plants, have true flowers and their seeds are enclosed in a fruit. Examples are grass, horse chestnut and daisy.

Animalia

The activity of animals is co-ordinated by a nervous system. Members of the animal kingdom reproduce using eggs and sperm. The animal kingdom can be subdivided into invertebrates and vertebrates.

Invertebrates

- **Coelenterates** have bodies with two layers of cells and radial symmetry. They often have tentacles, usually with stinging cells. Examples are jellyfish and sea anemones.
- **Platyhelminthes** are flat unsegmented worms and flukes. They usually have only one entrance to their digestive system. Parasitic members have suckers or hooks. Examples are tapeworms and roundworms.
- **Annelids** are segmented worms with no legs. Examples are earthworms and leeches.
- **Molluscs** have bodies clearly divided into a head, foot and a middle section and often live in a shell. Slugs, snails, mussels and squid are all molluscs.
- **Arthropods** have a hard external skeleton, bodies clearly segmented and jointed legs.
  Crustaceans are usually aquatic. Their head and body are not distinct. They possess two pairs of antennae, and often ten pairs of legs. Prawns, crabs and woodlice are crustaceans.
  Myriapods have a head with jaws, and legs on each body segment. Examples are centipedes and millipedes.
  Insects usually have wings as adults. The young may look very different from the adults as grubs, caterpillars or nymphs. An insect body is divided into three parts: head, thorax and abdomen. The thorax usually carries three pairs of legs and two pairs of wings. Bees, butterflies, dragonflies, ladybirds and ants are all insects.
  Arachnids have a head and thorax that are not distinct. They possess four pairs of legs. Arachnids kill their prey by injecting venom. Examples include spiders, harvestmen and scorpions.
- **Starfish** are marine animals that are radially symmetrical, usually forming a five-armed star. The arms carry tube feet. Examples are starfish and sea urchins.

Vertebrates (Chordates)

These are all animals with an internal skeleton and a spine housing a nerve cord. Most have a pentadactyl limb pattern. All vertebrates follow similar development patterns.

- **Fish** are aquatic animals that move using fins, breathe through gills and have scales to protect the surface. Fertilisation is external, with a large number of eggs. Examples include goldfish and sharks.
- **Amphibians** have soft unprotected skins and no scales. They breed in water using external fertilisation. Adults may live on land and use lungs. Examples are frogs and toads.
- **Reptiles** have scaly, dry skins and usually four legs. Eggs are laid with a leathery shell after internal fertilisation. Reptiles breathe with lungs. Examples are crocodiles and snakes.
- **Birds** are warm-blooded, insulated with feathers and fly using wings. They lay hard-shelled eggs after internal fertilisation and care for their young. Examples are sparrows and penguins.
- **Mammals** are warm blooded animals, insulated with hair. Fertilisation and development of young are internal and the young are fed on milk produced in mammary glands.

1 What important features separate whales and dolphins from fish?

2 Assign the animals shown in the photos to their appropriate groups.

Glossary/Index

LORETO COLLEGE LIBRARY MANCHESTER